HANDBOOK
OF USABILITY TESTING

WILEY TECHNICAL COMMUNICATION LIBRARY

DESIGN   EVALUATION   MANAGEMENT   RESEARCH   WRITING

SERIES ADVISERS:

JoAnn T. Hackos, Comtech Services, Inc., Denver, CO
William Horton, William Horton Consulting, Boulder, CO
Janice Redish, American Institutes for Research, Washington, DC

JoAnn T. Hackos — Managing Your Documentation Projects
Larry S. Bonura — The Art of Indexing
Jeffrey Rubin — Handbook of Usability Testing: How to Plan, Design, and Conduct
   Effective Tests
Karen A. Schriver — Dynamics in Document Design: Creating Texts for Readers

Other Titles of Interest

William Horton — The Icon Book: Visual Symbols for Computer Systems
   and Documentation
Deborah Hix and H. Rex Hartson — Developing User Interfaces: Ensuring Usability
   Through Product & Process
William Horton — Illustrating Computer Documentation: The Art of Presenting
   Information on Paper and Online
William Horton — Designing & Writing Online Documentation, Help Files
   to Hypertext
R. John Brockmann — Writing Better Computer User Documentation, From Paper
   to Hypertext, Second Edition
Tom Badgett and Corey Sandler — Creating Multimedia on Your PC
Robert Virkus — Quark PrePress: A Guide to Desktop Production
   for Graphics Professionals
Helena Rojas-Fernandez and John Jerney — FrameMaker for UNIX Solutions
Jim Mischel — The Developer's Guide to WINHELP.EXE: Harnessing the Windows
   Help Engine

HANDBOOK
OF USABILITY TESTING:
How to Plan, Design, and Conduct
Effective Tests

Jeffrey Rubin

JOHN WILEY & SONS, INC.
New York • Chichester • Brisbane • Toronto • Singapore

Publisher: Katherine Schowalter
Editor: Theresa Hudson
Managing Editor: Elizabeth Austin
Composition: Science Typographers, Inc.

This text is printed on acid-free paper.

This publication is designed to provide accurate and authoritative
information in regard to the subject matter covered. It is sold
with the understanding that the publisher is not engaged in
rendering legal, accounting, or other professional services. If
legal advice or other expert assistance is required, the services
of a competent professional person should be sought.

Library of Congress Cataloging-in-Publication Data:
Rubin, Jeffrey,
    Handbook of usability testing: how to plan, design, and conduct
effective tests / Jeffrey Rubin.
        p.   cm. — (Wiley technical communication library)
    Includes index.
    ISBN 0-471-59403-2 (alk. paper : pbk.)
    1. User interfaces (Computer systems)—Testing.   I. Title.
II. Series.
QA78.9.U83R82   1994
005.1′4—dc20   93-43038
                                                          CIP

Printed in the United States of America

10 9 8 7 6 5 4 3 2

To my wife Halice, and children, Dustin, Lance, and Mariel. Their unconditional love and support kept me going through an exhausting and difficult year, and spurred me on to greater heights. I would not and could not have done this without them.

To the memory of my spiritual teacher, the Venerable Chögyam Trungpa, Rinpoche, whom it was my great good fortune to meet in this lifetime.

To the memory of Ösel Tendzin, a fearless warrior if ever there was one.

Any perception can connect us to reality properly and fully. . . . There is some principle of magic in everything, some living quality. Something living, something real is taking place in everything.
　　—Chögyam Trungpa in *Shambhala, The Sacred Path of the Warrior*

CONTENTS

ABOUT THE AUTHOR

Jeff Rubin has more than 20 years experience as a human factors specialist in the computer industry. He is founder and owner of *J. Rubin Associates*, a human factors and technical communication consulting firm based in Morganville, N.J. While at the Bell Laboratories' Human Performance Technology Center, he developed and refined testing methodologies, and conducted research on the usability criteria of software, documentation, and training materials.

Presently, Mr. Rubin provides consulting services and workshops on the planning, design, and evaluation of user interfaces for new computer-based products for major corporations throughout North America, including Hewlett Packard, Texas Instruments, AT&T, the Ford Motor Company, and Bell Laboratories. His extensive experience in the application of user-centered design, along with the singular ability to communicate complex principles and techniques in non-technical language make him uniquely qualified to write on the subject of usability testing.

Mr. Rubin holds a degree in Experimental Psychology from Lehigh University. He resides near the Jersey Shore with his wife and three children.

PREFACE

THE USABILITY EXPLOSION

Usability is a business phenomenon. Whole industries and businesses have sprung up to help us operate computer-based products and systems, electronic equipment, and even household appliances that we own, but cannot use properly.

For example, there exists a third-party product for programming a video cassette recorder (VCR) to tape a future television show. With this product, you can program your VCR by entering the show's six-digit number found in your newspaper's television listings. All you need to know is how to enter that six-digit number. (This in itself could be a challenge). This simplified programming method enables VCR users to completely bypass the much more complicated method of programming built into the VCR by the manufacturer.

Other examples abound, such as the very successful industry that develops training videos that explain how to use specific software products. Ironically, these software products are often initially purchased because they are supposed to be easy to use. Or, consider the simplified remote control for television sets that is necessary because the original remote control that came with the T.V. remains a mystery to almost everyone in the household. Or, how about the thousands of third-party books on the market that explain how to master the complexities of popular software programs?

Amazingly, it is now an accepted and common practice to purchase products whose sole purpose is to help us master products that we own, but cannot use properly. While I applaud the entrepreneurs who seized this opportunity to provide a useful service (no pun intended), it is rather disconcerting that such a situation exists at all. But the fact is that hard-to-use products have become the norm.

Of course, it is not just the makers of third-party products who have been provided with a business opportunity here. Original manufacturers have the identical opportunity if they could just create products that are genuinely easy to learn and use *right out of the box*. For many of these manufacturers, the lure of usability as a market separator remains strong, even as they struggle to discover the magic formula for success.

Among those associated in some way with the development of computer-based or electronic products the recent interest and emphasis on usability is apparent. Many find that usability objectives are included in both their job descriptions and performance appraisals, and they are struggling to learn as much as they can as quickly as possible. To accommodate this growing need, usability oriented societies and associations have been growing by leaps and bounds.

Finally, what better proof of usability's maturation and growth than its descent into the realm of the superficial? Many companies simply jump on the usability bandwagon without first putting in the requisite effort to make genuinely usable products. Instead, they simply label and advertise their products as "user friendly," a term as devoid of meaning to every self-respecting usability specialist as the term "96% fat free" on a package of sliced ham, is to a nutritionist.

WHY THIS BOOK?

This explosion of usability has dramatically changed the way that products are designed and manufactured. Historically, the responsibility for usability in product development—when it was a concern at all—fell to the human factors or ergonomics specialist. This person typically possessed specialized training and education in either the social or behavioral sciences, was familiar with the literature on usability engineering principles, and had experience designing products from the end user's perspective. Today, however, with the demand for usable products far outpacing the number of trained professionals available to provide assistance, many product developers, engineers, system designers, technical communicators, and marketing and training specialists have had to assume primary responsibility for usability within their organizations. With little formal training and few guidelines upon which to rely, many are being asked to perform tasks related to usability engineering for which they are unprepared.

This book is intended to help bridge this gap in knowledge and training by providing a straightforward, step-by-step approach for evaluating and improving the usability of computer-based products, systems, and accompanying support materials. It is a "how-to" book, filled with practical guidelines, realistic examples, and many samples of test materials.

WHO IS THIS BOOK FOR?

This book is primarily intended for individuals (or even small groups) with little or no formal training in human factors or usability engineering, and with limited resources and facilities for conducting usability testing. It is targetted to those without a formal, well-equipped lab, or dedicated, multi-disciplinary test team on which to rely. Ironically, such modest resources, by forcing one to concentrate on the significant, and perform *all* the testing roles, can actually speed up one's learning, enhance one's creativity, and harden one's resolve to be successful.
The secondary audience is the more experienced human factors or usability specialist who may be new to the discipline of usability testing.

The intended audience includes (in alphabetical order):

- Human factors specialists
- Managers of product and system development teams
- Product marketing specialists
- Software and hardware engineers
- System designers and programmers
- Technical communicators
- Training specialists

In addition to the business professionals listed previously, this book is also intended for college and university students in the disciplines of computer science, technical communication, industrial engineering, experimental and cognitive psychology, and human factors engineering who wish to learn a pragmatic, no-nonsense approach to designing usable products.

WHAT DOES THIS BOOK COVER?

This book will teach you everything you need to know in order to plan, design, conduct, and analyze the results of a usability test within today's fast-paced production environment, where reducing "time to market" has become a prerequisite for survival. It proposes a series of iterative, small (four to ten subjects), usability tests throughout the product life cycle that are intended to gradually design and shape the product. This iterative approach features early qualitative research of users' conceptual model and thought process, leading to increasingly quantitative studies prior to product release. The common thread linking all of these studies is experimental rigor, which many of the guidelines within address.

HOW IS THIS BOOK ORGANIZED?

This book is organized into four parts, as follows:

PART	CONTENTS
One. Introduction to Usability Testing	*Chapter 1* explores the reasons for the proliferation of unusable systems, suggests as an antidote the methods and techniques of user-centered design, and provides the context for the discipline of usability testing.
	Chapter 2 proposes four types of usability tests that can be conducted throughout the development life cycle.
Two. Preparing for Usability Testing	*Chapter 3* explores several different testing environments, and recommends one for organizations just starting to test.
	Chapter 4 describes the different roles and responsibilities of testing, with special emphasis on the test monitor's role. One person may need to play many of these roles if resources are limited.
Three. Six Stages of Conducting a Test	*Chapters 5 through 10* comprise the heart of this book—a detailed, step-by-step approach to conducting a usability test, complete with many guidelines and examples.
Four. Expanding Usability	*Chapter 11* is a discussion of strategies and tactics for establishing a usability program within your own organization.

HOW IS THIS BOOK WRITTEN?

This is not a scholarly tome, although I have included references to other publications and articles that influenced my thinking, and for those readers who would like to learn more about a particular point or topic. I have used plain language, and have kept the reference to formulas and statistics to a bare minimum. While many of the principles and guidelines are based on theoretical and practitioner research, the vast majority have been drawn from my 20 years of experience as a human factors specialist designing, evaluating, and testing all manner of software, hardware, and written materials. Usability engineering is not an exact science. Wherever possible, I have tried to offer explanations for the methods presented herein. It is my intention that you, the reader might avoid the pitfalls and political landmines that I have discovered only through substantial trial and error.

LANGUAGE CONVENTIONS

Throughout this book I have used several terms in specific ways.

Product. I have used the term *product* in two ways. One, I use *product* to refer to the entire gamut of high-tech hardware and software, which can include a computer-based system or device, a piece of electronic equipment, or a household appliance. Second, I also use *product* to refer to the smaller components that make up the larger product, such as a user guide, a software user interface, a help system, or a control panel. When I refer to testing the product, the product is whatever specific component(s) for which you the reader are responsible.

Developer, designer, design team, and development team. I have used these four terms almost interchangeably to refer to any individual, team, or member of a team who designs and creates a product to be tested, whether it be software, hardware, or documentation. Designers, developers, design teams, and development teams, as I have used the terms, can be engineers, writers, trainers, interface designers, human factors specialists, product marketing specialists, and so on.

Participant or test participant. With a background in experimental psychology, I am very comfortable and very accustomed to using the term "test subject", to refer to those people who attend a usability test and try out the product in question. Other human factors professionals are equally at ease with this term. However, in seminars and talks that I have given, I have noticed a strong negative reaction to this term on the part of many in the audience. ("Strong" is too mild a term to describe the reaction in some cases. One gentleman approached me after a particular talk I gave, and told me I was evil for using that term; that it reminded him of testing rats). I also realized that I never used the term "test subject" when speaking directly to those who participated in the usability test, which I suppose says something important about how I thought it might be perceived. In seeking advice for a better, less intimidating term, some suggested I use the term "tester", but this is apt to be confused with the role of the person who conducts the test. So finally, after thrashing about, I opted for the term "participant", which I have used throughout the book to refer to the people who try out our products and let us know what they think. Please be advised however, that if a "test subject" or two accidentally slipped by our illustrious proofreader, I hope it does not reflect on my innate worth in your eyes.

CAVEAT

When it comes to usability, there is tremendous potential for self-deception, oversimplification, and a digression into superficiality. While I advocate the need for individuals and groups without formal training to take responsibility for their own product's usability, this responsibility must be applied intelligently, rather than through wishful thinking.

In lieu of enough trained specialists, some companies are granting the job title of "Human factors engineer" or "usability specialist" to those without the appropriate background and training, *and they are not allowing these individuals to grow into the job gradually*. Not only can this practice result in poorly designed products, but it can damage the progress and acceptance of usability engineering within the organization immeasurably.

In writing this book, I have placed tremendous trust in the reader to acknowledge his or her own capabilities and limitations as they pertain to usability engineering and to stay within them. Be realistic about your own level of knowledge and expertise, even if management anoints you as the resident usability expert. As you begin to design and conduct usability tests, start slowly with small simple studies, until you gain the necessary experience and confidence to expand further. Above all, remember that the essence of usability engineering is clear seeing, appreciation of detail, and trust in the ability of your future customers to guide your hand, if you will only let them.

ACKNOWLEDGMENTS

Every book is a collaboration of the efforts of many people, and this one is no exception. I would like to take this opportunity to thank those who helped me.

First and foremost, I would like to thank my associates Dean Vitello and Roberta Cross, who, as a team, edited and formatted the entire manuscript, and made many helpful suggestions regarding clearer communication. Both worked many evenings and even holiday weekends, and treated the book as if it were their own. I would also like to thank my administrative assistant, Michele Balestiero. Since I spend many days on the road, Michele typed several iterations of the manuscript from every manner of input, including dictation from airplanes and automobiles, facsimile documents, and even from my barely legible handwritten changes.

Thanks go to my old friend and colleague from my Bell Labs days, John Wilkinson. John reviewed the original outline and several chapters, offered many helpful suggestions, and, in general, kept me honest. Special thanks go to Pamela Adams, who reviewed the original outline and all but one chapter of the manuscript, and helped formulate the ideas on iterative testing in Chapter 2. Over the last three years, Pamela and I have worked together on a variety of usability engineering projects, several of which are reflected in this book.

I would also like to thank Terri Hudson from John Wiley who first approached me out of the blue with the idea for this book.

Lastly, I wish to thank my previous employers and clients, several of whom will recognize the thinly disguised examples and scenarios referenced throughout the text. I would especially like to thank Ellen Mason at Hewlett Packard with whom I have been implementing a usability engineering program. The program, which includes testing highly sophisticated equipment, has enabled me to refine many of the principles discussed within. Thanks especially to Hewlett Packard for its permission to use several examples of testing materials, and guidelines.

PART ONE

INTRODUCTION TO

USABILITY TESTING

THE PROBLEM OF

UNUSABLE PRODUCTS

AND SYSTEMS

1

INTRODUCTION

Why are so many high-tech products, such as computer-based systems, electronic equipment, and even everyday appliances, so hard to use?

In this opening chapter I would like to explore this question, discuss why the situation is exacerbated today, and examine the overall antidote to this problem of hard-to-use products. My primary focus will be on the field of computer-based products and systems, namely hardware, software and documentation, but even products such as the control panel for an ultrasound machine, or the user manual for a telephone answering machine will fall within the scope of this book.

For those of you who currently work in the product development arena, (as engineers, user-interface designers, technical communicators, training special-

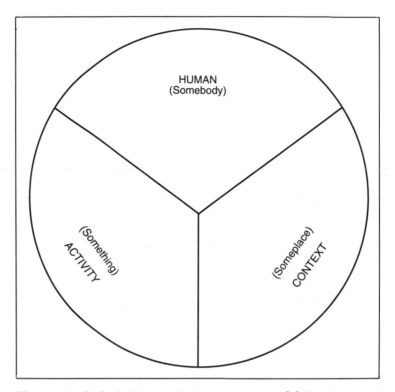

Figure 1.1 Bailey's Human Performance Model [7] (reprinted with permission of Prentice-Hall)

ists, or managers in these disciplines, I suspect that several of the reasons for the development of hard-to-use products and systems will sound painfully familiar.

FIVE REASONS FOR HARD-TO-USE PRODUCTS AND SYSTEMS

Reason 1. During product development the emphasis and focus have been on the machine or system, not on the person who is the ultimate end user. The generic model of human performance shown in Figure 1.1 will help to clarify this point.

There are three major components to consider in any type of human performance situation as shown in Bailey's Human performance model.

1. The human
2. The context
3. The activity

Since the development of a system or product is an attempt to improve human performance in some area, designers must consider these three components during the design process. All three will affect the final outcome of how well humans ultimately perform. Unfortunately, of these three components, designers, engineers, and programmers have traditionally placed the greatest emphasis on the *activity* component, and much less emphasis on the human and the context components. The relationship of the three components to each other has also been neglected.

There are several explanations for this unbalanced approach. First, there has been an underlying assumption that since humans are so inherently flexible and adaptable, it is easier to let them adapt themselves to the machine, rather than vice versa. Second, developers, almost invariably comprised of engineers, traditionally have been more comfortable working with the seemingly "black and white," scientific, concrete issues associated with systems, than with the more gray, muddled, ambiguous issues associated with human beings. Third, developers have historically been hired and rewarded not for their interpersonal, "people" skills but for their ability to solve technical problems. Finally, the most important factor leading to the neglect of human needs has been that in the past, designers were developing products for end users who were much like themselves. There was simply no reason to study such a familiar colleague. That leads us to the next point.

Reason 2. **As technology has penetrated the mainstream consumer market, the target audience has changed and continues to change dramatically. Development organizations have been slow to react to this evolution.**

The original users of computer-based products were "hackers," possessing expert knowledge of computers and mechanical devices, a love of technology, the desire to tinker, and pride in their ability to troubleshoot and repair any problem. Developers of these products shared similar characteristics. In essence, users and developers of these systems were one and the same [15]. Because of this similarity, the developers practiced "next-bench" design, a method of designing for the user who is literally sitting one bench away in the development lab. Not surprisingly, this approach met with relative success, and users rarely if ever complained about difficulties.

Why would they? Much of their joy in using the product was the amount of tinkering and fiddling required to make it work, and hacker users took immense pride in their abilities to make these complicated products function. Consequently, a "machine -oriented" or "system-oriented" approach met with little resistance and became the development norm.

Today, however, all that has changed dramatically. Whereas before it was very unusual for a nontechnical person to use electronic or computer-based equipment, today it is almost impossible for the average person *not to use* such a product in either the workplace or in private life. The overwhelming majority of products, whether in the workplace or the home, be they word processors, VCRs, or sophisticated testing equipment, are intended for this less technical, nonhacker user. Today's user wants a tool, not another hobby.

He or she is apt to have little technical knowledge of computers and mechanical devices, little patience for tinkering with the product just purchased, and completely different expectations. More important, *today's user is no longer even remotely comparable to the designer in skill set, aptitude, expectation, or in almost any attribute that is relevant to the design process.* Even companies that manufacture complex analytical systems for highly skilled engineers are finding that the skill and educational background of their customers has lessened considerably in the last three to five years. Where just recently they might find Ph.D. chemists using their products, today they will find high-school graduates performing similar functions. Obviously, "next-bench" design simply falls apart as a workable design strategy when there is a great discrepancy between user and designer, and companies employing such a strategy, even inadvertently, will continue to produce hard-to-use products.

Reason 3. **The design of usable systems is a difficult, unpredictable endeavor, yet many organizations treat it as if it were just "common sense."**

While much has been written about usability and usability engineering of systems, the concept remains maddeningly elusive, especially for those without a background in either the behavioral or social sciences. Part art, part science, it seems that *everyone* has an opinion about usability, and how to achieve it. That is, until it is time to evaluate usability, which requires an operational definition and precise measurement [117].

This trivializing of usability creates a more dangerous situation than if product designers freely admitted that usability was not their area of expertise, and began to look for alternative ways of developing products. Or as Will Rogers so aptly stated, "It's not the things that we don't know that gets us into trouble; it's the things we do know that ain't so." In many organizations usability has been approached as if it were nothing more than "common sense." But if that were the case, usable systems and products would also be common.

In a research study conducted several years ago, Gould and Lewis [49] determined that designers had erroneous notions of a user-centered approach to developing systems, and consequently of usability itself. When asked the question, "Which major steps are required to develop and evaluate a new computer for end users?" less than half of those polled (447 designers of computer-based systems) mentioned more than one of three very basic principles (to be reviewed shortly) required to design usable systems. In other words, while many of the principles of usability seem like common sense, it turned out that actual knowledge of usability was quite uncommon.

With the current emphasis on usability, it would seem that designers should be much more in tune with user-centered design principles than in the past. However, if my own and many of my colleagues' recent experiences working with designers is any indication, Gould and Lewis' research is as true today as it was in 1985. Usability principles are still not obvious, and there is still a great need for education, assistance, and a systematic approach in applying so-called "common sense" to the design process.

Reason 4. Organizations employ very specialized teams and approaches to product and system development, yet fail to integrate them with each other.

In order to improve efficiency, organizations have broken down the product development process into separate system components developed independently. For example, three components of a software product are *the user interface*, *the help system*, and *the written materials*. Typically, these components are developed by separate individuals or teams. Now, there is nothing inherently wrong with specialization. The difficulty arises when there is little integration of these separate components and poor communication among the different development teams.

Often the product development proceeds in very separate, compartmentalized sections. To an outsider looking on, the development would be seen as depicted in Figure 1.2.

Each development group functions rather independently, almost as an island, and the final product often reflects this approach. The help system will not

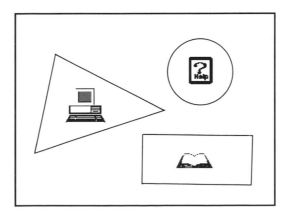

Figure 1.2 Nonintegrated Approach to product development

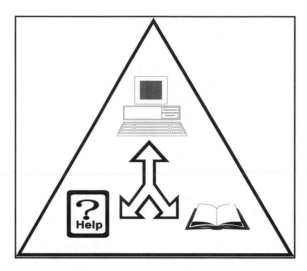

Figure 1.3   Integrated Approach to product development

adequately support the user interface or it will work very differently from the interface. Or documentation and help will be redundant with little cross-referencing. Or the documentation will not reflect the latest version of the user interface. I'm sure you get the picture.

The problem occurs when the product is released. The end user, upon receiving this new product, views it and expects it to work as a single, integrated product as shown in Figure 1.3. He or she makes no particular distinction between the three components, and each one is expected to *support and work seamlessly with the other*. When the product does not work in this way, it clashes with the user's expectations and whatever advantages accrue through specialization are lost.

Even more interesting is how often organizations unknowingly exacerbate this lack of integration *by usability testing each of the components separately*. Documentation is tested separately from the interface, and the interface separately from the help. Ultimately, this approach is futile, since it matters little if each component is usable within itself. Only if the components work well together will the product be viewed as usable and meeting the user's needs.

Reason 5. **The *design* of the user interface and the technical *implementation* of the user interface are different activities, requiring very different skills. Today, the emphasis and need are on the design aspect, while many engineers possess the mind set and skill set for technical implementation.**

Design in this case relates to how the product communicates, whereas implementation refers to how it works. Previously, this dichotomy between design and implementation was rarely even acknowledged. Engineers and designers were hired for their technical expertise (e.g., programming and machine-oriented analysis) rather than their design expertise (e.g., communication and human-oriented analysis). This is understandable, since with early generation computer languages the great challenge lay in simply getting the product to work. If it communicated elegantly as well, so much the better, but that was not the prime directive.

Now, with the advent of such tools as object-oriented programming languages and tools to automatically develop program code, the challenge of technical implementation has diminished. The challenge of design, however, has increased dramatically due to the need to reach a broader, less sophisticated user population and this population's rising expectations for ease of use. To use a computer analogy to illuminate this situation, the focus has moved from the inside of the machine (how it works) to the outside where the end user resides (how it communicates) [58].

This change in focus has altered the skills required of designers. However, many organizations still value the technical implementer's (machine) skills over the designer's (people) skills. In the future this evolution toward design and away from implementation will continue. Skills such as programming will be completely unnecessary when designing a user interface.

These five reasons merely brush the surface of how and why unusable products and systems became the norm and continue to flourish, and I do not wish to belabor the point. More important is the common theme among these problems and misperceptions; namely that too much emphasis has been placed on the product itself, and too little on the desired effects the product needs to achieve. Especially in the heat of a development process that grows shorter and more frenetic each year, it is not surprising that the user continues to receive too little attention and consideration.

It is easy for designers to lose touch with the fact that they are not designing products per se, but rather they are designing the *relationship* of product and human. Furthermore, in designing this relationship, designers must allow the human to focus on the task at hand, and not on the means with which to do that task. They are also designing the relationship of the various product components to each other, which implies excellent communication among the different entities designing the user interface, documentation, and help system. What has been done in the past simply will not work for today's user and today's technologies.

What is needed are methods and techniques to help designers change the way they view and design products—methods that work from the outside-in, from the end user's needs and abilities to the eventual implementation of the product. The name most recently given to this approach is *user-centered design* (UCD). Since it is only within the context of UCD that usability testing makes sense and thrives, let's explore this notion of user-centered design in more detail.

USER-CENTERED DESIGN

DEFINITION

User-centered design (UCD) is the recent term coined to describe an approach that has been around for decades under different names, such as human factors engineering, ergonomics, and, more recently, usability engineering. (The terms human factors engineering and ergonomics are almost interchangeable, the major difference between the two having more to do with geography than with real differences in approach and implementation. In the United States human factors engineering is the more widely used term, and in other countries, most notably in Europe, ergonomics is more widely used. In fact, the Human Factors Society only last year changed its name to The Human Factors and Ergonomic Society in deference to this fact.) UCD represents not only the techniques, processes, methods, and procedures for designing usable products and systems, but just as important, the philosophy that places the user at the center of the process.

Figure 1.4 depicts a user-centered design process. All development proceeds with the user as the center focus. A product's goals, objectives, context, and environment are all derived from the user's viewpoint, as well as all aspects of the tasks that the product supports.

One of the most cogent, concise, and clear definitions that I have seen of UCD is by Woodson [152] who defined human factors engineering as "...the practice of designing products so that users can perform required use, operation, service, and supportive tasks with a minimum of stress and maximum of efficiency." This is the essence of UCD. In elaborating, he goes on to say that this involves the "design from the human-out" and that a designer should "make the design fit the user," as opposed to "making the user fit the design." This definition is comprehensive, since it includes all the operations that a user needs to perform on a product or system, and not just the initial learning and usage of a product.

In a sense, though, even Woodson's definition is limiting, since it can be viewed as relating to the design process alone rather than the entire cycle of user ownership of a product. Ideally, the entire process of interacting with potential customers, from the initial sales and marketing contact through the entire duration of ownership through the point at which another product is pur-

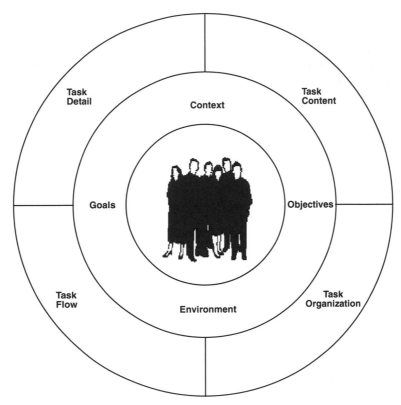

Figure 1.4 <u>User-Centered Design</u>

chased or the current one upgraded, should also be included in a user-centered approach. In such a scenario, companies would extend their concern to the user to include all prepurchase and postpurchase contacts and interactions. However, let's take one step at a time, and stick to the design process.

THREE PRINCIPLES OF A USER-CENTERED DESIGN

Numerous articles and books have been written on the subject of user-centered design (UCD) [48] [61] [96] [123], and it is not my intention to retread this ground. However, it is important for the reader to understand the basic principles of UCD in order to understand the context for performing usability testing. Usability testing is not UCD itself; it is merely one of several techniques for helping ensure a good, user-centered design. Gould and Lewis [49] in their work on human-oriented system design, posited three principles of a UCD.

These (three principles) are:

1. **An early focus on users and tasks.** This is more than just simply identifying and categorizing users. Gould and Lewis advocated direct contact between users and the design team throughout the development life cycle. However, I would caution the reader that direct contact itself can be hazardous if it is not structured. Designers, often lacking interpersonal skills, and visiting users, with nary a game plan, can come back with either their own ideas reinforced or with reams of unstructured data from both their own and their colleagues' interviews. In the worst cases, I have seen entire engineering teams trek across several continents on a tour of customer sites, only to return with a myriad of conflicting information documented and filed away on unstructured trip reports. Unfortunately, this volume of information and huge effort served little useful purpose.

   In an even worse prostitution of this principle, customer contact has become institutionalized in many organizations, with designers requiring customer visits merely to complete a checkoff box on their performance appraisal form.

   What is required is a systematic, structured, approach to the collection of information from and about users. Designers require training from expert interviewers before conducting a data collection session. Otherwise, the results can be very misleading.

2. **Empirical measurement of product usage.** Here, emphasis is placed on behavioral measurements of ease of learning and ease of use very early in the design process, through the development and testing of prototypes with actual users.

3. **Iterative design whereby a product is designed, modified, and tested repeatedly.** Much has been made about the importance of design iteration. However, this is not just fine tuning late in the development cycle. Rather, as Gould and Lewis advocate, true iterative design allows for the complete overhaul and rethinking of a design, through *early* testing of conceptual models and design ideas. If designers are not prepared for such a major step, then the influence of iterative design becomes minimal and cosmetic. In essence, true iterative design allows one to "shape the product" through a process of design, test, redesign, and retest.

ATTRIBUTES OF ORGANIZATIONS THAT PRACTICE UCD

User-centered design is an evolving approach and philosophy in the development of products and systems. As such, its implications on the design team and the overall development organization are worth exploring. It demands a rethinking of the way in which companies do business, develop products, and think about their customers. While there currently exists no cookie-cutter formula for success, there are common attributes that companies practicing UCD share. For example:

A PHASED APPROACH TO DEVELOPMENT THAT INCLUDES USER INPUT AND FEEDBACK AT ALL CRUCIAL POINTS

Unlike the typical phases we have all seen in traditional development methodologies, a user-centered approach is based on receiving user feedback or input during each phase, prior to moving to the next phase. This can involve a variety of techniques, usability testing being only one of these.

Today, most major companies that develop computer-based products or systems have product life cycles that include some type of usability engineering/human factors process. Invariably, with slight variations, these life cycles will include the processes or phases shown in the simplified life cycle of Figure 1.5.

Within each phase, there will be a variety of usability engineering activities. Figure 1.6 represents one company's attempt to define the human factors activities that need to occur during each phase.

Note that, although this particular life cycle is written from the viewpoint of the human factors specialist's activities, there are multiple places where collaboration is required among various team members, which leads to our next attribute of organizations practicing UCD.

A MULTIDISCIPLINARY TEAM APPROACH

No longer can design be the province of one person or even of one specialty. While one designer may take ultimate responsibility for a product's design, he or she is not all-knowing about how to proceed. There are simply too many factors to consider when designing very complex products for less technical end users. User-centered design requires a variety of skills, knowledge, and, most importantly, information about the intended user and usage. Today, teams composed of specialists from many fields, such as engineering, marketing, training, user-interface design, human factors, and multimedia, are becoming the norm.

CONCERNED MANAGEMENT

Typically, the degree to which usability is a true corporate concern is the degree to which a company's management is committed to following its own life cycle and giving its guidelines "teeth" by holding the design team accountable.

Booth [15] has coined the acronym OPTICS to represent this commitment to usability engineering activities, as shown in Figure 1.7.

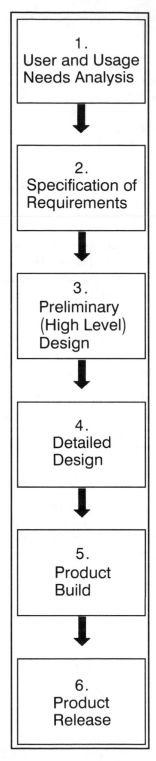

Figure 1.5   Product Development Life Cycle

	Phase 1 Needs Analysis	Phase 2 Requirements Specification
Objectives	Identify need for product by studying user, task, and work environment characteristics.	Specify requirements product must satisfy to meet user needs. Define system usability goals.
Human Factors Activities	Identify and characterize target user population. Identify and analyze user tasks. Identify users' physical and organizational environment. Identify usability problems on similar or existing products. Identify users' product feature list.	Identify ergonomic or market-based requirements. Define and develop product usability and acceptance goals. Define criteria for measuring usability and acceptance. Develop product localization plan. Develop usability testing schedule.
Human Factors Methods	Case Studies / Customer Visits Survey Focus Group Task Analysis User Diaries Conceptual Modeling Rapid Prototyping	Literature review of: - Previous product usability specifications. - Human Factors standards. - Market Research data. - Competitive research data.
Human Factors Collaboration	Assist Marketing in the identification and investigation of users and their needs.	Provide Marketing with information regarding product requirements that will satisfy user needs.
	Provide R&D with information on users/tasks and helps to scope the design, development, and test processes.	Work together with R&D to specify usability requirements, goals, and acceptance criteria.
	Assist Quality in the analysis of competitor products.	Work together with Quality to determine usability metrics for the product.
	Provide Learning Products with information on users/tasks and help to scope the design, development, and test processes.	Work with Learning Products to identify support materials that will facilitate learning and effective use of the product.

Figure 1.6   Hewlett Packard's Human Factors Activities During the Life Cycle (courtesy of Hewlett Packard, Inc.)

	Phase 3 Conceptual Design	Phase 4 Prototype, Development, and Test
Objectives	Develop product specifications to meet previously identified usability requirements and performance objectives.	Test product with target user population performing representative tasks to ensure a usable/functional product.
Human Factors Activities	Develop product interface requirements. Define mental models describing system from the user's perspective. Determine allocation of functions between user and system. Integrate Human Factors data, principles, and guidelines. Test conceptual models.	Provide technical support in the development of product prototypes. Review production prototypes for ergonomic compliance. Test usability of HW, SW, and Learning Products. Provide feedback (including design recommendations) to designers based on results of usability test.
Human Factors Methods	Incorporate previous usability test data, Corporate Human Factors specifications and Human Factors literature and standards. Observe/interview target users. Audio/Video taping. Structured walk-throughs (conceptual testing).	Usability test of: -Simulations or mock-ups. - Early prototypes. - Production prototypes. Early versions of Learning Products.
Human Factors Collaboration		Get assistance from Marketing to define target user population and identify representative tasks for usability testing.
	Work with R&D to explore the usability implications of proposed designs. R&D creates conceptual models for structured walk throughs.	Obtain HW and SW prototypes and technical support from R&D for usability testing.
	Help Learning Products to integrate support materials into the development process.	Obtain product setup guides, on-board documentation or online help messages/screens from Learning Products for usability testing.

Figure 1.6   (*Continued*)

	Phase 5 Product Evaluation
Objectives	Verify that the product meets previously identified customer needs. Gather information for future product development.
Human Factors Activities	Review final production specifications to ensure agreed upon usability recommendations have been satisfactorily implemented into the product design. Conduct on-site customer evaluations to determine product usability and how effectively the product meets user needs and expectations. Provide Marketing with usability advantages of the product. Analyze field data for next generation products.
Human Factors Methods	Beta-Site customer evaluations. Analyze Beta-Site data for future product specifications.
Human Factors Collaboration	Work with Marketing to collect field data regarding product usability in order to support the marketing, sale, and support of the product.
	Work with R&D to coordinate Beta-Site field testing. Obtain production HW and/or SW from R&D for Beta-Site evaluations. Obtain updated HW and SW as necessary/feasible from R&D and provide updates for field evaluation.
	Assist Quality in monitoring Beta-Site test data relative to previously set product usability metrics.
	Assist Learning Products in conducting Bete-Site customer evaluation. Obtain updated support materials as necessary/feasible from Learning Products and provide updates for field evaluations.

Figure 1.6 (*Continued*)

A "LEARN AS YOU GO" PERSPECTIVE

UCD is an evolutionary process whereby the final product is "shaped" over time. It requires designers to take the attitude that the optimum design is acquired through a process of trial and error, discovery and refinement. Assumptions about how to proceed remain assumptions and are not cast in concrete until evaluated with the end user. The end user's performance and preferences are the final arbiters of design decisions.

Activities	Description
Objectives	Management backing and clear objectives to produce a usable product.
Planning	Make plans and time to address the usability issue and apply human factors techniques and tools.
Techniques	Apply the relevant human factors tools and techniques (on a cost/benefit basis) at the right time in the development process.
Interest	Continually strive to put yourself in the user's position. Understand the user's needs. Involve representative users in design, review, and testing.
Care	Reflect concern for usability in all aspects of the product. Take care to fix important usability problems that are discovered.
Specialists	Make use of specialist human factors help.

Figure 1.7 Booth's Representation of Usability Commitment Activities [15] (reprinted with permission of Lawrence Erlbaum Associates)

USABILITY GOALS AND OBJECTIVES

The design of usability must be structured and systematic, beginning with high-level goals and moving to specific objectives. You cannot achieve a goal—usability or otherwise—if it remains nebulous and ill-conceived. Even the term *usability* itself must be defined. Although there is no broadly recognized definition that would be acceptable to all professionals in the usability community, it is generally accepted that an operational definition of usability include one or more of the following four factors, as outlined by Booth [15].

1. **Usefulness.** Usefulness concerns the degree to which a product enables a user to achieve his or her goals, and is an assessment of the user's motivation for using the product at all. Without that motivation, other measures make no sense, since the product will just sit on the shelf. If a system is easy to use, easy to learn, and even satisfying to use, but does not achieve the specific goals of a specific user, it will not be used even if it is given away for free. Interestingly enough, usefulness is probably the element that is most often overlooked during experiments and studies in the lab.

In the early stages of product development, it is up to the marketing team to ascertain what product or system features are desirable and necessary before other elements of usability are even considered. Lacking that, the development team is hard pressed to take the user's point of view, and will simply guess or even worse, use themselves as the user model. This is very often where a machine-oriented design takes hold.

2. **Effectiveness (ease of use).** The second element, ease of use or effectiveness, is usually defined quantitatively, either by speed of performance or error rate, and is tied to some percentage of total users. An example of such a measure would be "*95 percent of all users will be able to load the software correctly on the first attempt in less than 10 minutes.*"

3. **Learnability.** Learnability has to do with the user's ability to operate the system to some defined level of competence after some predetermined amount and period of training. It can also refer to the ability of infrequent users to relearn the system after periods of inactivity.

4. **Attitude (likability).** Attitude refers to the user's perceptions, feelings, and opinions of the product, usually captured through both written and oral interrogation. Users are more likely to perform well on a product that meets their needs and provides satisfaction than one that does not. Typically, users are asked to rate and rank products that they test, and this can often reveal causes and reasons for problems that occur.

Usability goals and objectives are typically defined in measurable terms of one or more of these four attributes. However, let me caution that usability is never simply the ability to generate numbers about usage and satisfaction. While the numbers can tell us whether a product "works" or not, there is a distinctive qualitative element to usability as well, which is hard to capture with numbers and is difficult to pin down. It has to do with how one interprets the usability data in order to know *how* to fix a problem, and the little subtleties that evade the untrained eye. Any doctor can measure a patient's vital signs, such as blood pressure and pulse rate. But interpreting those numbers and recommending the appropriate course of action for a specific patient is the true value of the physician.

Now let's review some of the major techniques and methods a usability specialist uses to ensure a user-centered design.

UCD: A BRIEF REVIEW OF TECHNIQUES, METHODS, AND PRACTICES

UCD is comprised of a variety of techniques, methods, and practices, each applied at different points in the product development life cycle. Reviewing the major methods will help to provide some context for usability testing, which itself is one of these techniques. Please note that the order of the techniques is more or less the order in which they would be employed during a product's development life cycle.

PARTICIPATORY DESIGN [49]

Less a technique and more an embodiment of UCD, participatory design employs one or more representative users on the design team itself. Typically used for the development of in-house systems, this approach thrusts the end user into the heart of the design process from the very commencement of the project by tapping the user's knowledge, skill set, and even emotional reactions to the design. The potential danger is that the representative users can become *too* close to the design team. They begin to react and think like the others, or by virtue of their desire to avoid admonishing their colleagues, withhold important concerns or criticism.

FOCUS GROUP RESEARCH

Focus group research is typically employed at the very early stages of a project in order to evaluate preliminary concepts using representative users. In some cases it is used to identify and confirm the characteristics of the representative user altogether. All focus group research employs the simultaneous involvement of more than one participant, a key factor in differentiating it from many other techniques [51].

The concepts that participants evaluate can be presented in the most preliminary form, such as paper-and-pencil drawings, storyboards, and/or more elaborate screen-based prototypes or plastic models. The objective is to identify how acceptable the concepts are, in what ways they are unacceptable or unsatisfactory, and how they might be made more acceptable. The beauty of the focus group is its ability to explore a few people's judgments and feelings in great depth, and in so doing learn how end users think and feel.

SURVEYS

Surveys are employed to understand the preferences of a broad base of users about an existing or potential product. While the survey cannot match the focus group in its ability to plumb for in-depth responses and rationale, it can use larger samples to generalize to an entire population. For example, the Nielsen ratings, one of the most famous ongoing surveys, are used to make multimillion dollar business decisions for a national population based on the preferences of fewer than 1500 people. Surveys can be used at any time in the life cycle, but are most often used in the early stages to better understand the potential user. An important aspect of surveys is that their language must be crystal clear and understood in the same way by all readers, a task impossible to perform without multiple iterations and adequate preparation time.

DESIGN WALK-THROUGHS OR STRUCTURED WALK-THROUGHS

Walk-throughs are used to explore how a user might fare with a product by envisioning the user's route through an early concept or prototype of the product. Usually the designer responsible for the work guides his or her colleagues through actual user tasks, while another team member records difficulties encountered or concerns of the team. In a structured walk-through, as first developed by IBM to perform code reviews, the participants assume specific roles (e.g., moderator, recorder) and follow explicit guidelines (e.g., no walk-through longer than two hours) to ensure the effectiveness of the effort.

PAPER-AND-PENCIL EVALUATIONS

In this technique users are shown an aspect of a product on paper and asked questions about it, or asked to respond in other ways. The questions can range from particular attributes, such as organization and layout, to where one might find certain options or types of information. In the example shown in Figure 1.8, the user is being asked to identify the pull-down menu of a word processing package under which he or she would look to perform each of 12 tasks. Data is collected and tabulated, and the intuitiveness of the menu organization or lack of same becomes apparent.

Paper-and-Pencil Simulation for Word for Windows

Next to each word processing task shown below, write in the name of the pull-down menu option under which you expect to find that task.

File	Edit	View	Insert	Format	Utilities	Macro	Window

1. Search for a word _____
2. Create a header _____
3. Create an index entry _____
4. Set up your document preferences _____
5. Repeat an annotation _____
6. Paste another file into your current file _____
7. Use italics _____
8. Show summary information about your document _____
9. Switch to another document _____
10. Show all annotations in the document _____
11. Repaginate the document _____
12. Annotate your document _____
13. Set up your printer _____

Figure 1.8 Paper-and-Pencil Simulation for Word™ for Windows™

The value of the paper-and-pencil evaluation is that critical information can be collected quickly and inexpensively. In the example given in Figure 1.8, one can quickly ascertain those menu names and structures that are intuitive and those that are not, *before one line of code has been written*. In addition, technical writers might use the technique to evaluate the intuitiveness of their table of contents before writing one word of text. The technique can be employed again and again with minimal drain on resources.

EXPERT EVALUATIONS

Expert evaluations involve a review of a product or system, usually by a usability specialist or human factors specialist who has little or no involvement in the project. The specialist performs his or her review according to accepted usability principles from the body of research and human factors literature. The viewpoint is that of the specific target population that will use the product.

Recent research [95] has indicated that a "double" specialist, that is, a specialist who is also an expert in the particular technology employed by the product, is more effective than one without such knowledge.

USABILITY AUDIT

This type of audit evaluates the product or system by comparing its design against checklists of standards. The standards could be taken from the body of research and literature, or from usability criteria established by the organization from successful predecessor products. The standards could relate to various product components, such as user interface, control panel, or documentation.

USABILITY TESTING

Usability testing, the focus of this book, employs techniques to collect empirical data while observing representative end users using the product to perform representative tasks. Testing is roughly divided into two main approaches. The first approach involves formal tests conducted as true experiments, in order to confirm or refute specific hypotheses. The second approach, a less formal one, employs an iterative cycle of tests intended to expose usability deficiencies and gradually shape or mold the product in question. In this book I will emphasize the latter type of testing, which I have divided into four types of tests.

1. Exploratory
2. Assessment
3. Validation
4. Comparison

FIELD STUDIES

A field study is a review of a product that has been placed in its natural setting, such as an office, home, or other type of realistic environment, just prior to release. Often a favored customer is used and offered some compensation to help evaluate the product. Data, such as patterns of use, difficulties, and user attitudes, is collected, and the results are used to refine the product prior to release. Typically conducted very late in the development life cycle, the information is rarely used to make significant changes, although the data can be extremely valuable when used for future releases. The benefit over a lab study is the exposure of the product to actual working conditions. The disadvantage is the loss of control over the data collection. Often these types of studies, known as alpha or beta tests, are conducted as rather unstructured, "try this and let us know what you think" affairs, which minimizes their effectiveness greatly.

FOLLOW-UP STUDIES [15]

A follow-up study is similar to the field study although it occurs after formal release of the product. The idea is to collect data for the next release, using surveys, interviews, and observations. Structured follow-up studies are probably the truest and most accurate appraisals of usability, since the actual user, product, and environment are all in place and interacting with each other. That follow-up studies are so rare is unfortunate, since designers would benefit immensely from learning what happened to that product that they spent two years of their lives perfecting. Sales figures, while helpful, add nothing to one's knowledge of the product's strengths and weaknesses.

This is not a definitive list of methods by any means, and is meant merely to provide the reader with an appreciation for the wealth of techniques available and the complexity involved in implementing a UCD approach. No organization performs all of these techniques, and just as few conduct them in their pure form [15]. Typically, they are used in altered and combined form, as the specific needs and constraints of a project dictate. Now let's take a closer look at probably the most renowned technique of all the ones discussed, and the focus of this book, usability testing.

OVERVIEW

OF USABILITY

TESTING

2

INTRODUCTION

I have noticed that the term *usability testing* is often used rather indiscriminately to refer to *any* technique used to evaluate a product or system. Many times it is obvious that the speaker is referring to one of the other techniques discussed in Chapter 1. Throughout this book I will use the term *usability testing* to refer to a process that employs participants who are representative of the target population to evaluate the degree to which a product meets specific usability criteria. This inclusion of representative users eliminates labeling as usability testing such techniques as expert evaluations, walk-throughs, and the like that do not require representative users as part of the process.

Usability testing is a research tool, with its roots in classical experimental methodology. The range of tests one can conduct is considerable, from true classical experiments with large sample sizes and complex test designs, to very informal qualitative studies with only a single participant. Each testing approach has different objectives, as well as different time and resource requirements. The emphasis of this book will be on more informal, less complex tests designed for quick turnaround of results in industrial product development environments.

GOALS OF TESTING

The overall goal of usability testing is to identify and rectify usability deficiencies existing in computer-based and electronic equipment and their accompanying support materials prior to release. The intent is to ensure the creation of products that:

✓ • are easy to learn and to use

✓ • are satisfying to use

✓ • provide utility and functionality that are highly valued by the target population [49]

More specific goals or benefits of testing are:

- **Creating a historical record of usability benchmarks for future releases.** By keeping track of test results, a company can ensure that future products either improve or at least maintain current usability standards.

✓ • **Minimizing the cost of service and hotline calls.** A more usable product will require fewer service calls and less support from the company.

✓ • **Increasing sales and the probability of repeat sales.** Usable products create happy customers who talk to other potential buyers or users. Happy customers also tend to stick with future releases of the product, rather than purchase a competitor's product.

- **Acquiring a competitive edge since usability has become a market separator for products.** Usability has become one of the main ways to separate one's product from a competitor's product in the customer's mind. One need only scan the latest advertising to see products described using phrases such as "easier to use" and "a baby could do it" among others. Unfortunately, this information is rarely truthful when put to the "test."

- **Minimizing risk.** Actually, all companies and organizations have conducted usability testing for years. Unfortunately, the true name for this type of testing has been "product release," and the "testing" involved trying the product in the marketplace. Obviously, this is a very risky strategy, and usability testing conducted *prior* to release can minimize the considerable risk of releasing a product with serious usability problems.

LIMITATIONS OF TESTING

Now, having painted a rather glorified picture of what usability testing is intended to accomplish, let's splash a bit of cold water on the situation. Testing is neither the end-all nor be-all for usability and product success, and it is important to understand its limitations. Testing does not guarantee success or even prove that a product will be usable. Even the most rigorously conducted formal test cannot, with 100 percent certainty, ensure that a product will be usable when released. Here are some reasons why:

- **Testing is always an artificial situation.** Testing in the lab, or even testing in the field, still represents a depiction of the actual situation of usage and not the situation itself. The very act of conducting a study can itself affect the results.

- **Test results do not prove that a product works.** Even if one conducts the type of test that acquires statistically significant results, this still does not prove that a product works. Statistical significance is simply a measure of the probability that one's results were not due to chance. It is not a guarantee, and is very dependent upon the way in which the test was conducted.

- **Participants are rarely fully representative of the target population.** Participants are only as representative as your ability to understand and classify your target audience. Market research is not an infallible science, and the actual end user is often hard to identify and describe.

- **Testing is not always the best technique to use.** There are many techniques intended to evaluate and improve products, as discussed in Chapter 1. For example, in some cases it is more effective both in terms of cost, time, and accuracy to conduct an expert evaluation of a product rather than test it. This is especially true in the early stages of a product when gross violations of usability principles abound. It is simply unnecessary to bring in many participants to reveal the obvious.

However, in spite of these limitations, usability testing, when conducted with care and precision, for the appropriate reasons, at the appropriate time in the product development life cycle, and as part of an overall user-centered design approach, is an almost infallible indicator of potential problems and the means to resolve them. It minimizes the risk considerably of releasing an unstable or unlearnable product. In almost every case, and this is an underlying theme of this book, it is better to test than not to test.

BASICS OF TEST METHODOLOGY

The origin of the basic methodology for conducting a test is taken from the classical approach for conducting a controlled experiment. With this formal approach, often employed to conduct basic research, a specific hypothesis is formulated, then tested by isolating and manipulating variables under controlled conditions. Cause-and-effect relationships are then carefully examined, often through the use of the appropriate inferential statistical technique(s), and the hypothesis is either confirmed or rejected. Employing true experimental designs, these studies require that:

- **A hypothesis must be formulated.** A hypothesis states what you expect to occur when testing. For example, "Help as designed in format A will improve the speed and error rate of experienced users more than help as designed in format B." It is essential that the hypothesis be as specific as possible.

- **Randomly chosen (using a very systematic method) participants must be assigned to experimental conditions.** One needs to understand the characteristics of the target population, and from that larger population select a representative random sample. Random sampling is often difficult especially when choosing from a population of existing customers.

- **Tight controls must be employed.** Experimental controls are crucial else the validity of the results can be called into question, regardless of whether statistical significance is the goal. All participants should have nearly the identical experience as each other prior to and during the test. In addition, the amount of interaction with the test monitor must be controlled as well.

- **Control groups must be employed.** In order to validate results, a control group must be employed, its treatment varying only on the single variable being tested.

- **The sample (of users) must be of sufficient size to measure statistically significant differences between groups [124].** In order to measure differences between groups statistically, a large enough sample size must be used. Too small a sample can lead to erroneous conclusions.

The preceding approach is the basis for conducting classical experiments, and when conducting basic research, is the method of choice. *However, it is not the method I will be emphasizing in this book for the following reasons.*

It is often impossible or inappropriate to use such a methodology to conduct usability tests in the fast-paced, highly pressurized development environment in which most readers will find themselves. It is impossible because of a myriad of organizational constraints, political and otherwise. It is inappropriate because the purpose of usability testing is not necessarily to formulate and test specific hypotheses, that is, conduct research, but rather to improve products.

In addition, the amount of prerequisite knowledge of experimental method and statistics required in order to perform these kinds of studies properly is considerable, and better left to an experienced usability or human factors specialist. Should one attempt to conduct this type of tight research without the appropriate background and training, the results can often be very misleading, and lead to a worse situation than if no research had been conducted.

Also, in the environment in which testing most often takes place, it is often very difficult to apply the principle of randomly assigning participants since one often has little control over this factor. This is especially true as it concerns the use of existing customers as participants.

Still another reason for a less formal approach concerns sample size. To achieve generalizable results for a given target population, one's sample size is dependent on knowledge of certain information about that population, which is often lacking (and sometimes the precise reason for the test). Lacking such information, one may need to test 10 to 12 participants *per condition* to be on the safe side, a factor that might require one to test 40 or more participants to ensure statistically significant results.

Lastly, and probably most important, the classical methodology is designed to obtain quantitative proof of research hypotheses; that one design is better than another, for example. It is not designed to obtain qualitative information on how to fix problems and redesign products. I assume that most readers will be more concerned with the latter than the former.

The approach I will be discussing and advocating is a more informal, iterative approach to testing, albeit with experimental rigor at its core. As the reader will see in later chapters of this book, experimental rigor is essential for *any* study that one conducts.

Current research [35] [95] [138] has shown that much can be achieved by conducting *a series* of quick pointed studies, beginning early in the development cycle. It is the intent of this book to present the basics of conducting this type of less formal, yet well-designed test that will identify the specific usability deficiencies of a product, their cause, and the means to overcome them. The basics of this approach are as follows.

BASIC ELEMENTS OF USABILITY TESTING

1. Development of problem statements or test objectives rather than hypotheses.
2. Use of a representative sample of end users which may or may not be randomly chosen.
3. Representation of the actual work environment.

4. Observation of end users who either use or review a representation of the product. Controlled and sometimes extensive interrogation and probing of the participants by the test monitor.

5. Collection of quantitative and qualitative performance and preference measures.

6. Recommendation of improvements to the design of the product.

I will discuss and detail the "how-to" of this approach in the chapters that follow. In the rest of this chapter, I will discuss the basics for conducting four types of specific tests, and then provide a hypothetical case study employing all four tests.

FOUR TYPES OF TESTS: AN OVERVIEW

The literature is filled with a variety of testing methodologies, each with a slightly different purpose. Often, different terms are used to describe identical testing techniques. Needless to say, this can be extremely confusing. In deciding which tests to discuss and emphasize, I thought the most beneficial approach would be to use the product development life cycle as a reference point for describing several different types of tests. I hope that by associating a test with a particular phase in the life cycle, it will help the reader to understand the test's purpose and benefits.

In this chapter I define and discuss three tests—exploratory, assessment, and validation tests—at a high level, according to the approximate point in the product development life cycle at which each would be administered. The fourth type of test, the comparison test, can be used as an integral part of any of the other three tests, and is not associated with any specific life cycle phase.

The basic methodology for conducting each test is roughly the same and is described in detail in Chapter 8. However, each test will vary by its emphasis on qualitative vs. quantitative measures, and by the amount of interaction between test monitor and participant. I should also add that the tests expounded here are definitely biased toward an environment of tight deadlines, limited resources, and with a keen eye on the bottom line.

My other purpose for presenting the test types in terms of the product development life cycle has to do with the power of iterative design. Usability testing is most powerful and most effective when implemented as part of an iterative product development process. That is, a cycle of design, test and measure, and redesign [49] throughout the product development life cycle has the greatest probability of concluding with a usable product. Even if important product flaws or deficiencies are missed during one test, another testing cycle offers the opportunity to identify these problems or issues.

An iterative design and testing approach also allows one to make steady and rapid progress on a project, to learn through empirical evidence, and to "shape" the product to fit the end users' abilities, expectations, and aptitude. I feel very strongly that such an approach provides the "best bang for the buck" when resources are limited, and that one will obtain the best results by conducting a series of short, precise tests that build one upon the other.

However, while the tests I am about to describe lend themselves to an iterative design process, one need not be concerned about applying the tests at *exactly* the correct moment. Rather, consider what it is that you need to understand about your product, and let that drive your test objectives and the appropriate application of a particular test method. Also, do not be put off if you are unable to conduct multiple tests. One test is almost always better than none, and it is better to focus on what you *can* do than on what you cannot do.

The first three tests, exploratory, assessment, and validation or verification, are shown in Figure 2.1 next to the approximate points in the life cycle at which they are most effectively conducted. Now let's review each in turn.

EXPLORATORY TEST

WHEN

The exploratory test is conducted quite early in the development cycle, when a product is still in the preliminary stages of being defined and designed. By this point in the development cycle, the user profile and usage model (or task analysis) of the product will have (or should have) been defined. The project team is probably wrestling with the functional specification and early models of the product. Or perhaps, the specifications phase is completed, and the design phase is just about to begin.

OBJECTIVE

The main objective of the exploratory test is to evaluate (although evaluate is too judgmental a term at this stage, examine or explore is a more accurate term) the effectiveness of preliminary design concepts, also known as the user's conceptual or mental model of the product. If one thinks of a user interface or a document as being divided into a high-level aspect and a more detailed aspect, the exploratory test is concerned with the former.

For example, designers of an object-oriented software interface would benefit greatly knowing early on whether the user intuitively grasps the fundamental

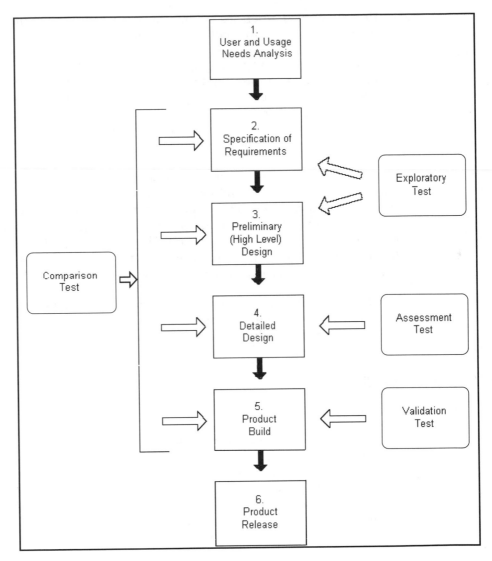

Figure 2.1   Product Development Life Cycle

and distinguishing elements of the interface. For example, designers might want to know how well the interface:

- Represents classes of objects
- Communicates the relationship between these objects
- Allows the user to manipulate these objects
- Allows the user to navigate from screen to screen and within a screen

Or using the task-oriented user guide of a software product as an example, technical writers typically might want to explore the following high-level issues:

- Overall organization of subject matter
- Whether to use a graphic or verbal approach
- Accessibility of the proposed format
- Anticipated points of help access
- How to address reference information

The implication of these high-level issues goes beyond the product, because you are also interested in verifying your assumptions about the *users*. Understanding one is necessary to define the other. Some typical user-oriented questions that an exploratory test would attempt to answer might include the following:

- What do users conceive and think about using the product?
- Does the product's basic functionality have value to the user?
- Are the operations and navigation of the user interface intuitive?
- Are former command line users able to grasp the basics of manipulating the product's new graphical user interface (GUI)? If not, why not, and where do they require assistance?
- What type of prerequisite information does a person need to use the product?
- Which functions of the product are "walk up and use" and which will probably require either help or written documentation?
- How should the table of contents be organized to accommodate both novice and experienced users?

I cannot emphasize enough the importance of this type of *early* analysis and research, for this is the point in time when critical design decisions set the stage for all that will follow. If the project begins with wrong assumptions and faulty premises about the user, the product is almost guaranteed to have usability problems later. Similar to building a house, once you lay the foundation for one type of model, you cannot simply build a totally different model without first ripping out the existing framework. The underlying structure determines all that will follow.

OVERVIEW OF THE METHODOLOGY

Exploratory tests usually dictate extensive interaction between the participant and test monitor to establish the efficacy of preliminary design concepts. One way to answer very fundamental questions, similar to those listed previously, is to develop preliminary versions of the product's interface and/or its support materials for evaluation by representative users. For software, this would typically involve a prototype simulation or mockup of the product that represents its basic layout, organization of functions, and high-level operations. Even prior to a working prototype, one might use static screen representations or even paper drafts of screens. For hardware representations, one might use two-dimensional or three-dimensional foamcore or plastic models. For user support materials, one might provide very rough layouts of manuals, training materials, or help screens.

When developing a prototype, one need not represent the entire functionality of the product. Rather, one need only show enough functionality to address the particular test objective. For example, if you want to see how the user responds to the organization of your pull-down menus, you need only show the menus and one layer of options below. If the user proceeds deeper than the first layer, you might show a screen that reads, "Not yet implemented," or something similar.

This type of prototype is referred to as a "horizontal representation," since the user can move left or right but is limited in moving deeper. However, if your test objective requires seeing how well a user can move down several menu layers, you will need to prototype several functions "vertically," so users can proceed deeper. You might achieve both objectives with a horizontal representation of *all* major functions, and a vertical representation of two of the functions.

During the test of such a prototype, the user would attempt to perform representative tasks. Or if it is too early to perform tasks, then the user can simply "walk through" or review the product and answer questions under the guidance of a test monitor. Or, in some cases, the user can even do both. The technique used is dependent on the point in the development cycle and the sophistication of the mockups.

The testing process for an exploratory test is usually quite informal and almost a collaboration between participant and test monitor, with much interaction between the two. Since so much of what you need to know is cognitive in nature, an exploration of the user's thought process is vital. The test monitor and participant might explore the product together, with the test monitor conducting an almost ongoing interrogation or encouraging the participant to "think aloud" about his or her thought process as much as possible. Unlike later tests where there is much less interaction, the test monitor and participant can sit side by side as shown in Figure 2.2.

Users are solicited for their ideas about how to improve confusing areas. Unlike later tests where there is more emphasis on measuring *how well* the user is able

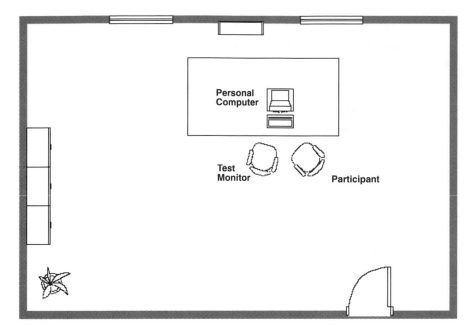

Figure 2.2 Test Monitor and Participant Exploring the Product

to perform by collecting quantitative data, here you strive to understand *why* the user performs as he or she does by collecting qualitative data. Regardless of whether you use a working prototype, static screens, early manuals, or whether the user performs tasks or simply "walks through" a product with the test monitor, the distinguishing feature of the exploratory test is its emphasis on discussion and examination of high-level concepts and thought processes.

EXAMPLE OF EXPLORATORY TEST

Since the nature of the exploratory test is often somewhat abstract, let's review how a typical exploration might proceed for a software product, such as a word processing package. Assume that you are exploring the main top-level screen, which consists of a graphical user interface (GUI) employing several pull-down menus. Assume also that this is a very early stage of development, so the user interface simply consists of a single screen without any underlying structure or connections. However, the pull-down menus function, so the user can view the menu options underneath each menu heading (File, Edit, etc.) as shown in Figure 2.3.

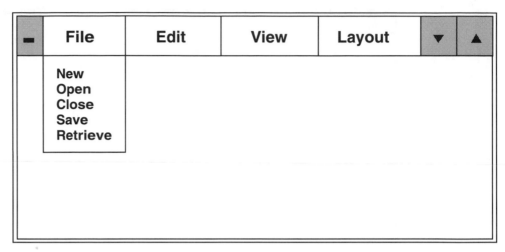

Figure 2.3   Pull-Down Menu Interface

Now let's look at Figure 2.4, which contains an excerpt of a test script for conducting an exploratory test, to see how the test might proceed. You might continue in this vein, having the user attempt to accomplish realistic tasks with much discussion about assumptions and thought process. Alternatively, though, if the software is in such a preliminary stage that the menus do not work, and you wanted to evaluate the effectiveness of the organization of the pull-down menus, you might ask the user to simply point to the pull-down menu under which he or she would expect to accomplish a particular task, similar to the paper-and-pencil evaluation in Figure 1.8 (Windows exercise in Chapter 1). This approach would establish which tasks were harder to initiate and less intuitive.

Exploratory tests are often conducted as comparison tests, with different prototypes matched against each other. This prevents the project team from committing too early to one design, only to find out later that the design has serious flaws and liabilities. An example of this type of test is shown later in this chapter.

The important point of exploratory tests is that you can be extremely creative in simulating early versions of the product. Paper screens, prototypes with limited functionality, and so on, all help to acquire important high-level information before the design is cast in concrete. It is never too early to learn how the user perceives the product and its fundamental presentation.

I cannot emphasize enough how much time can be saved by using exploratory research to establish the soundness of high-level design *prior* to fleshing out all the details. Explore very basic ideas and concepts as soon as you are able to simulate how they will work to users. Do not wait to take action until a very well thought-out, full-blown design takes shape.

The purpose of our session today is to review the design for a new word processing package and get your opinions about it. As we review this design together, I will be asking you a series of questions about what you see and how you expect things to work. Please feel free to ask any questions and offer any observations during the session. There are no wrong answers or stupid questions. This product is in a very preliminary stage, so do not be concerned if it acts in unexpected ways.

1. Let's begin with a hypothetical situation. You would like to find a letter you previously typed and stored on the system in order to revise it and send it to someone else. How would you go about fetching and reviewing that letter?

(User indicates how the task would be attempted, or attempts to do the task if the screen works.)

2. Okay, the letter is on the screen. Go ahead and remove the entire last paragraph.

(User indicates how the task would be attempted, or attempts to do the task if the screen works.)

3. Okay, now I'd like you to retrieve another file.

(User indicates how the task would be attempted, or attempts to do it if the screen works.)

etc., etc.

Figure 2.4 A Portion of an Exploratory Test Script

ASSESSMENT TEST

WHEN

The assessment test is probably the most typical type of usability test conducted. Of all the tests, it is probably the simplest and most straightforward for the novice usability professional to design and conduct. Assessment tests are conducted either early or midway into the product development cycle, usually after the fundamental or high-level design or organization of the product has been established.

OBJECTIVE

The purpose of the assessment test is to expand the findings of the exploratory test by evaluating the usability of lower-level operations and aspects of the product. If the intent of the exploratory test is to work on the skeleton of the product, the assessment test begins to work on the meat and the flesh. Assuming that the basic conceptual model of the product is sound, this test seeks to examine and evaluate how effectively the concept has been implemented. Rather than just exploring the intuitiveness of a product, you are interested in seeing how well a user can actually perform full-blown realistic tasks and in identifying specific usability deficiencies that are present.

OVERVIEW OF THE METHODOLOGY

Often referred to as an information-gathering test, the methodology for an assessment test is a cross between the informal exploration of the exploratory test and the more tightly controlled measurement of the validation test. Unlike the exploratory test,

- The user will always *perform* tasks rather than simply walking through and commenting upon screens, pages, and so on.
- The test monitor will lessen his or her interaction with the participant since there is less emphasis on thought processes and more on actual behaviors.
- Quantitative measures will be collected.

VALIDATION TEST

WHEN

The validation test, also referred to as the verification test, is usually conducted late in the development cycle and, as the name suggests, is intended to certify the product's usability. Unlike the first two tests, which take place in the middle of a very active and ongoing design cycle, the validation test typically takes place much closer to the release of the product.

OBJECTIVE

The objective of the validation test is to evaluate how the product compares to some predetermined usability standard or benchmark, either a project-related performance standard, an internal company or historical standard, or even a competitor's standard of performance. The intent is to establish that the product meets such a standard prior to release, and if it does not, to establish the reason(s) why. The standards usually originate from the usability objectives developed early in the project. These in turn come from previous usability tests, marketing surveys, interviews with users, or simply educated guesses by the development team.

Usability objectives are typically stated in terms of performance criteria, such as speed and accuracy; how well and how fast the user can perform various tasks and operations. Or the objectives can be stated in terms of preference criteria, such as achieving a particular ranking or rating from users.

It only makes sense then that the validation test itself can be used to *initiate* standards within the company for future products. For example, if one establishes that a setup procedure for a software package works well and can be conducted within 15 minutes with no more than one error, it is important that future releases of the product perform to that standard or better. Products can then be designed with this benchmark as a target, so that usability does not degrade as more functions are added to future releases.

Another major objective of the validation test is to evaluate, sometimes for the first time, how all the components of a product work together, for example, how documentation, help, and software/hardware are integrated with each other. The importance of an integrated validation test cannot be overstated. Since components are often developed in relative isolation from each other, it is not unusual that they do not work well together. It behooves an organization to discover this prior to release, since, from the user's viewpoint, it is all one product and it is expected to perform that way.

Still another objective of the validation test, or really any test conducted very late in the development cycle, has become known in the trade as "disaster or catastrophe insurance." At this late stage, management is most concerned with the risk of placing a new product into the marketplace that contains major flaws or that might require recall. If such a flaw is discovered, slipping the schedule may be preferable to recalling the product or having to send out "fixes" to every user. Even if there is no time to make changes before release, you are always at an advantage if you can anticipate a major deficiency in the product. There will be time to prepare a solution, train the support team, and even prepare public-relation responses. Even so, with all these advantages, there are companies that would rather not know about problems that exist in a product.

OVERVIEW OF THE METHODOLOGY

The validation test is conducted in similar fashion to the assessment test with three major exceptions.

- Prior to the test, benchmarks or standards for the tasks of the test are either developed or identified.

- Participants are given tasks to perform with either very little or no interaction with a test monitor.
- The collection of quantitative data is the central focus, although reasons for substandard performance are identified.

Since you are measuring user performance against a standard, you also need to determine beforehand how adherence to the standard will be measured, and what actions will be taken if the product does not meet its standards.

For example, if the standard for a task addresses "time to complete," must 70 percent of participants meet the standard, or will you simply compare the standard to the average score of all participants? Under what conditions will the product's schedule be postponed? Will there be time to retest those tasks that did not meet the standard? These are all questions that should be addressed and resolved *prior* to the test.

Compared to an assessment test, a validation test requires more emphasis on experimental rigor and consistency, since you are making important quantitative judgments about the product. Make sure that members of the design team have input and buy-in into developing the standards used during the test. That way they will not feel as if the standards were overly difficult or unattainable.

COMPARISON TEST

WHEN

The comparison test is not associated with any specific point in the product development life cycle. In the early stages, it can be used to compare several radically different interface styles via an exploratory test, to see which has the greatest potential with the proposed target population. Toward the middle of the life cycle, a comparison test can be used to measure the effectiveness of a single element, such as whether pictorial buttons or textual buttons are preferred by users. Toward the end of the life cycle, a comparison test can be used to see how the released product stacks up against a competitor's product.

OBJECTIVE

The comparison test is the fourth type of test and can be used in conjunction with any of the other three tests. It is used to compare two or more alternative designs, such as two different interface styles, or the current design of a manual with a proposed new design, or to compare your product with a competitor's. The comparison test is typically used to establish which design is easier to use or learn, or to better understand the advantages and disadvantages of different designs.

OVERVIEW OF THE METHODOLOGY

The basic methodology involves the side-by-side comparison of two or more alternative designs. Performance data and preference data are collected for each alternative, and the results are compared. The comparison test can be conducted informally as an exploratory test, or it can be conducted as a tightly controlled classical experiment, with one group of participants serving as a control group and the other as the experimental group. The form used is dependent on your goals in testing. If conducted as a true experiment, designed to acquire statistically valid results, the alternatives should vary along a single dimension, such as the way in which help is implemented, and the expected results of the test should be formulated as a hypothesis.

If conducted less formally as a more observational, qualitative study, the alternatives may vary on many dimensions. One needs to ascertain why one alternative is favored over another, and which aspects of each design are favorable and unfavorable. Invariably, when comparing one or more alternatives in this fashion, one discovers that there is no "winning" design per se. *Rather, the best design turns out to be a combination of the alternatives, with the best aspects of each design used to form a hybrid design.* I do not know why, but invariably this turns out to be the case.

For exploratory comparison tests, experience has shown me that the best results and the most creative solutions are obtained by including wildly differing alternatives, rather than very similar alternatives. This seems to work for several reasons:

1. **The design team is forced to stretch its conceptions of what will work rather than just continuing along in a predictable pattern.** With the necessity for developing very different alternatives, the design team is forced to move away from predictable ways of thinking about the problem. Typically, this involves revisiting fundamental premises about an interface or documentation format that have been around for years. The result is often a design that redefines and improves the product in fundamental ways.

2. **During the test, the participant is forced to really consider and contemplate why one design is better and which aspects make it so.** It is easier to compare alternatives that are very similar, but harder to compare very different ones. Why? Similar alternatives share the same framework and conceptual model, with only the lower-level operations working differently. Very different alternatives, however, are often based on different conceptual models of how each

works, and may challenge the user, especially one experienced with the product, to take stock of how the tasks are actually performed.

HYPOTHETICAL CASE STUDY USING THE FOUR TESTS

Now, having reviewed the basics of each type of test, let us explore how a series of tests might in fact work. Let's suppose that your company is developing a software product and its associated documentation, and that you intend to conduct three usability tests at three different times in the product develop-ment life cycle. Following is a hypothetical series of tests on this product throughout the life cycle, complete with hypothetical outcomes at the end of each test. Understand that I have greatly simplified the details in order to provide an overview of iterative design in action.

TEST 1: EXPLORATORY / COMPARISON TEST

THE SITUATION. Two early prototypes of the software interface have been developed (see Figures 2.5 and 2.6). The interfaces are both graphical-user interfaces (GUIs), although considerably different from each other.

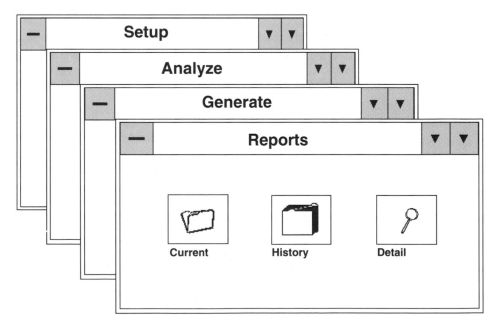

Figure 2.5   Card-Stack Interface

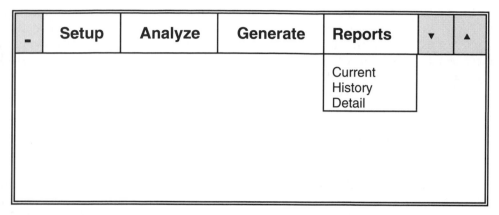

Figure 2.6 Pull-Down Menu Interface

The prototypes have very limited working functionality (e.g., about 30 to 40 percent of the proposed functions work). There is no documentation, but a technical expert will be available during the test to reveal limited but crucial information needed to use the product. (See the gradual disclosure technique in Chapter 8 for an explanation of how to use a technical expert in this way.) Primitive help, available on paper only, will be provided to the participant on demand; that is, when the participant chooses "help," the test monitor will provide the help text on paper as it would appear on the screen.

MAIN TEST OBJECTIVES

1. Which of the two interface styles/concepts is closest to the conceptual model of the proposed target population? In which is the user better able to remain oriented within the program?
2. What are the best and worst features of each approach?
3. What are the main stumbling blocks for the user?
4. After some period of initial learning, which style has the greatest potential for the power user?
5. For which tasks is help required?
6. What types of written information will be required?

   - Type of Prerequisite Information
   - Theoretical Information
   - Procedural Information
   - Examples
   - Training

BRIEF SUMMARY OF OUTCOME. The test was conducted. As is typical of comparison tests at this point, there was no "winner" per se. Rather, the result was an interface with the best attributes of both prototypes. The top-level screen will be the classic pull-down menu. However, the card stack will be used to represent underlying functions as appropriate. This interface will provide the most effective balance between ease of learning for a novice and ease of use by a power user.

For the targeted user, prerequisite and theoretical information in the user's particular discipline is required, rather than in the product's operations. Essentially, the users knew less about their area of expertise than the designers assumed. The documentation set will include, at minimum, a setup guide, some self-paced training on interface operations, and a procedural user guide arranged by everyday tasks and more advanced, less frequent tasks.

TEST 2: ASSESSMENT TEST

THE SITUATION. Two months have passed. A single prototype has now been expanded to approximately 60 to 80 percent of its eventual functionality. There are linked comprehensive help screens for working functions. A first draft, of simplified documentation, on 8 1/2" by 11" bond paper is available for the test, with a table of contents, but no index.

MAIN TEST OBJECTIVES

1. Confirm the findings of the original test as to the match of interface operations and the user's conceptual model.
2. Expose all major usability deficiencies and their causes for the most common tasks.
3. Determine if there is a seamless connection of software, help, and documentation. Can users move easily between the three elements? Are users more likely to access help or written documentation when confronted with difficulties?
4. Is the documentation being utilized as designed? Is it accessible? Are graphics understood and at the appropriate level of detail? Are certain sections not read at all? Are additional sections required? Is all terminology clear? Are there areas that require more explanation?
5. Is the help utilized as designed? Are all terms understood? Is it accessed without prompting? Is the level of detail appropriate? Are there difficulties in navigation, entry, or exit?

BRIEF SUMMARY OF TEST OUTCOME. Many difficulties in operations were identified, but the users' conceptual model of the product matched that employed by the design team for the product's interface operations. Essentially, the high-level interface "works," and the lower-level details remain to be implemented and refined. The help system worked when accessed, but users rarely invoked it unless prompted. There was a strong preference to use written documentation for this particular user audience. The organization of the documentation needs to be extensively revamped and made more task-oriented. Even more theoretical information needs to be included as the end users knew even less about their fields of expertise than was expected. This last issue turned out to be very controversial, as designers felt it was not their responsibility to teach users to do their jobs. It is possible that an entirely new section of the manual, or even a primer for users, may be required.

TEST 3: VERIFICATION TEST

THE SITUATION. Six months have passed. For this last test, a fully functional product with comprehensive linked help screens has been prepared. All sections of the documentation have been through one draft, with half of the sections undergoing a second draft. The documentation has a rough index for the test. A small primer for users about the actual subject matter was developed. For the major tasks of the product, specified measurable time and accuracy criteria have been developed. For example, one criterion reads:

Using the quick setup guide, a user will be able to correctly install and perform the check-out procedure within 20 minutes, with no more than two attempts required.

Unbelievably, and for only the first time in the recorded history of software development, there actually *will* be time to make minor modifications before release.

TEST OBJECTIVES:

1. Verify that 70 percent of participants can meet established criteria for each major task scenario. (The 70 percent benchmark is arbitrary, and is something that I have personally evolved toward over time. It provides a reasonably challenging test while still leaving the design team some work to do before product release to move that number toward a more acceptable and traditional 95 percent benchmark. A benchmark of 100 percent is simply not realistic except for tasks involving danger or damage to the system, and should never be used lightly. Achieving 100 percent performance has been shown to cost as much as 50 times the cost of achieving 95 percent performance. Therefore, only use the higher benchmark if you are willing to pay the piper.)

2. Identify any tasks and areas of the product that risk dire consequences (e.g., are unusable, contain destructive bugs) if the product is released as is.

3. Identify all usability deficiencies and sources of the problem. Determine which deficiencies must be repaired before release and which, if there is not time within the schedule, can be implemented in the next release.

BRIEF SUMMARY OF TEST OUTCOME. Every major task passed the 70 percent usability criteria with the exception of two. The team felt that the problems associated with those tasks could be corrected prior to release, and wanted to schedule a very quick test to confirm. A bug was found that destroyed previous files under certain conditions, but designers felt that a work-around could be put in place without slipping the schedule. Twenty recommendations from the test were identified for implementation prior to release, and at least fifteen recommendations were diverted to future releases.

Providing a primer prior to the test proved to be a stroke of genius. Participants loved it, and some even insisted on taking it back to their current jobs. One user suggested the company market the primer as a separate document for customers, and that is already in the works.

The revamped organization of the user guide was much more in tune with users' expectations than the previous one, although the index proved difficult to use. More task-oriented items must be added to the index to improve accessibility.

CONCLUSION

As you can tell from this condensed series of tests, the product evolved over time and reflected each test's findings. I strongly advocate such an iterative approach, but again, do not be discouraged if you can manage only one test to begin. Now let's discuss the details of the environment for conducting usability testing.

PART TWO

PREPARING FOR

USABILITY TESTING

SETTING UP

A TESTING

ENVIRONMENT

3

INTRODUCTION

For many of those contemplating the implementation of a usability testing program, the discipline has become synonymous with a high-powered, well-appointed, well-equipped, expensive laboratory. For some organizations, the usability lab (and by that I mean the physical plant) has become more prominent and more important than the testing process itself. Some organizations, in their zeal to impress customers and competitors alike with their commitment to usability, have created awe-inspiring palaces of high-tech wizardry *prior to laying the foundation for an ongoing testing program*. Not realizing that instituting a program of usability engineering requires a significant shift in the culture of the organization, these organizations have put the proverbial cart before the horse, in their attempt to create instant programs, rather than building programs over time.

This approach to usability testing is rather superficial and short-sighted, and has a high risk of failure. It approaches usability engineering as the latest fad to be embraced rather than as a program that requires effort, commitment, and time in order to have lasting effects on the organization and its products. I know of at least two organizations with newly built, sophisticated usability laboratories that unfortunately are now operating as the world's most elaborate storage rooms. (An analogy is a retail store that acquires and outfits a new store for business, only to realize that it does not have any interested customers.) Having succumbed to the misperception that equates the laboratory with the process itself, these organizations have discovered only too late that usability testing is much more than a collection of cameras and recorders. Rather, a commitment to usability must be embedded in the very philosophy and under-pinning of the organization itself in order to guarantee success.

In that vein, if you have been charged with developing a testing program and have been funded to build an elaborate testing lab as the *initial* step, resist the temptation to accept the offer. Rather, start small and build the organization from the ground up instead of from the top down. I will present some suggestions for how you go about that in Chapter 11.

Regardless of whether you will be initiating a large testing program or simply testing your own product, you need *not* have an elaborate, expensive lab to achieve your goals. In fact, starting small forces you to focus on all the other factors that make for a successful program.

SETTING UP THE TESTING AREA

In this chapter I describe five different testing setups/environments. They range from extremely simple, low-cost setups to more sophisticated expensive ones. Each setup has advantages and disadvantages, and each lends itself to a particular style or philosophy of testing, as well as to the degree of testing sophistication within the organization. Since this is a book for "beginners," I will recommend what I feel is the setup that provides the best value (e.g., objectives vs. cost) for a start-up testing enterprise.

SIMPLE SINGLE-ROOM SETUP

DESCRIPTION. The simple single-room setup, shown in Figure 3.1, is the most basic type of testing setup, both in terms of resources and the amount of space required. It represents the minimum environment required for testing that can accommodate observers; essentially a quiet secluded room. Within the room, the test monitor is located about four to six feet from the participant at about a 45 degree angle. As you can see from Figure 3.1, the idea is for the test monitor to be close but *not too close*. It is important to remain within the peripheral

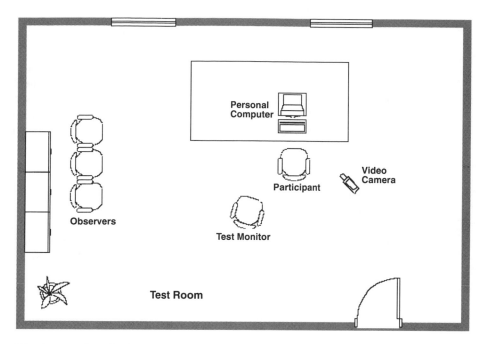

Figure 3.1   Simple Single-Room Setup

vision of the participant, so that the participant can sense where you are at all times, but not so close that your presence is distracting or anxiety-provoking.

The main concern with this type of positioning is that the test monitor might inadvertently bias the participant through subtle (or not so subtle) nonverbal cues. However, if such biasing can be minimized, there are real advantages to being close to the participant, and for very interactive testing, such as exploratory testing, this degree of intimacy is required.

ADVANTAGES

1. **The test monitor has an excellent sense of what is going on with the participant.** Not only can you read the typical verbal cues, but you have a much better sense of the participant's nonverbal cues and mannerisms, such as a slight frown or raising of the eyebrows. You can see exactly what the participant is doing down to small mannerisms and subtle changes in body language.

2. **During early phase exploratory tests, where much interaction is desired to interrogate the participant during the test, this position accentuates a sense of teamwork.** At this early stage of the life cycle, the participant is almost a partner who is helping to design the product or documentation. In fact, during

an exploratory test, you and the participant would be right next to each other, as shown previously in Figure 2.2.

3. **For difficult tests, where the participant has to struggle with the material, it enables you to encourage and overcome the participant's self-consciousness.** The participant does not feel nearly as alone or "on the hot-seat," as he or she would feel without you present in the test room. It is also more natural on the part of the participant to think aloud when the test monitor is in the test room.

DISADVANTAGES

1. **The test monitor's behavior can affect the behavior of the participant.** If you are not mindful of your speech, mannerisms, and so on, you will inadvertently and subtly react to what the participant is doing. Even if you do not make any outward remarks, the participant may pick up a sigh or a shift in your posture in response to what he or she is doing. That in turn can cause the participant to veer off from the direction in which he or she was going or look to another page. It is especially crucial to avoid making written notes when it appears the participant has finished a task. This can cue the participant that he or she has finished a task successfully even if the participant is not sure.

2. **There is very limited space for observers.** Obviously, the number of observers who can view the testing is dictated by the size of the room. If the room is really small, you probably would want to exclude observers entirely or include only one. It is never a good idea to crowd many observers around a single participant, as it can be very intimidating. Also, it is much harder for you as the test monitor to control the behavior of observers when they are so close to the proceedings.

MODIFIED SINGLE-ROOM SETUP

DESCRIPTION. This setup (Fig. 3.2) enables you to use a room large enough to position yourself at a workstation behind or to the side of the participant without impinging on the participant's "space." You view the proceedings via a TV monitor on your desk. This monitor is fed by the signal from a video camera that is focused on the participant's work area. Positioned at a desk outside of the line of sight of the participant, you are free to use a software data collection program running on a desktop computer. As with the previous setup, the accommodation of additional observers is dictated by the size of the room.

ADVANTAGES

1. **The test monitor is more free to move about, take notes, use data logging software while the test is going on, and yet is still within visual proximity of the participant.** Being somewhat removed from the participant, you need not

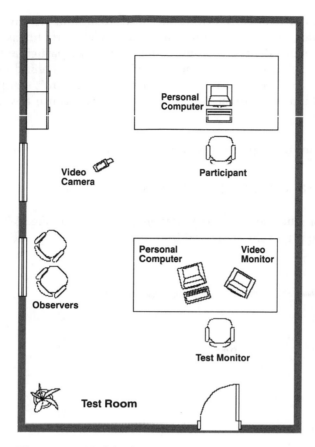

Figure 3.2 Modified Single-Room Setup

be as concerned about controlling body language, mannerisms, and so forth. In addition, you may use a computer without distracting the participant.

2. **The participant does not have a complete sense of isolation, since the participant is still in the room with the test monitor.**

3. **This setup is also more likely to encourage the participant to think aloud, than if left alone in the test room.**

DISADVANTAGES

1. **Loss of proximity to the participant limits what the test monitor can see directly of the proceedings.** It is possible to miss subtle behaviors. It is crucial to have a good angle via the video camera on what the participant is seeing and doing, since you may be blocked from seeing directly.

2. **If the test monitor is directly behind the participant and within ten feet or so, the test monitor could make the participant feel very uneasy and overly self-conscious, since the test monitor is not within the participant's peripheral vision.** The guideline here is to remember when you are behind the participant but within ten feet, you must stay within the participant's peripheral vision. Further back than approximately ten feet should not cause any discomfort to the participant.

3. **As with the simple single-room setup, there is limited space for observers.**

ELECTRONIC OBSERVATION ROOM SETUP

DESCRIPTION. The electronic observation room setup (Fig. 3.3) enables the observers to be physically separated from the testing activities. From a separate

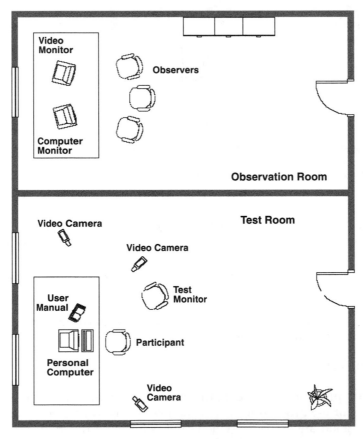

Figure 3.3   Electronic Observation Room Setup

observation room, they are able to watch but not communicate directly with the test monitor. The signal from the video camera(s) as well as the CRT image (if the test involves software) are both directed to video monitor(s) in the observation room. The room could be in a completely different part of the building or adjacent to the testing area. Audio is also piped in to the observation room, but there is no reciprocal communication going to the test area. Any communication between the test monitor and observers must occur either face to face, via notes, or in some cases via an earplug that the test monitor wears.

ADVANTAGES

1. **All the advantages of the simple single-room setup also accrue to this setup.**

2. **Observers get to view the test as much as they like without having to worry about interfering.** They are free to come and go as they please without distracting anyone. This is especially crucial for very lengthy tests, where observers may be interested only in certain portions. More important, they are able to talk among themselves, discussing test observations and even thinking ahead to possible remedies.

DISADVANTAGES

1. **As with the simple single-room setup, the test monitor's behavior can adversely affect the test.**

2. **Unless you have a permanent setup, you will need to tie up two conference rooms for up to a week.**

CLASSIC TESTING LABORATORY SETUP

DESCRIPTION. This setup (Fig. 3.4) consists of one room designated as the testing room and a second room designated as an observation and control room. The only individual inside the testing room is the participant. All other test personnel, including the test monitor, observers, camera operator, etc., are stationed inside the control room viewing the proceedings through a one-way mirror. All communication between the test monitor and participant occurs through an intercom and speaker arrangement, and, in the more elaborate laboratories, the test is extensively monitored with multiple video cameras, audio tape recorders, data loggers, and other modern electronic equipment. However, as an alternative, depending on the type of test, the test monitor could also be in the test room with the participant.

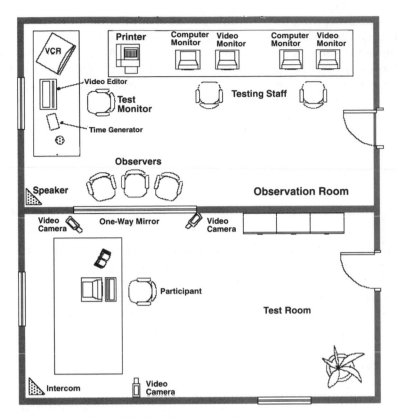

Figure 3.4   Classic Testing Laboratory Setup

This setup requires a large capital outlay and commitment to testing by management. However, if you are interested in trying out such a setup for a test that you are conducting, you may do so for a modest rental fee. Simply locate a marketing firm in your area (there are many throughout the country) that uses this type of facility to conduct focus groups and other marketing research. A marketing firm would be more than happy to rent you the space including all equipment for a per-diem rate. You could also use its personnel to recruit participants at the same time.

ADVANTAGES

1. **It allows unparalleled unobtrusive data collection.** Since the test monitor is not in the room, this eliminates almost entirely any possible biasing effects due to inadvertent non-verbal communications or mannerisms.

2. **Being in a soundproof room, the testing staff and observers can easily communicate among themselves about the proceedings and discuss possible product improvements.**

3. **This environment can accommodate many observers viewing the test at one time.**

DISADVANTAGES

1. **Depending on the skill of the testing staff, the control room setup can create a very impersonal environment.** This is sometimes referred to as the "guinea pig" syndrome, with the participant feeling overly self-conscious during the test. (This effect can be exacerbated by the type of intercom system used, some of which make the test monitor's instructions sound like the "voice of God.") This self-consciousness is worse for less sophisticated (in terms of exposure to high-tech equipment) participants who are insecure about their abilities. The test monitor may need to mitigate the effects of this setup by staying in the room with a less sophisticated participant.

2. **Unless you have ideal camera placements, you may not be able to see exactly what the participant is viewing or experiencing.** For example, sometimes you may not be able to tell where in a document or on a screen a participant is looking unless there is a dedicated and well-placed camera. To compensate, you may need to utilize a "thinking aloud" protocol which may not fit in with your test design.

3. **For exploratory tests, the control room setup may offer little advantage to monitoring the test, since you will need to be next to the participant in any case.** However, for observers, it is still superior to the other types of setups.

MOBILE, OR TRAVELING, LAB

DESCRIPTION. The mobile lab setup has no room or rooms designated for testing. Rather, the testing equipment, such as cameras, PCs, and VCRs, is carted around to different available locations or sometimes even taken off site to actual customer sites. This is a very cost-effective way to begin a testing program if management has neither the inclination nor space to dedicate a permanent location for holding the tests. Eventually, some of the same equipment can be utilized when a permanent "home" is acquired.

Figure 3.5 lists the inventory for a mobile setup that was created at one organization that performed testing at both on-site and off-site locations [89]. The equipment that you choose to equip such a lab need not be the best equipment, but it should not be the cheapest equipment either. The equipment needs to be rugged and be able to sustain movement from location to location.

This list represents the basic equipment that you can use for setting up a mobile lab. The approximate cost for this setup ranges from $10,000 to $15,000, with prices dropping consistently from year to year. There are other components you

Equipment	Description
Hi8 Video Camera	The 8 millimeter camcorders now on the market are small, easily managed with excellent quality images.
Color Video Monitor (13" - 27") larger, if needed.	The video monitor is used to view the image that is projected from the camcorder. If viewing from an observation room, purchase one large enough to be seen by all in the room.
Hi8 Video Cassette Recorder/Player/Editor	This is the main component of the mobile lab. You can record, play, and edit from the same small package. You can edit from the source side and then use the edited version to make a copy to a VHS recorder for general distribution. The disadvantage is that the Hi8 video tape is fragile and can break or jam.
VHS Recorder/Player	This is used to record from the 8 or Hi8 format to VHS format for distribution.
Microflex Microphone	You should get either a table-mounted version with good omni directional pick up or a wireless version for a bit more money that does not need a wire to the camcorder.
Video Tripod	Used to hold the camcorder in place during filming.
Video Cart	To protect your investment and make it easier to transport the equipment, buy a decent video cart complete with powerstrip. Acquire one that locks securely.

Figure 3.5   Mobile Setup Equipment List

can add as you grow, such as additional video cameras, audio/video mixers, and so on, but the setup listed in Figure 3.5 will suffice quite nicely.

ADVANTAGES

1. **This is a very cost-effective solution since no costs are incurred for a physical location.**

2. **Since the equipment is portable, you are free to rent space near existing customers, such as a hotel conference room or a company sales office.** Essentially, you can bring the test to the field.

3. **Storing all equipment in a lockable cart decreases the probability of equipment becoming damaged or misplaced and makes it very easy to "set up" the test site in very little time.**

DISADVANTAGES

1. **Not having a permanent space means having to settle for whatever space is available.** This lends a very tentative "air" to the discipline of testing altogether.

2. **If you will be doing a lot of testing, moving around delicate equipment can play havoc on that equipment.** In addition, it requires you to retest the equipment before each test to ensure that it works.

SUMMARY

The electronic observation room setup shown in Figure 3.3 is the setup I recommend for organizations just beginning to test and for those with limited resources. It provides for the best tradeoff of test monitor access to the participants, accommodation of observers, and cost (since there is very little revision of the physical plant required). Since direct viewing of a test by observers is one of the great benefits of testing, this setup is strongly recommended for project teams that need to view the test. Electronic observation is almost as effective as one-way-mirror observation. The downside is the necessity to commandeer two rooms for up to a week. To mitigate this, look for rooms in your company that are not fully utilized such as training areas, labs, or two adjoining offices. Management will look favorably on such a situation, if it makes more efficient use of existing facilities.

Eventually, if your organization adopts a full-scale testing program, you will want to switch to a dedicated lab similar to the classic testing laboratory setup shown in Figure 3.4.

TESTING ROLES

WITH SPECIAL EMPHASIS

ON THE TEST MONITOR

4

INTRODUCTION

A professional testing staff consists of a group of people who are trained to plan, set up, conduct, analyze, and report the results of a usability test. Each member generally performs a variety of functions. This division of labor is intended to collect and record the greatest amount of information possible. However, since this book's focus is a fledgling organization or individual that will be conducting a test, many of the testing functions or roles described will be handled by just one or two individuals, not by an extensive team. Regardless of the size of your testing team, the roles that follow describe the main testing activities that need to be accomplished [65].

THE DIFFERENT TESTING ROLES

TEST MONITOR / ADMINISTRATOR

The test monitor is in charge of the actual test, and as such has primary responsibility for all that occurs. The test monitor oversees the testing team and works with the developers to design the test. The test monitor will, at minimum, greet, interact with, and debrief each participant, and take ultimate responsibility for compiling and communicating test results to the development team. Since this is such an important role and the person so designated will most likely perform the majority of testing activities in many organizations, an entire section is dedicated to the test monitor later in this chapter.

DATA LOGGER

A data logger classifies the expected critical activities and events of a test into coded categories. For example, if the participant is expected to access four screens during a test, each screen could be categorized with a different letter, A, B, C, or D. During the test, when the participant accesses a particular screen, the data logger need only record a letter for that action. At the same time the data logger could also note the time in order to cross-reference with the videotape record.

Before the test, the data logger assigns codes to expected activities of interest and makes sure that these actions are easily identifiable during the test. In the previous situation, the data logger would need to distinguish the different screens.

There are also data logging programs available to expedite this whole process and cross-reference to the videotape time automatically. Such a program is discussed in Chapter 7.

TIMERS

Timers are responsible for (you guessed it) keeping track of the beginning, ending, and elapsed time of test activities. Typically, the timing of each task will be recorded separately. This can be done in real time as the test proceeds, or after the fact by reviewing each videotape and noting the times. This function is often performed by the camera operator, especially if the camera setup is a simple one. I recommend that the test monitor *not* be the one who tracks the timings as it is very labor intensive and distracts one from capturing the *what* and *why* of the participant's activities.

VIDEO RECORDINGS OPERATOR

The video recordings operator is responsible for recording a permanent unbiased account of the entire test proceedings, including comments made by the participants, instructions given by the test monitor, and all interactions between the test monitor, participant, and the product being tested. This job is extremely critical for one main reason. Human memory is simply not a reliable substitute for a video or audio tape recording.

The video recordings operator's responsibilities include:

- Adjusting the equipment for optimum recording
- Testing the camera angles to ensure that the participant and product are clearly visible
- Ensuring that test materials have identifying characteristics (such as a tab) that are visible

During the test, the operator monitors the audio and video taping, zooming and focusing on the central activities as appropriate. It is important, therefore, that the operator have a sense of the flow and sequence of activities before the test begins. After the test, the operator is responsible for rewinding and clearly labeling the tapes, making copies as needed, and maintaining the tapes in a safe, secure environment. The operator would also take responsibility for editing the tapes after the test to show to developers, use in a presentation, and so on.

If you have limited resources, the responsibilities of the timer, data logger, and video recordings operator can all be assumed by one person.

PRODUCT / TECHNICAL EXPERT(S)

This is one or more individuals who know the technical aspects of the product being tested. Their role is to ensure that the product does not malfunction during the test. For example, if a system crashes and jeopardizes the test, someone needs to be available to restore it or provide a working backup. This is crucial if you are testing at an early stage of development when the product is temperamental and "buggy". You should have at least one product expert available at every test session to troubleshoot. If there is a group of people on the development team who can take on this role, it makes sense to coordinate their time so at least one is always present.

ADDITIONAL TESTING ROLES

Additional testing roles will depend on the nature of the test. One or more people might be needed to simulate different roles during the test, as part of the test design. You might need someone to staff a hotline in order to simulate "help" calls during the test. Or, you might need someone to mimic a mail delivery or a repair person sent out by the company.

TEST OBSERVERS

A test observer is not particularly a testing role per se. Rather, it refers to anyone else who attends a test, whether members of the development team, members of other projects, managers, or even members of other companies who are developing products that interact with yours. While not strictly a testing role, observation of the test by a variety of people helps the product and the organization immensely. The product benefits because the people responsible for product development get direct feedback. In addition, testing often brings a positive change in perspective toward user-centered design which can help the development of future products. All development team members should be encouraged to attend as many test sessions as possible.

ROLE OF THE TEST MONITOR

The role of the test monitor or test administrator is the most critical of all the test team members, presuming you even have the luxury of a test team. In fact, the monitor is the one team member that you absolutely must have in order to conduct the test. The monitor is ultimately responsible for all preparations including test materials, subject arrangements, and coordination of the efforts of other members of the test team.

During the test, the monitor is responsible for all aspects of administration including greeting the participant, collecting data, assisting and probing, and debriefing the participant. After the test, he or she needs to collate the day's data collection, meet with and debrief other team members, and ensure that the testing is tracking with the test objectives. If the usability test were an athletic contest, the monitor would be the captain of the team. As such, he or she has the potential to make or break the test. An ineffective monitor can seriously negate test results and even waste much of the preliminary preparation work. In this section I will discuss several alternatives for acquiring test monitors from inside and outside your organization, as well as the desired characteristics of an effective test monitor.

WHO SHOULD SERVE AS A TEST MONITOR?

One of the basic tenets of usability testing—and of this book—is that it is almost impossible to remain objective when conducting a usability test of your own product. There is simply too strong a tendency to lead participants in a direction that you wish the results to go, rather than acting as a neutral enabler of the process. This is even true for experienced test monitors who conduct the test from an external control room. In fact, asking someone to test his or her own product is like asking parents to objectively evaluate the abilities of their child. It is an impossible endeavor.

Having said that, let me add that having only yourself available to test your product should not prevent you from testing altogether. In almost every case, it is still better to test than not to test, even if you must do the testing yourself. However, for the long term, you would want to be out of the self-testing business as soon as possible.

WHO THEN SHOULD CONDUCT THE TEST?

Imagine that you want to conduct a test on a product for which you have primary responsibility, and if possible you would like someone less involved with the product to conduct the test. You can help develop the test materials, make arrangements, and select participants, but you need a more objective person to handle the actual test monitoring. Suppose also that your organization currently has no in-house testing staff and does not plan to introduce one shortly. To whom should you look for help?

The following sources represent a number of areas from which you can find candidates who possess the requisite skills to conduct a test, or who could head up the beginnings of an internal testing group. They may or may not already be working on your product.

HUMAN FACTORS SPECIALIST

A human factors specialist is the most likely candidate to conduct a usability test. This type of person typically has an advanced degree in psychology, industrial engineering, or similar discipline, and is familiar with experimental methodology and test rigor. Just as important, the human factors specialist is grounded in the basics of information processing, cognitive psychology, and other disciplines related to the development of usable products, systems, and support materials. This grounding is crucial in differentiating the important from the superficial usability factors in a product and ultimately in designing and conducting the test.

With the current focus on usability engineering and testing, it is highly probable that human factors specialists within your organization are already involved with testing in one form or another.

MARKETING SPECIALIST

A marketing specialist is typically customer-oriented, user-oriented, or both, has good interpersonal and communication skills, and would be very interested in improving the quality of products. This type of specialist may already be involved with your product, but usually not to the detailed level that would tend to disqualify him or her from conducting the testing.

TECHNICAL COMMUNICATOR

Technical communicators, including technical writers and training specialists, often make wonderful test monitors. Many technical communicators already serve as user advocates on projects, and their profession requires them to think as a user in order to design, write, and present effective support materials.

ROTATING TEAM MEMBERS

Let's suppose that no one from the disciplines listed previously is available to help on your project, and you are still determined not to test your own materials. Another alternative is to draw upon colleagues of similar disciplines, who are *not* working on the same product. An example of this approach is for technical communicators to test each other's manuals or for software engineers to test each other's program modules.

In such a scenario, the person whose product is being tested could help prepare many of the test materials and make the pretest arrangements, then turn over the actual monitoring of the test to a colleague. One of the advantages of this approach is that two (or more) heads are better than one, and it is always beneficial to have someone other than yourself help prepare the test. The person acting as the test monitor would need time to become familiar with the specific product being tested and to prepare to test it in addition to the time required to actually monitor the test.

Should you decide to implement this approach, you must plan ahead in order to build the test into your mutual schedules. You cannot expect your colleague to drop everything he or she is working on to help you. Of course, you would reciprocate and serve as test monitor for your colleague's product.

EXTERNAL CONSULTANT

Another option is to hire an external consultant. Many human factors, industrial design, market research, and usability engineering firms now offer usability testing as one of their services, including the use of their test laboratories. You may simply want to outsource the usability test to such a firm, or use such a firm to "kick off" a testing program in your organization.

Using an external consulting company guarantees the objectivity that testing requires. Even some organizations that employ internal human factors specialists to work on the design and development of products still outsource the testing work for the greater sense of impartiality it provides.

If you know your organization is committed to eventually forming a long-term testing program on site, then seek out a consulting company that will work with you to transfer the technology of testing into your organization. Even if you are unsure about the long-term prospects for testing in your company, it still might be easier to have outside help with an initial test. Just make sure that if you conduct the test off site, its location is physically close enough to allow development team members to attend the test sessions. Do not simply farm out the test to a remote location. Viewing tests in person is much more effective than watching a videotape, especially for those who are skeptical about the value of testing.

CHARACTERISTICS OF A GOOD TEST MONITOR

Regardless of who conducts the test, either yourself or internal or external staff, and regardless of the background of that person, there are several key characteristics that the most effective test monitors share. These key characteristics are listed and described in the paragraphs that follow. If you are personally considering taking on the role of test monitor in your organization, use these key characteristics as a checklist of the skills you need to acquire. If you are considering using either an internal person or hiring an external person to perform this role, use these key characteristics to help evaluate the person's capabilities.

GROUNDING IN THE BASICS OF USABILITY ENGINEERING

Grounding in the basics of human information processing, cognitive psychology, and user-centered design (essentially the domain of the human factors specialist) helps immensely because it enables the test monitor to sense, even before the test begins, which interactions, operations, messages, or instructions are liable to cause problems. Test monitors with this background have a knowledge of which problems can be generalized to the population at large and which are more trivial. This helps to ascertain when to probe further and what issues need to be explored thoroughly during the debriefing session. Additionally, this background can also prevent the need to test situations that are known to cause problems for users, such as the inappropriate use of color or the incorrect placing of a note in a manual. Lastly, a strong background in usability engineering helps the test monitor to focus on fixing the important issues after a test is complete.

QUICK LEARNER

An effective test monitor need not be expert in the intricacies of the specific product being tested. For example, if the product is a database management system, the monitor need not be an expert in database management. However, he or she must be able to absorb new concepts quickly and to integrate these concepts into his or her thinking and vocabulary. The monitor also needs to absorb all the peripheral issues surrounding a product, such as its positioning in the marketplace, competitors, and historical problems. During the test itself, the monitor must be able to understand the actions and comments of the participant quickly, as well as the implications behind those actions and comments. Being a quick learner enables the monitor to probe and question effectively.

INSTANT RAPPORT WITH PARTICIPANTS

Bringing in participants to evaluate your product is an auspicious and very opportune point in the development cycle that should not be squandered. If for some reason a participant is not at ease and is not able to function as he or she normally would, it represents a lost opportunity and potentially misleading results. If you are able to test only five participants, one uneasy participant represents a potential loss of 20 percent of your test data. The test monitor's ability to quickly size up each participant's personality, make friends, and put the person at ease is essential to getting the most from the testing process. Some participants need coddling, some need stroking, and some are businesslike and require a more formal approach. Whichever the case, the test monitor must make each person feel comfortable and secure.

EXCELLENT MEMORY

Some might believe that since usability test sessions are videotaped, the test monitor need not rely on memory for conducting and evaluating a test session. Actually, memory is called into play well before a test session has ended. Since a test session can be two to three hours or even longer, the test monitor needs to remember behaviors or comments that took place earlier in the session in order to cross-check and probe those behaviors later in the session. For example, a participant may attempt to perform the same task in two or three different ways, and the test monitor may want to probe to understand why the participant performed the task differently each time.

Memory is also required to recall the results of a test session after its completion. Since there is often very little time to devote to searching the videotapes after a test, except as insurance against missing some point entirely, the test monitor often must rely heavily on memory and notes.

GOOD LISTENER

Listening skills involve the test monitor's ability to hear with "new ears" during each session and to lay aside personal biases and strong opinions about what he or she is seeing and hearing. The test monitor needs to understand both the content and the implication of a participant's comments, as there are often mixed messages of all kinds during testing. The test monitor must pick up on the subtle nuances of speech and emphasis, as a participant's comments are often indirect and less than forthcoming. It is so important to understand the rationale behind the participant's behavior, because the rationale often signals whether a change in the product is required or not.

COMFORTABLE WITH AMBIGUITY

Usability is not a precise science consisting of formulas and black and white answers. Even if a usability test is conducted under the most rigorous conditions, which is atypical, you are still not assured that all of the results are valid and generalizable to your entire user population. Instead usability testing can often be an imprecise, ambiguous enterprise, with varying and sometimes conflicting observations, not surprising for any venture that has human beings as its focus. A test monitor, then, must understand and be comfortable with ambiguity.

For example, prior to testing you may think that there are only two ways to perform a particular task. During testing though, you discover that the participants have found *four other ways* to perform the same task. Or, you discover that you are no closer to a clear-cut resolution of a product's problems after a week of testing than you were before you began. Or, when testing multiple versions of a product, no clear winner emerges. The versions are all equally bad or, if you are lucky, equally good. These situations require patience, perseverance, and very often skill at negotiation. Without tolerance for ambiguity and the patience to persevere, the test monitor tends to rationalize and to blame the participants for making unplanned choices during the test.

FLEXIBILITY

Another related characteristic of an effective test monitor is flexibility, which has to do with knowing when to deviate from the test plan. There are times when a particular participant does not have the expected skills or simply views the task in a completely different way than was originally intended. I recall an instance when I was conducting a test when the entire high-level design of an interface became questionable after testing only two participants. I could see immediately that the premise for the design was flawed. At that time, I recommended that the company halt testing and go back to the drawing board. To continue ferreting out minor problems with the product would have been a waste of everyone's time. While this is an extreme case, the point is that one needs to be prepared for the unexpected, even if that has serious consequences.

LONG ATTENTION SPAN

Experienced test monitors share a secret: Usability testing can be tedious and boring. There are long stretches when seemingly nothing is happening, when participants are reading and absorbing, thinking, and sometimes just resting. The monitor cannot possess the type of personality that needs new stimulation every five to ten minutes. The monitor must be able to pay attention for long periods of time because there is no predicting when a gem of a discovery will arise during a test session. In addition, since the monitor may view up to 10, 15, or 20 sessions, all of which involve observing the same or similar tasks, the ability to stay focused is extremely vital.

EMPATHIC ''PEOPLE PERSON''

Participants will relate more readily to a test monitor who is an empathic individual. This may not be all that critical during the test session itself, especially if the session requires little probing or exploration on the part of the test monitor. However, empathy can play a major part during the debriefing session when the test monitor is trying to elicit a participant's innermost thoughts and feelings about the previous two hours of work. Participants will tend to hold back if they feel that the test monitor cannot relate to their particular situation, this being especially true if the session was unusually frustrating or difficult.

''BIG PICTURE'' THINKER

There is so much data collected during a usability test and there is so much data that *could* be collected during a test that it is very easy to lose sight of the forest for the trees. The test monitor must be able to weed out the significant from the insignificant, and this ability takes two concrete forms.

1. The ability to draw together all of the various inputs, comments, and data from a *single* test to form a cohesive picture of a participant's performance.
2. The ability to draw together the varied inputs from *different test sessions* and focus on the most important and critical findings.

It is very easy to get lost in the details and focus on trivial observations. It is also easy to be influenced by the last participant and forget all that has come before.

An effective test monitor, however, avoids these difficulties by staying focused on the big picture.

GOOD COMMUNICATOR

Good communication skills are essential in usability testing. The test monitor must communicate with individual members of the development team, participants, observers, and other individuals who may be helping to administer the test in one way or another. The test monitor must be skillful at persuading others to make changes that are in their best interest, and he or she must be able to explain the implications behind the test results. Good writing skills are also essential because the test report is often the sole means of communicating test results to those who did not attend the test sessions. The written report is also the important historical document that is relied upon months or years later to review or revisit the test results.

GOOD ORGANIZER AND COORDINATOR

A usability test is a project within a project. Even a simple test requires the management of an astonishing number of small details, events, and milestones. Ensuring that equipment is in running order, getting all participants to the site on time, and making sure that the product is ready for testing are ultimately the responsibility of the test monitor. In addition, the test monitor is the focal point for the other test team members, and must coordinate their activities as well as those of any outside consultants into a unified effort. Therefore, the test monitor should be a good organizer and coordinator.

TYPICAL TEST MONITOR PROBLEMS

Now that you have reviewed some of the important characteristics that a test monitor should possess, let's review some of the behaviors that test monitors should avoid. In this section I will cover the most common "errors" that test monitors make while conducting a test, many of which I have learned from experience. Consider it a list of "what not to do." Even experienced test monitors can benefit from taking a few moments just prior to testing to review this list. As with the previous list of characteristics, you can use this list to evaluate and improve your own performance or to evaluate the performance of someone you hire to conduct usability testing for you.

LEADING RATHER THAN ENABLING

Behavior that leads rather than enables is usually caused by the test monitor being too close to the product and unintentionally providing cues to the participant about correct performance. The test monitor's tone of voice, a nod of the head, cutting short tasks when the participant struggles, even the type of question the test monitor asks can all influence the participant and the test results. This potential problem is the main reason why professional testing is often conducted from a control room, although subtle hints are still possible even from there. To avoid the problem of leading rather than enabling, remember that you are there to collect data and to ensure that the test environment remains as neutral as possible.

TOO INVOLVED WITH THE ACT OF DATA COLLECTION

While the purpose of the test is to collect as much information as possible, the act of collecting that information should not interfere with direct observation of what is occurring. The test monitor needs to stay aware of what the participant is doing at all times, even if that means that every aspect of the participant's behavior is not written down. That's the purpose of videotaping the test, of developing coding categories, and of having others help with the more rote collection of such things as timings and number of references to an index. All of these aids help ensure that the test monitor does not become so engrossed in the collection process that he or she misses important behaviors.

ACTING TOO KNOWLEDGEABLE

This problem occurs when the test monitor and participant are in the same room during the test. Participants will tend to defer to the test monitor and ask many questions if they feel that the test monitor knows all the answers. Being too knowledgeable can also intimidate a participant who may be somewhat nervous and self-conscious about his or her abilities.

One simple way to counteract the problem of acting too knowledgeable is for the test monitor to "play dumb." That is, the test monitor downplays any knowledge of the product and takes on the role of a research technician who is simply collecting data. I have seen participants change their entire demeanor when it became clear that they were not going to receive any assistance from the test monitor. They began to try harder and to behave as if they were alone in their own home or office.

TOO RIGID WITH THE TEST PLAN

An experienced test monitor will know when to deviate from the test plan. It is important for the monitor to sense when the test design is not achieving its objectives and is not exposing the product's deficiencies to the fullest extent. At those times, it is up to the monitor to make the appropriate changes so that a participant's time and efforts are not wasted. Sometimes a participant with a different background than what was expected will appear. Sometimes the tasks are the wrong ones for addressing the problem statements. Whatever the case, it is up to the monitor to revise the plan accordingly.

NOT RELATING WELL TO EACH PARTICIPANT

Participants come in all shapes, sizes, and demeanors. Regardless of whether a particular participant is shy, arrogant, moody, intimidated, self-conscious, or whatever, the test monitor needs to adjust his or her style in order to allow the participant to be comfortable and at ease. The test monitor should not get involved with battling, belittling, or in any way making a participant feel like anything but a guest. As far as the test monitor is concerned, the participant is always right.

JUMPING TO CONCLUSIONS

Inexperienced test monitors tend to overreact to early results. This can cause other members of the test team to act on the data prematurely. It is up to the test monitor to maintain a cool, steady demeanor and remind everyone to avoid forming conclusions until all of the results are in. One of the reasons for testing multiple participants is just for that purpose: to get a rounded, comprehensive view of the product through the eyes of different types of people with different types of backgrounds. While it is important for the test monitor to pick up patterns in the behavior of participants as early as possible, this does not necessarily mean reacting to that behavior. Avoiding premature conclusions will help to keep members of the test team from making major product changes before all the data is in.

GETTING THE MOST OUT OF YOUR PARTICIPANTS

Now that you have reviewed some of the more notorious things that inhibit the testing process, let's explore some things that the test monitor can do to enhance the process. One of the best things a test monitor can do is to develop increased sensitivity to the plight of the participants. What does it feel like to be on the other side of the glass? Figure 4.1 shows a hypothetical example of one participant's point of view compiled from many of the participants I observed over the years. While it is written tongue in cheek, its point is not. Participants are often placed in awkward, stressful situations where they have little control over events. The more you put them at ease, the greater are your chances for accurate results that are applicable to real-world situations. I would also suggest becoming familiar with the portion of the Human Factor Society's Code of Ethics that refers to participants. It can be found in Appendix A.

A Day in the Life of the Participant

Well, today's the day. I received the confirmation letter yesterday and I'm supposed to report to some building over on 14th Street, some sort of research facility. I have to admit that I'm a little nervous about this. When I spoke to the woman on the phone, she asked me a whole lot of questions about my background and experience. She seemed particularly gleeful that I wasn't very competent using computers and equipment. I'm glad that she's so happy, but for me it's kind of a recurring problem.

I feel kind of intimidated when I have to use a computer. In fact almost any kind of electronic equipment sort of throws me for a loop. It's always been that way, ever since I can remember I seem to be all thumbs. And now she wants me to perform with some people watching me. Well, it's an easy 35 bucks, I guess, and seeing as how I don't really know these people it can't be too embarrassing.

So, I head over to the building where I'm supposed to report and a man meets me at the front door. He ushers me into this room, hands me a questionnaire, and begins asking me the same questions that I answered on the telephone. I guess they want to make sure I'm really not some kind of ringer. I'm starting to get that nervous feeling in the middle of my stomach. That same feeling I used to get when I took those exams in fifth grade with Mrs. Bealer. That kind of feeling that I'm going to be put on the spot and I'm not quite sure how this is going to pan out. My palms are really starting to sweat, and maybe I should have stayed home and painted the garage floor.

I'm probably being silly, so I complete the questionnaire and begin making small talk with some of the people in the room. I'm just starting to relax when I'm ushered into another room. The room is empty, and I begin to wonder where everybody is. I just assumed there would be a lot of people watching. The room is large, with a table, desk, computer, and a piece of equipment I've never seen before. I'm told to sit down. That's when somebody else comes into the room and begins to explain that I'll be working in this room by myself and some people on the other side of the glass will be watching me.

Now my palms really begin sweating. They can see me but I can't see them? This is definitely worse than with Mrs. Bealer. What if I can't do this? What if I totally bomb? What if I'm the first person that has ever tried this that can't use it? Oh boy, if one more person tells me "Remember, we're not testing you," I'm going to walk out. The next thing I know, they'll be telling me this is for my own good. Well, at least I still have my sense of humor and I'm $35.00 to the good.

Figure 4.1   A Day in the Life of the Participant

HANDLING FRUSTRATION

Keeping in mind that the participant may be very nervous is the first step. Skillfully working with the person's sense of frustration is the next step. There will be times when the participant becomes exceedingly frustrated during the course of a test. When you see that this is occurring, recognize this as a critical point which can be advantageous. Many test monitors, at the first sign of user frustration, will immediately tell the participant to give up and go on to the next task. They do this in order to avoid confrontation, keep things on an even keel, and maintain the participant's interest. However, since the frustration is usually related to a critical deficiency in the product, moving on too quickly misses an important opportunity. *The participant's behavior at this point can be more revealing than at any other time* and can help the test team to understand how the participant learns to use the product. It is important to encourage the participant to continue rather than cutting the task short too quickly. The trick is to find just that point when the participant is frustrated but is still willing to try.

Another reason for encouraging the participant to keep trying is to show designers and developers watching the usability test the dire consequences of certain difficulties experienced by participants. It is important to let them see just how painful and frustrating the process of using their product can be. Actually seeing the participant struggle and get very frustrated and observing the serious consequences firsthand will do more to convince a designer to revise a product than weeks of discussions and negotiations. Sometimes just that extra amount of human struggle will convince a product designer that a change is needed and that the product should not be released as is.

So how should you encourage the participant? One way is to empathize with the participant and provide an end goal or end time frame. For example, you might say, "I can sense you're getting frustrated, but this is a particularly crucial part of the software/documentation, would you please try a little bit longer?"

You might try stating that other participants in the past have also had their share of difficulty. While this runs the risk of slightly biasing the participant, you may lose the participant in any case, if he or she has already experienced great difficulty. You might say, "I see you're having a difficult time with this. This isn't the first time that I've seen someone experience some difficulty here. Would you please continue on for five more minutes?"

The most skilled test monitor can encourage a participant to work with a smile. Make it seem like you and the participant are in this together, and that what is happening in the test is not a reflection of the participant's abilities. Often times, the frustration level builds due to a sense of self-consciousness and a loss of self-esteem on the part of the participant. The test monitor can help immensely by deflecting the problem back to the product. For example, the test monitor might say, "Boy this sure is turning out to be a tough section. I really appreciate your efforts in trying to get through this." Don't be afraid to encourage the participant to verbalize what's happening. Very often, if a participant is allowed to vent while performing, frustration can be minimized. It is up to the test monitor to gauge that fine line between rescuing the participant too early and pushing him or her beyond the point at which continuing the test is no longer possible. Through practice and experience, one can find the middle road between pushing too hard and giving up too early in order to get the best results.

HOW TO IMPROVE YOUR TEST MONITORING SKILLS

Conducting a usability test is an extremely challenging and worthwhile endeavor on a variety of levels. On the most ordinary level, you are working very closely with people in an attempt to design a product for maximum utility and benefit. On a deeper level, it is a very profound experience that forces you to confront your own mind and its tendency to be biased, distracted, and flighty. Monitoring a test puts you on the spot and forces you to be extremely mindful and disciplined. You spend long periods of time maintaining concentration while observing people, all the time being as unobtrusive as possible. Speaking from my own experience, I have found it to be delightful, frustrating, boring, exhausting, and sometimes these feelings result from working with *just the first participant*.

If you are seriously considering acting as a test monitor on a regular basis in either some official or unofficial capacity, it can be a very rewarding and enlightening experience. Let's look at some ways for growing into this job.

LEARN THE BASIC PRINCIPLES OF HUMAN FACTORS / ERGONOMICS

Learn the basic principles of human information processing, experimental psychology, cognitive psychology, statistics, interface design, and usability engineering. Subscribe to and read the proceedings from the major societies (listed in Chapter 11). Attend seminars and study basic psychology courses. The University of Michigan has been hosting an excellent two-week "Introduction to Human Factors" program every summer for over 20 years. Other universities, such as Stevens Institute in New Jersey, offer certificate programs in human factors. Attend conferences hosted by professional societies, such as CHI, STC, and the Human Factors Society. (See Chapter 11 for additional suggestions.)

LEARN FROM WATCHING OTHERS

Watching other test monitors is a key to success. When you have an opportunity to watch an experienced test monitor at work, you get to see what works and what doesn't firsthand. If the opportunity presents itself, ask the test monitor why he or she uses a particular technique that caught your interest. Take notes about particular techniques and behaviors, and so forth, that seem particularly effective and try them out yourself. Again, do not let your concern for making mistakes prevent you from exploring new techniques.

WATCH YOURSELF ON TAPE

One of the benefits of taping your test sessions is that you have an ideal medium for reviewing your own performance. Take advantage of this technology by reviewing your sessions with the intent of improving your skills. Take notes on what you do well and on behaviors that need improvement. That way you will remember to work on those aspects the next time you monitor a test.

WORK WITH A MENTOR

Work closely with an experienced test monitor. Help the test monitor work on a test and have that monitor do the same for you. If it is a test with many participants, perhaps you can conduct some of the sessions. Have your mentor watch you and critique your performance. If you hire a consultant to help conduct a test, arrange for the consultant to work closely with you in a mentor/coaching relationship, so that you can learn faster than by just observing.

PRACTICE MONITORING

Start with the right attitude. Do not be a perfectionist. You are going to make mistakes, bias participants, reveal information you should not, and invent new ways to invalidate a test session's results. This is just par for the course. Usability testing has a twofold saving grace—testing multiple participants and iterative design. Testing multiple participants means that if you invalidate one session, there is always another opportunity to do it right. Iterative design also makes up for any mistakes you might make, because you have several chances throughout the product development life cycle to catch problems with the product. The important thing is not to get discouraged. Continue to practice, continue to learn, continue to improve. Even the most experienced test monitors make mistakes.

LEARN TO MEDITATE

Meditation practice, specifically the type of meditation that fosters mindfulness and awareness, can be a valuable aid in learning to see clearly and in observing subtle nuances in behavior. This type of discipline is based on the belief that to understand another's mind, you first have to master your own.

Meditation practice or mindfulness training involves setting aside a period of time to sit down on a cushion and practice a simple breathing technique, while at the same time acknowledging thoughts that arise and letting them be. Over time, the result of this practice is a very personal and heartfelt recognition of how everything we perceive is filtered and biased by our version of things. Through continual practice, one's thoughts become more transparent, which in turn frees one to perceive more clearly and directly [130] [133]. During a test session, this is exactly what an excellent test monitor attempts to do; observe the participant's behavior free from the tyranny of his or her own expectations and biases.

I am not suggesting that one take up meditation strictly to become a better test monitor; that would be missing the point. However, if you are already inclined toward a discipline to quiet the mind and gain a clearer perception, meditation practice is a natural complement to the testing discipline.

PRACTICE ''BARE ATTENTION''

"Bare attention" practice is an adjunct to meditation practice, except it is done within one's normal daily routine. Practicing "bare attention" can heighten your ability to concentrate during test sessions. To practice "bare attention," set aside a period of time (15–30 minutes is more than enough to begin) when you intentionally and very deliberately heighten your awareness of whatever you happen to be doing and of your surroundings. For example, if you are working at a computer, experience very deliberately the sense of your fingers hitting the keys, of your eyes looking from the paper to the screen, of your thought process. Notice when (and how often) your mind wanders from what you are doing, and when it does, gently bring it back to the present task at hand. The intent is to stay in the present moment 100 percent of the time. Try it sometime just to see how difficult it is. This practice, as with the previously described meditation practice, helps to foster mindfulness and awareness.

PART THREE

SIX STAGES OF

CONDUCTING A TEST

DEVELOPING

THE TEST

PLAN

5

INTRODUCTION

The test plan is the foundation for the entire test. It addresses the how, when, where, who, why, and what of your usability test. Under the sometimes unrelenting time pressure of project deadlines, there could be a tendency to forego writing a detailed test plan. Perhaps, feeling that you have a good idea of what you would like to test in your head, you decide not to bother writing it down. This informal approach is a mistake, and invariably will come back to haunt you. Following are some important reasons why it is necessary to develop a comprehensive test plan, as well as some ways to use it as a communication vehicle among the development team.

1. **It serves as the blueprint for the test.** Much as the blueprint for a house describes exactly what you will build, the test plan describes exactly how you will go about testing your product. Just as you would not want your building

contractor to "wing it" when building your house, so the exact same logic applies here. The test plan sets the stage for all that will follow. You do not want to have any loose ends just as you are about to test your first participant.

2. **It serves as the main communication vehicle among the main developer, the test monitor, and the rest of the development team.** The test plan is the document that all involved members of the development team as well as management (if it is interested and involved) should review in order to understand how the test will proceed and to see whether their particular needs are being met. Use it to get buy-in and feedback from other members to ensure that everyone agrees on what will transpire. Since projects are dynamic and change from day to day and from week to week, you do not want someone to say at the end of the test that his or her particular agenda was not addressed. Especially when your organization is first starting to test, everyone who is directly affected by the test results should review the test plan. This makes good business sense and political sense as well.

3. **It describes or implies required resources, both internal and external.** Once you delineate exactly what will happen and when, it is a much easier task to foretell what you will need to accomplish your test. Either directly or by implication, the test plan should communicate the resources that are required to complete the test successfully.

4. **It provides a focal point for the test and a milestone for the product being tested.** Without the test plan, details get fuzzy and ambiguous, especially under time pressure. The test plan forces you to approach the job of testing systematically, and it reminds the development team of the impending dates. Having said all that, it is perfectly acceptable and highly probable that the test plan will be developed in stages as you gradually understand more of the test objectives and talk to the people who will be involved. Projects are dynamic and the best laid plans will change as you begin to approach testing. By developing the test plan in stages, you can accommodate changes.

For example, as your time and resource constraints become clearer, your test may become less ambitious and simpler. Or, perhaps you will not be able to acquire as many qualified participants as you thought. Perhaps not all modules or sections of the document will be ready in time. Perhaps your test objectives are too imprecise and need to be simplified and focused. These are all real-world examples that force you to revise the test and the test plan.

A sound approach is to start writing the test plan as soon as you know you will be testing. Then, as the project proceeds, continue to refine it, get feedback, buy-in, and so forth. Of course, there is a limit to flexibility, so you need to set a reasonable deadline prior to the test *after which the test plan may not change*. Let that date serve as the point at which the product can no longer change until after the test. You may find that the test is the only concrete milestone at that point in time in the development cycle and, as such, serves an important function.

Once you reach the cutoff date, do all that you can to freeze the design of the product you will be testing. Additional revisions may invalidate the test design you have chosen, the questions you ask, even the way you collect data. If you are pressured to revise the test after the cutoff date, make sure everyone understands the risks involved. The test may be invalidated, and the product may not work properly with changes made so close to the test date.

Remember to keep the end user in mind as you develop the test plan. If you are very close to the project, there is a tendency to forget that you are not testing the product—you are testing its relationship to a human being with certain specific characteristics.

SUGGESTED FORMAT

Test plan formats will vary according to the type of test and the degree of formality required in your organization. However, following are the typical sections to include, along with a description of each one. At the end of this chapter is a sample test plan.

- Purpose
- Problem statement/test objectives
- User profile
- Method (test design)
- Task list
- Test environment/equipment
- Test monitor role
- Evaluation measures (data to be collected)
- Report contents and presentation

PURPOSE

Describe at a high level the reason for performing this test at this time. You need not provide the very specific objectives or problems to be explored here—rather, the major focus or impetus is the key point, often from the viewpoint of your organization. For example:

- Is the test attempting to resolve problems that have been discovered from the company's hotline?
- Have returned warranty cards of your product recently been directed toward one aspect of the product, an understanding of which needs clarification?
- Has a new policy recently been instituted stating that all products must be tested before release?
- Does management feel it is critical for the development team to see real customers at this time?

It is okay if the test purpose remains at a high level, since the problem statements will reduce the goal(s) into measurable statements. The important point is that the testing be tied to business goals within the organization and that testing be the most appropriate technique for addressing the problem or opportunity.

Following are some rather vague, inappropriate reasons for testing a product. These are rarely placed on paper, but are usually communicated via word of mouth. They are *not* sound reasons for testing, and invariably they often come back to sabotage the project.

- Everyone else has a testing program (everyone else has many things).
- The conference area used for testing is available the third week of the month (so is the cafeteria every evening).
- Lou just went to the latest CHI meeting and learned about this really neat testing technique (let Lou evaluate the technique's benefits to the organization first).
- You want to see if there is a need for this type of product in the marketplace (backwards logic; a focus group or survey is a more appropriate technique early on).

You might say to yourself, especially if you are eager to begin testing, "As long as we test, I don't care what the reasons are. We'll worry about the consequences later." And for the short term, there is no problem with any of the reasons stated previously. However, for the long term, if you want testing to become an integral part of the way your organization develops products, you must tie testing to the needs of the product and to the organization's overall business needs. Else, you run the risk of testing becoming one more fad, one more of the latest approaches that come and go with the seasons.

Following are some more rational reasons for holding a test that stand a better chance of resulting in a successful outcome and that pave the way for future tests.

- You want to understand whether both of your major customers can use the product equally well.

- You want to know whether or not the documentation is able to compensate for some acknowledged problems with the interface.

- You have received numerous complaints associated with using the control panel. You are interested in determining the exact nature of the problem and how you will fix it within your development budget for this year.

PROBLEM STATEMENTS / TEST OBJECTIVES

This section is the single most important one in the test plan, because it describes the issues and questions that need to be resolved and focuses the research, as well as the rest of the activities associated with planning, designing, and conducting the test. It is essential that the problem statement be as precise, accurate, clear, and measurable (or observable) as possible. Even when conducting exploratory testing in the early stages, which is typically less structured, you still need to accurately describe what you hope to learn.

Without a clear succinct problem statement(s), you might find yourself in the unenviable position of conducting a wonderful test that neglects to answer the key concern of developers on the project team. Or, you might find yourself with a test whose development bogs down in controversy because no one can agree on what to test. Speaking from my own experience, I have seen test preparations move in circles and the test itself result in controversy because the test objectives were never committed to paper.

Following are two examples of unfocused and vague problem statements.

EXAMPLE 1. *Is the current product usable?*

EXAMPLE 2. *Is the product ready for release or does it need more work?*

The difficulty with these statements is *not* that they do not make sense. Rather, they are incomplete and vague. They neither state nor imply how to measure or quantify the results. A test based on these statements will invariably bias the results favorably. Why? If those involved cannot agree on what problems or issues need to be resolved, how do you know when you have found one? Of course, in those circumstances, the tendency will be *not* to find any problems.

Figure 5.1 shows an example of several more appropriately focused problem statements for hardware, documentation, and software products. If you find that you are having unusual difficulty designing the test and/or appropriate measures, or deciding on the appropriate end users, or even designing the data

PRODUCT	PROBLEM STATEMENTS
Hardware	1. Is a one-line, 20-character display adequate to communicate all messages? 2. Are all buttons on the control panel able to be used correctly without documentation? 3. Will the end users use the shortcut keys or will they prefer the more intuitive but clearer scaling method? 4. Is there a need for the LCD arrow keys or can that space on the panel be used for another function?
Online and Written Documentation	1. Can end users install the software using the quick setup guide? 2. Is the on-line reference section adequate or will a written reference manual also be required? 3. Do the end users reference the on-line help during error conditions? 4. Once they reference help, is it adequate to correct errors? 5. Is the index being used as the main entrance into the user manual? 6. Do the three user groups vary in their desire to use hypertext help? 7. Do end users read the new "theory" section as requested?
Software	1. Are end users able to move freely between the two major modules? 2. Do novice end users inadvertently wander into the advanced features screen? 3. Is the response time a cause of user frustration or errors? 4. Is help easier to access via a "hot key" or via a mouse selection? 5. Do the screens reflect the end user's conceptual model?
General	1. What obstacles prevent completion of setup tasks? 2. Can end users perform common tasks within established benchmarks? 3. Does the product contain major usability flaws that prevent completion of the most common tasks? 4. Is the new release harder to use than its predecessor? 5. Is there an appropriate balance of ease of use and ease of learning?

Figure 5.1   Problem Statements

collection form, you might return to the problem statement to see if it is clear or needs further clarification.

The problem statement(s) should originate with discussions with the development team or with individual developers, technical writers, marketing personnel, and so on. Do not be surprised if they have difficulty in pinning down the test objectives and if they can communicate only the most general questions or objectives. This may be an indication that:

- They are not quite ready to test.
- They need a greater understanding and education of the goals, intent, and process of testing.
- They need help in formulating their objectives into statements that can be measured or observed. Do not be afraid to jump in and help.

USER PROFILE

This section of the test plan describes the end user(s) of the product/document that you will be testing. It is important to work closely with marketing to determine the target population. For detailed procedures on how to establish the user profile and acquire participants, see Chapter 6.

Figure 5.2 shows a sample user profile for a chemical analysis software product.

METHOD (TEST DESIGN)

This section of the test plan is a detailed description of how you are going to carry out the research with the participants, and how the test session will unfold. Essentially, it is a synopsis of your test design. It should provide an overview of each facet of the test from the time the participants arrive until the time they leave, in enough detail so that someone observing the test will know roughly what to expect. If you are questioning why this amount of detail is necessary in the test plan, the following reasons should satisfy your curiosity.

- It enables others to understand and visualize what will happen so that they can comment and make suggestions accordingly.
- It enables you as the test developer to focus on what has to be done and the types of materials that have to be developed prior to the participants arriving.
- It reveals the need to communicate your plans to additional resources whom you might have forgotten, such as a receptionist who will greet the participants in a corporate lobby when they first arrive.
- It allows multiple test monitors (if that is required by the test design) to conduct the test in as similar a manner to each other as possible.

Test design is one of the more highly specialized skills required of a usability professional, often requiring knowledge of experimental design and method and basic statistical analysis. Designing a test requires one to clearly identify and understand the test objectives, and then to select the test design that will effectively ferret out the answers to the questions posed. If the test design is flawed or if the test is carried out with little attention to experimental rigor,

Characteristic	Range	Frequency Distribution
General Computer Experience	None to two years	10% have never used computer. 35% have 1 year experience. 55% have 1+ years experience.
Education Level	High School	10% High School
	College	60% B.A.
	Graduate	20% Masters
	Post Graduate	10% Ph.D.
Age	18–55 Years	85% ages 25–50 15% other
Gender	Male/Female	85% Male
Learning Style Preference	Trial and error Consult with others Read documentation	Unknown
Education Major	Chemistry, Math, MBA, others	75% Chemistry 10% Math 5% MBA 10% other
Operating System Experience	DOS, UNIX	75% DOS 25% UNIX
Computer Interaction Experience	Graphical user Interface (GUI) DOS-based Command Line Fill-in fields	25% GUI 75% other

Figure 5.2   Sample User Profile

then the results will be suspect. Not only can this result in faulty recommendations, but it sabotages the progress of usability engineering per se within the organization. Therefore, for the first few times you conduct a test, get advice and feedback on your test design from someone more experienced than yourself.

SOME EXAMPLES OF TEST DESIGN. The test design is mainly predicated upon your test objectives; what you need to learn about the product and its audience. The design will be greatly affected by your resources, your constraints, and your creativity. Constraints are time, money, management backing, development team support, ability to acquire participants, and other real-world concerns. Following are several examples of test designs for some of the most common situations you will face. Following that, I will present some guidelines for ensuring experimental rigor.

The simplest test design, which is represented in Figure 5.3 for a software communications package, will consist of testing several different users, all from one type of user group (e.g., managers), and having them perform a series of representative tasks on different modules of a system.

INDEPENDENT GROUPS DESIGN. This is called an independent groups design since each module of the product is tested by a unique set of users. This design will require 12 participants and will mitigate the potential transfer of learning effects caused by doing one set of tasks prior to performing similar tasks. In other words, performing Module A may help one to perform Module B, and mask any usability problems associated with Module B. This design could also

Module A Setup	Module B Establishing Communication	Module C Creating and Editing Messages
Bob	Toni	Lucius
Mary	Pam	Alaya
Halice	Gene	Dustin
Bill	Lance	Mariel

Figure 5.3 Independent Groups Design

Module A	Module B	Module C
Bob	Bob	Bob
Mary	Mary	Mary
Joan	Joan	Joan
Bill	Bill	Bill

Figure 5.4   Within-Subjects Design

be used if the modules are extremely lengthy and there is a possibility that the participants may become fatigued.

WITHIN - SUBJECTS DESIGN. Perhaps though, testing 12 participants is simply out of the question. Instead of 12, you could get by with only 4 participants by having each one perform all three modules as shown in Figure 5.4.

This method is called a within-subjects design. However, you have the same problem of transfer of learning effects to consider. To mitigate these effects, you must use a technique called *counterbalancing*, whereby the order of tasks is either randomized or balanced out. By varying the order of the presentation of tasks, one can limit the effects of learning transfer.

In this case, you would vary the presentation order of modules as shown in Figure 5.5, with each participant performing modules in a different order. By randomizing the order of the modules, you minimize the transfer effects while requiring only four participants. However, there are still some issues to resolve. If the order of modules would normally be sequential in real life (e.g., the modules required to set up a piece of hardware), then you have an important decision. Is it more critical to provide a realistic task order for users and possibly mask some usability problems on later tasks, or is it more crucial to provide a random order of tasks (which is possible in the lab) and risk confusing and alienating the participant? I think most would argue that you should retain the sequential order. If you decide to do so, you will still need to address possible transfer effects, possibly by using prerequisite training to equalize participants' experience before performing. In addition, you may need to conduct each session with breaks to allow participants to rest.

Subject	Module Sequence
Bob	A, B, C
Mary	B, A, C
Joan	C, B, A
Bill	A, C, B

Figure 5.5 Randomized Order of Module Presentation

TESTING MULTIPLE PRODUCT VERSIONS. Now let's look at another common situation. Suppose that you want to compare two different versions of a product, Version A and Version B, to see which one shows more promise as your ultimate design. Additionally, you want to see whether performance varies for either of two groups, call them supervisors and technicians. This will result in a 2 × 2 matrix design as shown in Figure 5.6.

If you use an independent groups design whereby each cell is populated by a different set of participants, then this design will require 16 participants; four supervisors will use Version A and four technicians will use Version A, and so on. Suppose though that you only want to use eight participants. You could simply populate each cell with only two participants, but that is increasing the risk that the data for any one group will be meaningless. Instead, let each person in the two groups, supervisors and technicians, try each of the versions, one after the other. As with the previous example, there may be an unfair advantage for the version that is tested last, since the participant may learn to perform the tasks while using the first version. On the other hand, it may even

Group	Version A	Version B
Supervisors	4	4
Technicians	4	4

Figure 5.6 2 × 2 Matrix

Supervisors	Module	Technicians	Module
Lou	A, B	Howard	A, B
Tracie	B, A	Susan	B, A
Ellen	A, B	Steve	A, B
Dean	B, A	Roberta	B, A

Figure 5.7   Example of Counterbalancing the Order of Presentation

reverse the effect; the participant may learn the first version and have difficulty adapting to the second version because it is so different. In either case, your results may be biased.

To account for these potential differences, you will again counterbalance the order of presentation of the versions. As shown in Figure 5.7, for eight participants, some participants will do Version A first, and others will do Version B first. Note that each version is performed as many times in the first position as it is in the last position, which negates the potential biasing effects.

TESTING MULTIPLE USER GROUPS. Now let's look at a slightly more complex, yet realistic scenario. Suppose your user profile consists of two different user groups, managers and clerks, who will be using your product. One of your test objectives is to see if there are differences in their ability to use the product. In addition, you also want to see if there are differences in novice and experienced users within each group. You will therefore need to vary experience and job type, each of which will have two levels. Once again, you will use a matrix design, as shown in Figure 5.8.

Group	Novice	Experienced
Managers	4	4
Clerks	4	4

Figure 5.8   2 × 2 Matrix

Each one of the four conditions or "cells" shown in Figure 5.8 will be populated with a different set of participants. If you want to acquire at least four participants per cell, as shown, you will need a total of 16 participants. If this is too many participants for your budget and time, (and is also the bare minimum required to evaluate group differences), then you *cannot* simply apply a within-subjects design. Instead, you will either have to limit each cell to fewer participants or simplify the study. Remember, limiting a cell to less than four participants severely limits the conclusions you can make about each group. You will probably need to simplify the research to exclude a study of group differences.

GUIDELINES FOR ENSURING EXPERIMENTAL RIGOR. The other aspect of establishing the method is designing and conducting the test to ensure experimental rigor. Following are some guidelines for ensuring that your study is not compromised through lack of rigor.

EMPLOY AN ADEQUATE NUMBER OF PARTICIPANTS. When it comes to selecting the number of participants to employ for a test, the overriding guideline is "You cannot have too many participants." For achieving statistically valid results, small sample sizes lack the statistical power to identify significant differences between groups. For a true experimental design, a minimum of 10 to 12 participants per condition must be utilized [124].

However, for the purpose of conducting a less formal usability test, recent research has shown that four to five participants will expose 80 percent of the usability deficiencies of a product, and that this 80 percent will represent most of the major problems [138]. Of course, if you have the time and resources to study more than four or five participants, by all means do so. It is possible that the additional 20 percent of deficiencies you might find could be important for your product.

Recently, I conducted a test that held true to the preceding principle. We tested eight participants and discovered about 80 percent of the problems within the first four participants. However, participant 8, our last one, performed a particularly grievous error on one task that would have required a service call for the product. This would never have been uncovered had we only tested four participants. Until you become experienced at testing, employing more participants decreases the probability you will miss an important problem, while providing additional opportunities to practice your monitoring skills.

BE CONSISTENT. Consistency is the underlying theme behind experimental rigor. It is important to conduct tests in as identical a way as possible from session to session, so that each participant works with the same materials in the same way under the same conditions. How can you help to ensure that this happens? Here are a number of ways.

1. Use scripts.

   Whenever it is necessary to provide instructions to the participant, read them off of a test script verbatim. This prevents you from adding any new information, omitting information, or providing your own personal twist to the subject matter.

2. Use checklists.

   Testing is composed of a wealth of details, and it is very easy to forget one of them during the often frenetic time of running a test. By using checklists, you ensure that you do not miss any activities or instructions and that all participants are performing the same activities.

3. Have the same person, if possible, conduct all test sessions.

   Obviously, if you are conducting lengthy sessions over a long period of time, this may be impossible. That is where the scripts and written procedures come into play.

CONFIRM THE CHARACTERISTICS OF YOUR PARTICIPANTS. Do not just trust that the right people showed up. Have them fill out a background questionnaire and look it over to make sure that the people with the correct characteristics will be participating. If not, you have an important decision to make: to either send them home or to use them and make a note that they were not the right people. This decision is often a difficult one depending on many circumstances, such as time frame, relationship with the participants, or relationship with a procurement agency.

NOTE ANY UNUSUAL PROBLEMS WITH THE TEST. Invariably, something is going to go wrong or some event will occur that may skew the results of one particular test session. If that is the case, simply note what occurred and decide later whether that disqualifies the participant's results from being part of the overall test results.

In addition, make minimal changes to the products and test materials between sessions. However, there is an exception to this rule of minimal changes when conducting "fast iteration" exploratory tests. During such a study, you test, make changes to the product in between sessions, and then retest. For the "fast iteration" test, you may test as many as 10 or more participants and change the product three to four times in the course of a week.

If you find you are having problems during a test, do all you can to shield the participant from whatever event is occurring. For example, if you need to make repairs to a product in the middle of a session, usher the participant out to a waiting area so that he or she is not exposed to information that other participants have not seen.

HAVE SPECIFIC GOALS OR OBJECTIVES IN MIND. Testing should not just simply be a fishing expedition. It is important that you search for specific deficiencies, flaws, or problems. If not, there is a tremendous tendency to find whatever results one would like to find. Without some type of framework, even an exploratory test becomes too informal and unfocused.

CONDUCT A PILOT TEST. I cannot emphasize enough the importance of conducting a pilot test before the main test. Not only does this get the "bugs" out of the product you are testing, but it also enables you to debug your experimental method and your test design. You will be able to see where questions you are asking are biased or where you are presenting one prototype to the detriment of another inadvertently. In essence, the pilot test enables you to tighten up your experimental design before the results actually count.

KEEP IT SIMPLE. Especially if you are new to the game and are not confident that you can conduct a test with experimental rigor, then by all means keep the test simple. The simpler the test, the easier it is to keep everything consistent from session to session. It is better to attain meaningful results from a smaller, simpler study than to acquire a wealth of meaningless data from a larger study. Do some usability testing as early and often as possible. It need not be elaborate to be useful or cost effective.

MAKE THE TESTING ENVIRONMENT AS REALISTIC AS POSSIBLE. As much as possible, try to maintain a testing environment that mimics the actual working environment in which the product will be used. This means that if the product will be used in a busy office, you should try to simulate that kind of business with phones ringing off the hook, interruptions, and so on. If a person may be calling the help desk, simulate the help desk. This helps to ensure that the results you find will be transferable to the true environment.

Once you have established the method for the test, summarize it in the test plan so that designers will have a chance to review it. Figure 5.9 shows an example of the high-level description of the test method for a test that includes hardware, software, and documentation. As you can see, a narrative description is quite appropriate, and at this point, all the details are not required.

TASK LIST

The task list is comprised of those tasks that the participants will perform during the test. The list should consist of tasks that will ordinarily be performed during the course of using the product, documentation, and so on.

Eight to ten participants will be evaluated based on availability and time requirements. They will first receive prerequisite training on the system, and if appropriate, complete a criterion test to exhibit mastery of training objectives. Prerequisite training will consist of orientation to the equipment, and training on the basic functionality of the system. The training will attempt to reflect the typical training a customer receives when purchasing a new system, but will not reflect an in-depth XYZ training course that is optional and for which customers pay.

The criterion test will consist of machine-related tasks and paper-and-pencil questions that the participants must complete. The criterion test will establish how well the training achieved its objectives, and will help to evaluate the test results.

The test setup will consist of the ABC system and all support material (e.g., documentation, quick-reference, etc.) that a new customer uses on the job. The test itself will consist of a series of tasks of varying complexity that the participants will perform. The tasks will be typical of those performed by XYZ's customer base.

Prior to the test, the test monitor(s) will orient the participants on the nature of their participation, and will then observe them throughout the test. The test monitor will record his or her observations, noting such items as errors of commission and omission, excessive time to search through the documentation, requests for additional information or other questions, points of confusion or hesitation, etc. The test will be videotaped with a standard video recorder at a viewing angle that reveals the buttons and keys that each participant presses.

After the test, the participants will be given a short break. They will then be asked to complete a questionnaire which collects subjective data about their performance and equipment. The questionnaire will explore their perceptions about high-level topics like workstation data handlers, and system compatibility. While the participants are filling out the questionnaire, the test monitor will review his or her notes of the test in order to ask the participants about unresolved errors or activities during the debriefing session.

After each participant completes the questionnaire, the test monitor will debrief the participant, answering any questions the participant might have and clarifying unresolved issues about the participant's performance that are not obvious. For example:

▸ Why did a particular participant update the customer's file three times?

▸ What was a particular participant thinking when he or she deleted a customer from the database?

The debriefing session is an opportunity to collect information about each participant's thought process, and also leave the participants with a good feeling about their participation. The debriefing session will be audiotaped, and the participants will receive a token of appreciation before they leave.

Figure 5.9   Sample Description of a Generic Test Method

There are two stages to developing these tasks. In the early stages of developing the test, the task list description is intended only for members of the project team and not for eventual participants. You need to supply only enough detail so that reviewers of the test plan can judge whether the tasks are the correct ones and are being exercised properly.

Later, you will expand the tasks into full-blown task scenarios which are presented to the participants. The scenarios will provide the realistic details and context that enable the participants to perform tasks with little intervention from the test monitor. Expanding the initial tasks into task scenarios is covered in Chapter 7. For now, your task list need only include the following.

- **A brief description of the task.** Include only enough detail at this time to communicate the task to the project team. A one-line description is usually enough.

- **The materials and machine states required to perform the task.** Context is everything in usability testing. As the test monitor, you may actually be providing these materials or simulating the machine states if the product is in an early stage. For example, if you were testing software before the screens were coded or prototyped, you might provide drafts of the screens. Or, if the screen were available in a file on the computer but not hooked up as part of a working prototype yet, you (or the participant) might bring that file up to the screen for viewing at the appropriate time.

  Or, perhaps parts of the test will be performed with documentation, while other sections will not. For example, if you are testing how well a participant performs after a certain period of time using the documentation, and the later tasks will be done without documentation, this needs to be specified. If it is appropriate and helpful, you might also include in the task list the components of the product that are being exercised for that particular task.

  For example, in a task that asks a participant to enter a customer name into a database, you might specify as part of the task the screens that the participant will be navigating during completion of that task. This helps to give you a sense of whether the full system is being exercised or not.

- **A description of successful completion of the task.** How will you measure success? It is amazing how much disagreement there can be over this question and how often developers have differing opinions on what represents successful completion of a task. Including successful completion criteria (SCC) with the task description adds precision to what you are measuring and how you view the task. SCC define the boundaries of your task and help to clarify test scoring. Sometimes difficulty ascertaining the SCC reflects the development team's confusion about the product design. Establishing and documenting the SCC is a good exercise just for that reason alone.

- **Benchmark timings that establish the maximum time limits for performing.** If applicable, establish benchmarks that represent either the average or maximum time to perform the task. Benchmarks help to evaluate participant performance during a test. While they are not absolutely necessary, they can help to monitor and evaluate the results of a test session more precisely, since successful participant performance is a reflection of both correct behavior and timely completion.

  For example, if a participant takes 15 minutes to correctly enter his or her name and address on an E-mail system, the design is obviously flawed from almost anyone's standards, and you need to know that. During the test then, you need to track when a participant is outside the boundaries of some designated maximum time. You may choose to intervene at that point, or let the participant continue and note on your data collection form that he or she "maxed out." You will certainly have to stop the participant eventually, if he or she cannot complete the task correctly.

  It is important to determine and arrive at fair and reasonable benchmarks. There are a number of ways to do this, but before describing them, let me emphasize that they need not be deadly accurate. In fact, if you are conducting iterative, ongoing testing, you will be revising the benchmarks from test to test as you learn more about realistic time frames for task completion.

  One source for benchmark times is any original case studies, interviews, or customer visits you may have performed or been privy to. Not only should you note what tasks the end users perform but typically how long they take. It goes without saying that not only is task definition essential for testing, but it should have been an integral part of the design process as well. (Better late than never if you are the first to ascertain the tasks that your end users will perform.)

  Another source for benchmark times is any usability objectives that were included as part of the product or functional specification. Typically, the usability objectives will include targets for time to complete functions or tasks. Any usability data from previous tests that were performed is also a source.

  Another source is polling in-house end users who fit the user profile in one's own company. Simply asking them how long it takes them to perform common tasks will get you on the right track.

  Since time benchmarks are subjective, they may be controversial. Product developers may feel, and rightfully so, that the benchmarks should be longer than the test monitor has provided. In order to anticipate this potential controversy before the test has even begun, I have found that it pays to give developers the benefit of the doubt by erring on the side of overly generous benchmarks.

Here is how I established benchmarks for one test for an organization that had not done usability testing before. The test was for a hardware product that would be tested with documentation. I had three engineers provide estimates of the maximum time that they felt a user would need to correctly perform each task on the test. I also had three technical writers on the project provide the same estimates, since their perspective on the end user was different.

I then averaged all estimates, and, in order to give everyone the benefit of the doubt, *I multiplied the average for each task by a constant of 2.5 to come up with the maximum time for a participant to complete the task*. The constant of 2.5 was rather arbitrary and quite generous. I simply wanted everyone to feel that the participants were being given ample time before I classified the task as "incomplete" on my scoring sheet. I felt confident about being this generous because I was familiar with the design of the product and its potential flaws. I was confident that participants would expose the prob-lematic areas, even with the generous time allotments.

As it turned out, some of the tasks took up to three times longer than even these generous benchmarks, which really drove home the point about difficulties. Experience has taught me that poor product design will make itself known eventually.

TIPS ON DEVELOPING THE TASK LIST

While the development of the tasks for the test may seem straightforward, it is a very subtle process at the same time. The trick is to *indirectly* expose usability flaws by having the participants perform tasks that use the parts of the product in question. What you are really testing is the *relationship* of your product to the end user. From the end user's viewpoint, your product and its associated documentation are a means to an end, either used to solve a problem or provide a service.

The tasks that you develop for the test need to reflect this relationship and, as much as possible, allow the test to expose the points at which the product becomes a hindrance rather than a help for performing a task. Let's look at a simple example of a task to satisfy a test objective and, in so doing, review some possible pitfalls.

SAMPLE TEST OBJECTIVE. Suppose one of your test objectives is to test how easy it is to understand a label that will appear on your product, in this case a copier machine used primarily in a corporate setting. The test objective is written as, "Establish whether users can understand the meaning of the XYZ label."

There are four labels on the product, but the XYZ label is the problematic one. It reads:

Please fan the paper before loading for optimum results.

On the current version of the copier in the marketplace, end users are either not responding to or not understanding the label, and they are experiencing excessive jams and misfeeds.

If you simply take the objective at face value ("Establish whether users can understand the meaning of the XYZ label."), you might decide to have a task that has the test monitor:

Show the participants the XYZ label and have them explain its meaning to you.

In other words, the test monitor will get feedback about the label. This seems simple and direct, since the label is the offending aspect of the product. However, this is oversimplifying the situation. By performing a simple analysis, you ascertain that there are actually three discrete processes associated with correctly using the simple label.

1. Noticing the label
2. Reading the label
3. Processing the information and responding correctly

In addition, these three processes occur within the very specific context of using the copier to make copies.

If you simply show the participants the label, you will only address the second and third processes, at best. You will not know if the participants even notice the label, which precedes the other behaviors. You will also be negating the entire context as well. In the course of using the copier, the participants will be performing a particular task(s) at the time when they are supposed to be reading the label, not having someone point out the label and ask them what they think. This "context" is critical as it will dramatically affect their ability to process information.

The other aspect that you need to address concerning context has to do with the physical location of the label. If it resides in the midst of three other labels, you will need to see how the participants perform with those potential distractions in place.

Now, having done analysis of the label usage and having accounted for context and physical location, you know that merely asking the participants to explain the meaning of the label does not really suffice. Instead, you have to provide a task during which they are expected to use the label, and ascertain whether they notice, read, and use the label correctly. In fact, the label is actually secondary to the task of loading paper that it supports.

The actual task, then, that will expose the label's usability is:

Load paper into the copier.

Notice that the task description does not even mention the label. The label usage is explored indirectly by the test monitor while the task is performed. The test monitor must note where the participants look, and so forth, and then question them during the debriefing session.

Having arrived at the correct task to meet your objective, let's classify it according to the fourfold logic previously discussed. See Figure 5.10.

Now that you have reviewed an example of developing a task, the next issue is ascertaining what tasks you need to include. It is very rare when you can actually test the full range of tasks that comprise an entire interface, documentation, or both together. There is simply not enough time during the test. (It is

TASK COMPONENT	DESCRIPTION
Task	Load paper into the copier.
Machine State	Copier with four labels attached and an empty cassette tray.
Successful Completion Criteria	Test subject loads paper into cassette after first fanning the stack of paper.
Benchmark	Loads correctly within one minute.

Figure 5.10 Task Component and Description

impractical to conduct test sessions that last for days at a time, unless you are willing to commit an inordinate amount of resources.) Instead, you are typically faced with a situation of having to test a representative sample of the product's functions.

When choosing this sample of tasks, it is important that you exercise as many of the most important aspects of the product as possible and address all test objectives. Filter or reduce your task list to something manageable, while ensuring that you capture as many of the usability deficiencies as possible. Following are some common methods used to prioritize or pare down the task list while sacrificing as little as possible.

- **Prioritize by frequency.** Select those tasks that comprise the most frequently performed tasks of your end user population. The most frequent tasks are the ones that the typical end user would access day to day, possibly up to 75 to 80 percent of the time when using the product. For example, if you were testing a word processing package, you would want to make sure, for starters, that the end user could easily perform the following tasks before you concern yourself with the more esoteric tasks like, "how to hide a comment that does not print out."

  1. Open a file.
  2. Save a file.
  3. Edit a file.
  4. Print a file.

  Often times, tests are filled with a series of obscure tasks that less than 5 percent of the end user population will ever find, never mind use. Why does this happen? My main theory is that the development team finds those "5 percenters" the most interesting and challenging tasks to implement, since they are usually the leading edge of the product. Unfortunately, the typical end user does not share the developer's priority or enthusiasm for these obscure tasks.

  If, after applying the "75 percent usage guideline," there is still time to test more tasks, then include tasks that at least 25 percent of your end user population will perform regularly. The point is not to bother testing infrequently used tasks at the expense of tasks that will be used consistently. Only when you are sure that the frequent tasks are covered should you include the less frequently performed tasks.

- **Prioritize by criticality.** Critical tasks are those which, if performed incorrectly or missed, have serious consequences either to the end user, to the product, or to the reputation of the company. For example, let's say that there is a task that if done incorrectly will limit proper use of the product, and cause a phone call to the support line. Or, there is a task that if done incorrectly will cause grave damage to the company's reputation for reliability. Or, there is a task that involves the possible loss of data, or that might cause damage to the machine if performed incorrectly. In short, you want to make sure you catch those tasks that result in the most pain and potentially bad publicity.

- **Prioritize by vulnerability.** By vulnerability, I am referring to those tasks that you suspect, even before testing, will be hard to use, or that have known design flaws. Often, the development team will have a good handle on this. When asked, the development team will voice concern for a new feature, process, interface style, section of a document, and so on. If so, include tasks in the test that address these major areas.

Sometimes, developers will pretend, in the interest of being unbiased, that all functions work equally well (or poorly), and that none are particularly problematic. They do this for a valid reason, not wanting to bias the test with their own preconceptions. Or, they do this for a less noble reason; they do not want known problems exposed during the test. Consequently, tasks that are obviously hard to use and that represent whole components, screens, or sections of a document are left out of the test and prove to be albatrosses much later when there is no time to fix them. To avoid that, use *your* critical judgment about which tasks/features are not quite worked out, are new or never-before-tested features, or have been difficult for in-house personnel to perform. If you are unsure, a human factors specialist can help determine the vulnerable aspects of the product by performing an evaluation. (An expert evaluation can also help you to tighten your test objectives in general.)

- **Prioritize by readiness.** If you are testing very late in the development cycle, you may simply have to go with functions that are ready to be tested or forego testing entirely. While this is not ideal, it is sometimes your only choice. You will not always have the luxury of waiting for every last component, screen, and user manual section to be completed. *Remember, it is always better to test something than nothing*.

An example of a comprehensive task list can be found in the sample test plan at the end of this chapter.

TEST ENVIRONMENT / EQUIPMENT

This section of the test plan describes the environment you will attempt to simulate during the test and the equipment that will be required by the participants. For example, you might want to simulate a sales office for a product that is used by insurance agents. Or, perhaps your product is used by chemists in an environmental laboratory. Or, suppose you simply want to test the product in a very noisy, somewhat crowded office where phones are constantly ringing. Whatever the typical operating environment, try your best to simulate actual conditions. Not only does this help the participants to take on the role of actual end users, but it also means the test results will be a better predictor of the product's performance in the workplace.

The equipment described here only includes the equipment that will be used by the participants. Examples of equipment are phones, computers, printers, and so forth. It is not necessary to describe data collection equipment or cameras you will be using to monitor the test. A sample test environment description appears in the test plan at the end of this chapter.

TEST MONITOR ROLE (OPTIONAL SECTION)

This is listed as an optional section although I always try to include it in my test plans. It helps to clarify what you as a test monitor will be doing, and it is especially important when there will be observers of the test who are unfamiliar with the testing process. Specify when the test monitor will be doing something out of the ordinary which may be confusing. For example, sometimes it is unclear why and under what circumstances the test monitor is probing and intervening. This is especially true when the test monitor may be role playing or intentionally playing devil's advocate with an overly acquiescent participant.

See the test plan at the end of this chapter for a sample description of the test monitor's role.

EVALUATION MEASURES (DATA TO BE COLLECTED)

This section of the test plan provides an overview of the types of measures you will be collecting during the test, both performance and preference data. Performance data, representing measures of participant behavior, includes error rates, number of accesses of the help by task, time to perform a task, and so on. Preference data, representing measures of participant opinion or thought process, includes participant rankings, answers to questions, and so forth. The data collected should be based on your problem statement/test objective. Sometimes these measures will have already been alluded to in a previous section of the test plan such as the methodology section. Both performance and preference measures can be used either quantitatively or qualitatively, depending on the test objectives.

Listing the evaluation measures you will use enables any interested parties to scan the test plan to make sure that they will be getting the type of data they expect from the test.

Following is a sample of the types of measures you might collect during a typical test:

Sample Performance Measures

Time to complete each task
Number and percentage of tasks completed correctly with and without assistance
Number and percentage of tasks completed incorrectly
Time required to access information in the manual
Time required to access information in online help
Time needed to recover from error(s)
Time spent reading a specific section of a manual
Time spent talking to help desk

Count of all incorrect selections (errors)
Count of errors of commission
Count of errors of omission
Count of incorrect menu choices
Count of incorrect icons selected
Count of calls to the help-desk

Count of user manual accesses
Count of visits to the index
Count of visits to the table of contents
Count of "negative comments or mannerisms"

Sample Preference Measures

Ratings and rationale concerning:

   Usefulness of the product
   How well product matched expectations
   Appropriateness of product functions to user's tasks
   Ease of use overall
   Ease of learning overalll
   Ease of setup and installation
   Ease of accessibility
   Usefulness of the index, table of contents, help, graphics, and so on
   Help desk replies to inquiries

Preference and rationale for:

   One prototype vs. another prototype
   This product vs. a competitor's product
   This product's conceptual model vs. the old model

Quotable quotes: (For example)

"I loved it—when can I get one?"
"You guys have done it again—you're **still** not listening to customers"
"Wow, I'm very, very impressed"
"Can I please leave now—keep my money and the product"

REPORT CONTENTS AND PRESENTATION

This section provides a summary of the main sections of your test report and the way in which you intend to communicate the results to the development team. For the report contents section, simply list the sections that will appear in your test report.

For the presentation section, describe how you will communicate results to the development team both prior to and following the report. For example, you might hold an informal meeting with those on the critical path of the project just after the test is completed and prior to analyzing all the data. Then, following completion of all analyses and the test report, you might follow that with a formal presentation to the entire project team, as well as other interested parties, management, and so forth.

SAMPLE TEST PLAN

Following is an example of a test plan with all sections intact. The product being tested is a printer for a home or small office. The test includes taking the product out of the box and setting it up to print. Documentation is included in the form of a setup guide and a small pamphlet that is stored on the printer.

SAMPLE

TEST PLAN FOR EZ-TECH'S PRONTO

PRINTER

INTRODUCTION

Following is the test plan for conducting usability tests of the prototype of EZ-Tech's new home office printer, known internally as Pronto. The plan covers the following sections:

- Purpose
- Problem statements
- User profile
- Methodology
- Task list
- Test environment and equipment requirements

- Test monitor role
- Evaluation measures
- Test report contents and presentation

PURPOSE

The main purpose of the test is to predict the expected performance of an actual customer using the current product and materials and to remedy serious problems prior to release. The usability test will measure the time to complete tasks and will identify errors and difficulties involved in using the printer and rough prototypes of the on-board manual and quick setup guide. Simulated tasks include setup, routine operations, and selected troubleshooting tasks.

PROBLEM STATEMENTS

The specific questions that need to be answered:

1. Are all terms on the keypad intuitive? If not, are terms learned through performing typical printing tasks?
2. Do users recognize the functionality of the vertical paper tray? How can it be improved?
3. Does the on-board manual support the critical setup and maintenance tasks?
4. Are users able to set dip switches from the new location?

USER PROFILE

A total of 10 participants will be tested during the week of September 25, 1995 at the Market World facility in New York City. Two participants will be tested per day. Two alternate participants will be acquired in case one of the participants is unable to attend at the last minute. The participants will be divided according to background as follows:

- Two participants who are both computer and printer novices. While these participants are not necessarily the intended buying audience, they represent the least competent user who will use the product. If they are able to perform, that is a strong indicator that more qualified end users will also be able to perform.

- Eight participants who have previous computer and printer experience. Participants in this group will have the following characteristics:

  - Work with a computer on a regular basis or plan to purchase one within three months.

  - Have previously purchased 0 to 2 printers.

  - Have never purchased or used a laser printer on a regular basis.

  - Have limited font sophistication (i.e., do not use more than three fonts at a time).

  - Spend the majority of computer usage performing word processing tasks. Do not perform spreadsheet or desktop publishing tasks more than 20 percent of their computer usage time.

  - Do not require a wide-carriage printer, or one that can print multipart forms.

METHODOLOGY

The usability test will consist of the main performance test designed to gather extensive usability data via direct observation, as well as a paper-and-pencil test designed to gather information about keypad terminology. Each is discussed next.

The main performance test is composed of the following four sections:

1. Participant greeting and background questionnaire

Each participant will be personally greeted by the test monitor and made to feel comfortable and relaxed. The participants will be given a name tag and asked to fill out a very short questionnaire that gathers basic background information. At this time the issue of confidentiality will be broached, and participants will be asked to sign nondisclosure statements.

2. Orientation

The participants will receive a short, verbal, scripted introduction and orientation to the test, explaining the purpose and objective of the test, the need for product anonymity until after the test, and additional information about what is expected of them. They will be assured and reminded that the product is the center of the evaluation and not themselves, and that they should perform in the way that is typical and comfortable to them. The participants will be informed that they are being observed, videotaped, and audiotaped.

3. Performance test

The performance test consists of a series of tasks that the participants will be asked to carry out while being observed. The scenario is as follows:

- After the orientation is complete, the participants will be asked to sit down at their desks (see description of test environment). A staff member simulating a mail delivery will drop off a box containing Pronto and all associated documentation. The participants will be told that the printer they ordered last week has just been delivered and to set it up for immediate operation. The participants will be asked to set up the equipment as if they were in their own office. They will be observed to see the techniques they use for opening the box and how closely they follow the quick setup guide which leads them through the entire setup process.

- After completion of the setup process or expiration of the time limit (each task will have upper time limits), each participant will then be guided through a series of routine operations and troubleshooting tasks by the test monitor. The participants will be encouraged to work without guidance save for the documentation and the product itself. The test monitor may ask a participant to verbalize his or her thoughts if the participant becomes stuck or hopelessly confused. This will help to pinpoint the reason for the problem and will be noted by the test monitor.

During the main performance test, elapsed time and errors will be noted for each unique task on the task list. The test monitor will also make notes about relevant participant behavior, comments, and any unusual circumstances that might affect the result (e.g., the printer malfunctioned). The participants will be videotaped in order to get a permanent record for verification.

4. Participant debriefing

After all tasks are complete or the time expires, each participant will be debriefed by the test monitor in one of the side rooms and the debriefing session audiotaped. The debriefing will include the following:

- Filling out a brief preference questionnaire pertaining to subjective perceptions of usability and aesthetics of the printer
- Participant's overall comments about his or her performance
- Participant's responses to probes from the test monitor about specific errors or problems during the test

The debriefing session serves several functions. It allows the participants to say whatever they like, which is important if tasks are frustrating. It provides important information about each participant's rationale for performing specific actions, and it allows the collection of subjective preference data about the printer and its support.

After the debriefing session, the participants will be thanked for their effort, and then released. A small token of appreciation will be extended before they leave.

TERMINOLOGY EVALUATION

This is the printer's secondary evaluation designed to gather information about the self-evidence of keypad terminology. The objective is to evaluate whether the terms are inherently understood prior to usage and to identify the amount of learning that takes place through typical printer setup, usage, and reading of the quick setup guide and on-board manual. Ordinarily, end users would also have the larger reference manual as well.

The paper-and-pencil evaluation consists of two parts:

Part 1. Just after the orientation and prior to the performance test, the participants will be handed a paper representation of the keypad and asked to briefly define the terms shown. The participants need only write a sentence or two—enough to reveal whether they understand the term or not. This part evaluates the self-evidence of the terms for the first-time user.

Part 2. Just after the performance test and prior to the debriefing, the participants will be handed an identical paper representation of the keypad and asked to define the terms once again. Participants will not be allowed to see their original definitions. This part evaluates the influence of using the product and its associated documentation on a participant's understanding of the keypad terminology.

The preliminary task list for the main performance test is attached. This list will be refined and transformed into a data collection form to be used during the test.

Timings shown in the MTC (maximum time to complete) field were compiled from two sources of subject matter experts. These judgments are estimates that have been adjusted by a multiple of 2.5, and do not necessarily reflect the actual time to complete tasks. They are useful as benchmarks in evaluating participant performance and in establishing upper time limits for the completion of each task.

TEST ENVIRONMENT AND EQUIPMENT REQUIREMENTS

We will need to create an environment approximating a home office, including a desk, computer, chair, typical supplies such as pencils, pens, phones, and so on. The desk will be somewhat cluttered and have an IBM-compatible PC sitting on it ready to be attached to the printer. The machine will contain MS DOS and Wordperfect software. The computer should be prominently labeled as to its type (e.g., IBM PC) for the task requiring hooking up the printer and verifying communication.

The lighting should approximate an office environment and at the same time, allow for clear videotaping. On a side table in proximity to the desk will be the following items:

1. White bond paper for loading into the printer. This paper should be stacked in a pile of no less than 150 sheets in order to ascertain if the participants attempt to overload the paper tray.

2. Letterhead paper (not from company).

3. Four different interface cables, each prominently labeled. One cable should be the appropriate parallel interface for attaching the printer to the computer on the desk, another should be a serial interface cable. The other two cables can be any other type.

4. Two or more print cartridges (without company labels). Each cartridge should be placed in its original packaging prior to each test. Since the cartridge instructions refer to the company's product, the instructions should be removed from the box. The participants must rely on the quick setup guide and on-board manual entirely for cartridge installation and removal.

5. A box of #10 envelopes.

6. A stack of at least five pages of address labels that have been designed for this printer.

The prototype must be in working order and be able to accomplish all functionality required by the tasks on the task list. While the availability of a second prototype on site at Market World would be ideal, having one available at the company site for immediate backup is the next best option.

The prototype will be repackaged in its original package prior to each test, complete with all support materials. The package should appear to have come "off the shelf." It is imperative that at least one qualified engineer remain on site to repair the prototype printer should it malfunction while being tested.

TEST MONITOR ROLE

The test monitor will sit in the room with each participant while conducting the test. The test monitor will initiate tasks after initial setup, simulate the particular scenarios necessary for each task, and record timings, errors, and observations.

The test monitor will also control printing of files from the computer, since software knowledge is not considered part of the test. The test monitor will not help any of the participants unless a question about the test procedure arises. Participants will be asked to rely on the printer, its documentation, and their own abilities to perform the required tasks.

In addition to the test monitor, a variety of observers will be present during the course of the testing period. The Market World facility can easily accommodate unobtrusive observation by up to 25 people, as it allows one-way viewing and separate entrance.

EVALUATION MEASURES

The following evaluation measures will be collected and calculated:

1. The average times to complete each task, and each grouping of tasks, across all participants.
2. The percentage of participants who finished each task successfully versus those who had errors from which they could not recover.
3. Error classification: to the degree possible, each error will be classified and a source of error indicated. Error classes are as follows:

   Observations and Comments—The test monitor notes when participants have difficulty, when an unusual behavior occurs, or when a cause of error becomes obvious.
   Noncritical Errors—An individual participant makes a mistake but is able to recover during the task in the allotted time.
   Critical Errors—An individual participant makes a mistake and is *unable* to recover and complete the task on time. The participant may or may not realize a mistake has been made.

Note: Typical sources of error are: design of the keypad, instructions in the on-board manual, and so on.

4. Paper-and-pencil measures:

   • Percentage of participants who gave the correct definition of the keypad terms during Part 1.

- Percentage of participants who gave the correct definition of the keypad terms during Part 2.
- Comparison of Part 1 and Part 2 scores for each definition.

5. Participant rankings of usability and aesthetics of the product. (Some questions may be essay-type questions, rather than rankings.)

TEST REPORT CONTENTS AND PRESENTATION

The report will include the following sections:

1. Test Plan (including variations)
2. Results (this section will present summaries of all results in tabular form. Raw data will be included in the appendix)
3. Findings/recommendations and discussion (this section will summarize the results, and make recommendations to designers and learning product developers about possible changes and additional research if appropriate)

The results of the usability test will be presented first in preliminary form through a meeting with concerned parties on October 4. These results will be composed of the most important findings that can be compiled quickly. It is understood that such findings are preliminary in that it will not be possible to complete all analyses.

Final results composed of findings and recommendations will be presented in the form of a report approximately two weeks after the test. These will include any revisions to the preliminary findings, as well as completion of all proposed analyses.

ATTACHMENT: Preliminary Task List for Pronto Printer Usability Test

Task List Legend

MTC	= Maximum time to complete
OBM	= On-board manual
QSG	= Quick setup guide
Req's	= Requirements to perform the task
P	= Participant
SCC	= Successful completion criteria
TM	= Test monitor

The first set of tasks is associated with setting up the printer using the quick setup guide.

TASK NO.	TASK DESCRIPTION	TASK DETAIL	
1	Unpack the printer.	Req's:	Unopened box, QSG.
		SCC:	Printer removed from box and ready for further preparation.
		MTC:	5.0 min.
2	Install the on-board manual.	Req's:	On-board manual, QSG.
		SCC:	On-board manual placed in its slot.
		MTC:	2.0 min.
3	Connect power cord.	Req's:	Power cord, QSG, printer.
		SCC:	Power cord placed in its socket correctly.
		MTC:	3.0 min.
4	Choose appropriate interface cable.	Req's:	Four (4) cables clearly marked on the table (include serial cable as one choice), QSG (cable table).
		SCC:	Correct cable chosen from the four and P indicates it is the correct one.
		MTC:	2.5 min.
5	Connect interface cable.	Req's:	Interface cable, QSG, printer, PC.
		SCC:	One end of cable placed firmly in its seat in the printer, and the other end seated firmly in computer's port.
		MTC:	6.0 min.
6	Install the print cartridge.	Req's:	Cartridge pack (instructions removed), QSG, printer. Note: Cartridge should be stripped of any company markings to ensure anonymity of company.
		SCC:	Cartridge placed firmly in its housing directly against the green dot. (Also self test will serve as dual SCC).
		MTC:	5.0 min.
7	Load the paper.	Req's:	Box of paper, printer paper tray, QSG.
		SCC:	Paper placed correctly in paper tray underneath two corners. Note: Could ask them to form feed to test if paper is placed correctly.
		MTC:	3.0 min.
8	Turn the printer on.	Req's:	Printer with all connections, paper, cartridge, etc., QSG.
		SCC:	Participant slides switch to on position. Printer powers on.
		MTC:	1.0 min.
9	Print the self test.	Req's:	Printer keypad, QSG.
		SCC:	Self test comes out of paper tray.
		MTC:	3.0 min.

TASK NO.	TASK DESCRIPTION	TASK DETAIL	
10	Prepare PC to talk to the printer.	Req's:	Printer on line, MS-DOS loaded on PC, QSG instructions for paralll interface.
		SCC:	Types correct sequence of commands on computer.
		MTC:	3.0 min.
11	Verify communication of printer and PC.	Req's:	Printer on line, MS-DOS loaded on PC, QSG.
		SCC:	Printer busy light comes on, followed by printing of a listing of files on disk.
		MTC:	3.0 min.

The next set of tasks represents routine operations after the setup is completed. They will exercise any remaining buttons on the control panel that have not been used.

TASK NO.	TASK DESCRIPTION	TASK DETAIL	
1	Place the printer in a pause state.	Req's:	Printer keypad, OBM.
		SCC:	The participant presses the Status button and the Offline indicator lights.
		MTC:	2.5 min.
2	Change the quality of the print to a lesser quality.	Req's:	Printer keypad, OBM.
		SCC:	The participant presses the Quality button and the Draft indicator lights.
		MTC:	1.5 min.
3	Change the font setting to Times Roman.	Req's:	Printer keypad, OBM.
		SCC:	The participant presses the Font button and the Times Roman indicator lights.
		MTC:	1.5 min.
4	Change the printer settings to emulate an XYZ printer.	Req's:	Printer Dip Switches (DIPS), OBM, pen or similar implement for manipulating DIPS. Note: The participant will have to select the correct implement.
		SCC:	DIP settings exactly match XYZ configuration as shown in the OBM.
		MTC:	4.0 min.
5	Load a #10 envelope as if you wanted to print an address on it.	Req's:	#10 envelope with orientation markings for TM use, OBM, printer paper tray.
		SCC:	Envelope is seated within the envelope guide. Participant presses Forms Feed button to load the envelope.
		MTC:	4.0 min.
6	Load several pages of labels as if you wanted to print addresses on them.	Req's:	Several address labels, OBM, printer paper tray.
		SCC:	Labels are placed correctly in paper tray. Note: Could ask the participants to perform a form feed to test if the labels are placed correctly.
		MTC:	2.0 min.
7	Replace the existing cartridge with a new one.	Req's:	Correctly seated cartridge in printer, cartridge pack, OBM.
		SCC:	Old cartridge removed without damage. New cartridge is inserted and correctly seated in housing.
		MTC:	2.0 min.

TASK NO.	TASK DESCRIPTION	TASK DETAIL	
8	Clear a printer jam.	Req's:	Jam situation initiated by TM via either the PC or the printer, OBM. Note: The participant may or may not witness the jamming process.
		SCC:	Participant clears the jam and either prints via software or presses the Forms Feed button to verify that the jam is cleared.
		MTC:	3.0 min.
9	Find the information that refers to "wrong font printing" error condition.	Req's:	TM indicates error condition has occurred, OBM.
		SCC:	Participant moves to the correct page to shoot the trouble in the OBM and announces same to the TM.
		MTC:	5.0 min.
10	Repeat above scenario for the following error conditions. Each participant will receive three conditions. 1. Printer will not print. 2. Print quality is poor. 3. Characters are printing lighter. 4. Error indicators are lit on keypad.		
11	Place a sheet of letterhead into the paper tray so that it will print at the correct orientation.	Req's:	Several sheets of letterhead on the table, printer with loaded paper tray, OBM.
		SCC:	Participant removes other paper or places letterhead over original sheets in correct orientation. (TM will print a page of text to prove the orientation. If incorrect, the participant will get two more attempts to correct the orientation.)
		MTC:	2.0 min.
12	Move the letterhead paper so that printing begins after the letterhead information.	Req's:	Letterhead paper resides in paper tray, OBM.
		SCC:	Participant presses the Line Feed key x times.
		MTC:	5.0 min.

SELECTING AND

ACQUIRING

PARTICIPANTS

6
___

INTRODUCTION

The selection and acquisition of participants whose background and abilities are representative of your product's intended end user is a crucial element of the testing process. After all, your test results will only be valid if the people you test are typical end users of the product, or as close to that criterion as possible. If you test the "wrong" people, it does not matter how much effort you put into the rest of the test preparation. Your results will be questionable and of limited value.

In this chapter I address the major activities of selecting and acquiring participants. Selecting participants involves identifying and describing the relevant skills and knowledge of the person(s) who will use your product. This description is known as the user profile or user characterization of the target population and should have been developed in the early stages of the product development. Then, once that has been determined, you must ascertain the most effective way to acquire people from this target population to serve as participants within your constraints of time, money, resources, and so on.

CHARACTERIZE THE USER

Let's begin by discussing how to document the user profile of the target population; a description of the most crucial skills, knowledge, demographic information, and other relevant factors required of the people who will be using your product. If possible, the profile should describe for each major skill the range of experience and percentage (approximately) of end users residing at low and at high levels of experience. This is important because if you anticipate that 75 percent of your end users will have extensive experience for a particular skill, such as word processing, the product should be designed and your participant selection weighted toward these highly experienced end users.

The specific characteristics that make up the user profile will of course depend on your product. However, Figure 6.1 shows the categories for a generic user characterization for a typical computer-based product. You will characterize your own end user in a similar fashion albeit with factors that represent your own end user(s) and that speak directly to your own product.

Note that the characterization in Figure 6.1 includes items such as "Learning style" and "Attitude toward high technology." While it is worthwhile attempting to obtain such information about your end user, do not be discouraged if you are unable to ascertain it. As long as you can capture the basic skill and knowledge set, you will still be ahead of the game.

In order to make the concept of a user profile or user characterization more concrete, let's discuss the profile for a company's hypothetical software product whose primary audience will be C+ programmers. This information is typically acquired in consultation with product marketing. To keep it extremely simple, let's start by looking at only one particular skill of this intended user profile, C+ programming experience. In terms of the *range* of programming experience, your target population will consist of programmers who have from zero to more than five years of experience programming in a C+ environment. More precisely, you anticipate that the *frequency distribution* of users of your product with regard to C+ programming experience will break down as follows:

- 10 percent of programmers will have 0 to 6 months of C+ experience.
- 75 percent will have 6 to 24 months of C+ experience.
- 15 percent will have more than two years of C+ experience.

Personal History	Age Gender Attitude toward computers or your type of product Left or right handed (could affect mouse usage for example) Learning style (read then do, try then read, or learn by doing, etc) Attitude toward high technology
Education History	Highest grade completed Subjects studied Major
Computer Experience	Total time using Frequency of use Types of computers/peripherals used Operating systems used Types of screen interaction used (GUI vs. DOS)
Product Experience	Total time used Frequency of use Types of tasks performed and frequency Types/brands used (are they users or non-users of your company's product?)
Occupation History	Current and past job titles Responsibilities Training Classes taken Time with current company

Figure 6.1   Generic User Characterization

This breakdown has implications for the test design and implications for the acquisition of participants. From the preceding frequency distribution it is apparent that you should really bias the design of this product (and consequently any usability tests) toward the person who has an intermediate level of C+ experience. Both the novice and the very experienced programmer will be less frequent users.

C+ programming experience is only one factor, however, that will affect an end user's ability to master this product. Typically, the user profile will include many factors from a user's background that you expect the user to possess (or not possess as the case may be).

Let's look at a full-blown user profile that includes a number of different factors. Figure 6.2 shows the projected user profile for a new chemical analysis software product that is intended for chemists and chemical engineers. This information is being used to design the product, and of course is the basis for testing the product as well.

From this information about whom you expect will be using the product, you would attempt to acquire several participants who are representative of this market. The information also enables you to create a snapshot of your "typical" participant; someone who at least in theory represents the average end user. This snapshot is not only beneficial for designing a usability test, but also helps developers to "visualize" the person for whom they are designing the product, another benefit of doing this type of analysis. I use the term *person* in the singular, simply because developers are more likely to have one person in mind, when they are designing, rather than many different types of people. Unfortunately, the "person" they visualize, in lieu of real data, is often themselves, even though they, the developers, may not even remotely reflect an actual end user. So, an accurate snapshot of the end user can be a real boon to the design process because it helps to keep the developers on track.

If you review the categories in the preceding example, you will see that your so-called typical end user would be a middle-aged male with a degree in chemistry, who is experienced with DOS-based programs and is a novice at using GUI. If you are very limited in the amount of participants you can bring in for a test, then you had better make sure that at least *that* person is represented in your test.

Now your first thought might be that the information describing the user profile should already exist and be written down somewhere within your organization, since the design and makeup of any product is *supposed to be* predicated on knowing the end user. While this is so in theory, my own experience has been that this information is rarely collected systematically or written down. Or, if it is written down, it does not quite make it to the desks of the developers, the people who really need it. Or, if it makes it to the desks of the developers, they either pay it little mind or have a distorted version of the information.

To test this premise in your own development organization, go around and ask three or four different staff members in the development group to describe the user profile of the current product they are working on. Most likely, you will receive three or four very plausible, but very different descriptions of the end user. Or, you will get a vague answer such as "small business owners" or "accountants." This simply means you will have to dig further to find the correct, more detailed information that will enable you to bring in a representative cross section of the right end users.

Characteristic	Range	Frequency Distribution
General computer experience	None to two years	10% have never used computer. 35% have 1 year experience. 55% have 1+ years experience.
Education level	High school	10% high school
	College	60% B.A.
	Graduate school	20% Masters
Age	18–55 Years	85% ages 25–50 15% other
Sex	Male/Female	85% male
Learning style preference	Trial and error Consult with others Read documentation	Unknown
Education major	Chemistry, math, MBA, others	75% chemistry 10% math 5% MBA 10% other
Operating system experience	DOS, UNIX	75% DOS 25% UNIX
Computer Interaction Experience	Graphical user interface (GUI). DOS-based command line Fill-in fields.	25% GUI 75% other

Figure 6.2 User Profile for Chemical Analysis Software Product

By the way, as long as I am discussing this topic, let me add that it is just this lack of a clear delineation of the characteristics of the end user that contributes to usability deficiencies of products in the first place. Since developers do not know or do not agree on the characteristics of the end user, it is difficult for them to develop a consistent, well-designed product that meets the end user's needs. Testing just happens to be one of the first activities that makes this lack of a clear end user characterization so painfully obvious.

WHERE TO LOOK FOR INFORMATION ABOUT THE END USER

So, where shall you look for this information? Let's look at some of the potential sources of this type of information in your organization. Following is a list of some typical places and people from whom to ascertain the user profile.

THE FUNCTIONAL SPECIFICATION

The functional specification or product requirements document is the blueprint for the product. It describes the product's intended functionality, as well as the tasks that the end user will perform. Most functional specifications include a comprehensive description of the intended user population (if an internal product) or market (if an external product) for the product, which is the basis for your user profile.

STRUCTURED ANALYSES OR MARKETING STUDIES

Task analyses or similar analyses may have already been completed by developers, technical writers, or human factors specialists prior to any design work. These usually include the skill and knowledge set required to use the product effectively. In larger corporations there is almost sure to have been a marketing study conducted for each unique product which has a similar breakdown.

PRODUCT MANAGER (R & D)

If you are unable to get your hands on specific documents, analyses, or reports, there are certain individuals who should be able to help determine the user profile. Among them is the product manager who should have his or her finger on the pulse of the marketplace and should have a clear understanding of the end users for whom the product is intended. The product manager may also have access to reports and surveys that describe the user profile in detail.

PRODUCT MANAGER (MARKETING)

Marketing may have done some in-depth analyses that have not yet been distributed to the development team. These could be the results of surveys or focus groups similar to the ones to which the product manager has access. Very often all the information you need is contained in reports of this type, but in a form that is not all that accessible. (This is one of the reasons it often goes unused. The development team has more than enough to do without reading through a long report.) You may have to distill much of the information into a more concise form. If you do end up condensing this information, by all means make it available to the development team for its design work, as well as using it for setting up the usability tests. Having a simple one-page depiction of the end user on every developer's desk would be a boon to product development.

COMPETITIVE BENCHMARKING AND ANALYSIS GROUP

Some organizations assign a group (or an individual) to do extensive benchmarking of their own and competitor's products. Consequently, they will have a good handle on not only who is using their product but who is using their competitor's products as well. This can be a wonderful source of information for establishing the user profile.

If you can, interview these sources yourself rather than through a third party, so that you can probe and elicit the type of information you need. If they do not have the information you require, you may be forced to acquire that information directly from the end user, via surveys and phone calls. In fact, a clear depiction and understanding of the end user is so crucial that even if you have that information, you may *still* want to verify it with phone calls or visits to user sites or by conducting a quick survey.

DIFFERENTIATE BETWEEN PURCHASER AND END USER

When determining the user profile, make sure to differentiate between the purchaser or buyer of the product and the actual end user. Often times the user profile is slanted toward the person who makes the buying decision in an organization but who knows very little about the problems that the end users face. You certainly would not want to bring in "purchasers" to test the product that will give you a very slanted view of how the product is performing.

Another potential pitfall is the fact that the end user of the product and the end user of the documentation may differ. This is especially true for large systems that are being developed for internal end users, where only one or two people, such as the system administrator, will receive documentation. The rest of the end users will be left to their own devices or will have to specifically ask for the documentation. Fortunately, this occurs much less frequently than in the past.

DIVIDE THE USER PROFILE INTO DISTINCT END USER CATEGORIES

The user profile describes the range of skills that make up the entire universe of target end users. Every end user should fall somewhere within that spectrum. However, you are not interested in individuals alone. Instead, identify entire groups of end users, who share many of the same characteristics on the user profile. These groups, usually identified by similar occupations or job titles, will use the product and its support materials in different ways and for different purposes. It is important that you include a representative sample of each of these groups. For example, the product for the chemical industry previously mentioned is intended for both managers and their staff, each group using the product differently and for different purposes. If you were testing that product, you would want to select a representative sample of managers and a representative sample of their staff members in proportion to their likelihood of using the product.

Or, suppose you were responsible for testing a banking system that will be used by both tellers and "back office" staff members. You will want to test some tellers who will use the system for performing daily customer transactions. You will also want to test some "back office" staff members who will use the system to generate reports and conduct different analyses.

Each group will have similar characteristics when compared to other members of their group, although with varying levels of experience. With each group, make sure that you are representing these varying experience levels, if any. For example, test some novice tellers, some experienced tellers, some novice "back office" staff, and some experienced "back office" staff. To represent these different skill levels, you may want to use a matrix test design.

CONSIDER A MATRIX TEST DESIGN

Since you want to make sure that you are representing the entire population, consider a matrix design for the test that balances these different variables in such a way that no particular user group or *cell* of the matrix is left out. In the banking example, unless you take experience level into consideration, you could end up only acquiring tellers who are novice PC users, or only "back office" personnel who are all experienced PC users. That would mean that for your test, experienced tellers will simply not be represented, and the test results will be slanted toward novices alone. Maybe experienced end users would have different problems with the product.

Good test design means that you balance the mixtures of user groups and user characteristics in such a way that the major categories or cells are all represented. For the banking example, you might test a total of 16 participants whose job and experience level look like the ones in Figure 6.3.

Category	Novice	Experienced
Teller	4	4
Back office	4	4

Figure 6.3 Job and Experience Levels Matrix

OPERATIONALLY DEFINE AND DOCUMENT THE CRITERIA FOR EACH GROUP

When classifying a group, it is important to be crystal clear about the meaning of such terms as "novice," "experienced," and so forth. Often these terms are bandied about so indiscriminately that everyone concerned with the product has a different understanding of their meaning. In actuality, unless you define these categories you almost assuredly are *not* speaking of the same thing. Novice can mean many things to many different people, and it is important that you take responsibility for translating buzzwords into operational definitions. Therefore, when talking to the people who supply you with information about the end user, beware of words such as "novice" and "expert," unless you define them.

An operational definition should quantify an end user's experience in terms of some objective reference point such as elapsed time spent using a product or the frequency with which a specific task is performed. For example, an operational definition for "novice" might be anyone with less than six months' experience using a particular product. I have found it more accurate to use criteria that are measurable, objective "facts" rather than subjective self-classifications on the part of potential end users. A self-classification will have the end user rate his or her own abilities and skill level, which is more subject to misinterpretation and wide variance. (For information on the difference between self-rating and frequency of usage questionnaires, see Chapter 7.)

For example, when attempting to classify a group of end users as "novice," before using them in a usability test, do not simply accept their own rating of themselves as "novice," "expert," and so on. Instead, ask them how often (e.g., daily, weekly, monthly) they perform the task, or how long they have been performing the task (e.g., never, six months, one year, etc.). This latter method has the advantage of using a criterion on which everyone can readily agree. With self-rating, however, you run the risk of each end user having different interpretations of what is meant by such terms as novice or expert. You are dependent on the user's self-image to guide the classification.

CHOOSE THE NUMBER OF PARTICIPANTS TO TEST

The number of participants you choose to test depends on many factors, including:

- The degree of confidence in the results that you require
- The number of available resources to set up and conduct the test
- The availability of the type of participants you require
- The duration of the test session
- The time required to prepare for the test

Ultimately, you have to balance your need for acquiring participants with these practical constraints of time and resources. If you require statistically valid results, you will need to test enough participants to conduct the appropriate analyses and generalize to your specific target population, as well as to rigorously control for potentially biasing conditions and factors.

If however, you are simply attempting to expose as many usability problems as possible in the shortest amount of time, then test at least four to five participants. The latest research indicates that testing four to five participants will expose the vast majority of usability problems. However, I must add that I am a bit uncomfortable testing only four participants, and I try to test at least eight participants if at all possible. While you may expose most of the usability problems with four participants, there is still a good chance you may overlook a problem that could have severe ramifications.

An important consideration is whether you will conduct more than one test during the product development life cycle. If you are going to conduct multiple tests, then you can feel confident testing fewer participants. For example, if you conduct three tests with five participants each, you end up testing fifteen people. If you will be conducting a single test, however, then you will be better served by having more participants for that lone test.

If you use a matrix design, try to test at least four participants per treatment group (one cell of the matrix equals a treatment group). If you cannot fill all cells with four participants, then bias toward the end users who will represent the most users in your target population. In the banking example, if you suspect that 75 percent of eventual end users would be novices, make sure that most of your participants fit that category.

INCLUDE A FEW LEAST COMPETENT USERS IN EVERY TESTING SAMPLE

I have found that I learn an extraordinary amount by including one or more least competent users (LCUs) among my participants, *even if they do not make up a significant percentage of my eventual end users*. An LCU is defined as an end user who represents the least skilled person who could potentially use your product. In the previous example of the user profile for the chemical engineering market, the LCU is a person with no computer experience, who has never used even a word processor, who is a high-school graduate, and so on. The LCU need not fall at the bottom of *all* the scales, but the LCU should be at the bottom of the majority of them. Why include LCUs even if the user profile is projected at mostly experienced users? Simply for the following reason. If your least experienced group can successfully use the product, if *they* can muddle their way through the usability test, then you can assume that most other groups will also be able to use the product. Of course, there are exceptions to every rule, but by and large, I have found the LCUs to be excellent indicators of a product's overall usability and ease of learning.

On the other hand, if the LCUs cannot get through the test, that is *not* necessarily an indictment. It does, however, reveal clues on how to fix fundamental problems of intuitiveness, orientation, or organization through redesign, more information in the documentation, and so forth. In addition, during early product development and exploratory tests, you learn much about the end user's conceptual models through the eyes of the LCU, before the LCU has been "polluted" by previous experiences with similar products. If your product is targeted toward new audiences, the LCU test can obviously help predict problems for those folks.

SOME OTHER CONSIDERATIONS FOR PARTICIPANT SELECTION

WHAT ABOUT USING INTERNAL PARTICIPANTS?

Internal participants are those participants who fit the criteria of the rest of your user profile with one exception; they also happen to work for the company that is manufacturing or developing the product. Many usability tests are conducted using internal participants exclusively. This is problematic since, by virtue of their affiliation, these participants are "different" from typical end users. They are part of the corporate culture and they have inside information that others do not have. They also have a vested interest in seeing that the product is successful.

Does this mean that you should never use internal personnel as participants? No, not at all. It simply means that you should never use them as your *primary* participants. There are many ways, however, that you can use internal participants to good advantage. Let's discuss a few of these.

- **To test the test.** When you are in the early stages of coming up with your test and want to pilot it, internal participants are a valuable resource. Your main focus should *not* be in gathering usability information during the pilot test. Instead, use the test to make sure that your materials are clear and understandable, that the test design is sound, that you have not forgotten any important tasks, and that your hardware, software, and documentation are in order and ready for testing.

- **To conduct early exploratory research.** Internal participants make good exploratory participants as long as they are unfamiliar with the product. With early exploratory research, you are not as concerned with the subtle issues of later validation tests. Instead, you are more concerned with gross problems of the product such as the conceptual model, primary navigation techniques, organization of the manual, organization and navigation of an on-line help system, and so on. Internal participants can quickly help to determine whether you are on the right track, without the expense and time necessary to recruit outside participants.

- **To conduct "best case" testing.** In "best case" testing, which is often employed at an early stage of development, you see how someone who is very experienced and more familiar with the culture (i.e., a ringer) uses the product. The idea is that if this best case user has trouble, you have *serious* design problems. In some cases the internal participant will be more critical than the external participant, more willing to point out problems and not hold back. If the product passes the best case scenario, you should quickly follow with a less experienced end user to verify the soundness of the design. If it does not "pass" the best case scenario, do not bother with further testing. Instead, head back to the drawing board for further development work before testing again.

Of course, in some cases the internal participant *is* the end user. By all means, in that case, use them exclusively for your test.

BEWARE OF INADVERTENTLY TESTING ONLY THE ''BEST'' PEOPLE

Very often when acquiring participants, and especially when you do not have primary control of participant selection, you will be sent only the very "best" people by your procurement agent. By "best," I mean that regardless of the category of end user, whether it be a novice, an experienced person, whomever, you are sent the cream of the crop, the high achievers. Your first reaction to this might be very positive, but on close inspection it is easy to see the potential problem here. The "best" end users typically possess the skills to plow through even the most hard-to-use products and perform admirably. Consequently, the product "tests out" much better than it should, and provides a false sense of confidence to the design and marketing team. Later, after release, when average and poor performers use it, many of the design flaws that exist, but did not come out during the test, are exposed.

This situation is especially apt to occur when you are acquiring participants under the following conditions:

- **When you will be testing end users from within your own company, usually from a department with which you are not familiar.**
- **When you are acquiring people directly from an established customer and participation is seen as an enviable perk.** In this case the manager responsible for providing people sends participants to your company as a reward for a job well done at their company. Invariably, these are their best performers.
- **When you are acquiring people from an established customer through your own sales force.** In this case, similar to the previous one, there is also a hidden agenda. Your sales rep very often has strong relationships which he or she would like to further by using the testing as a perk. These relationships are often with the best performers and most influential people in your customer's organization. You never see the average or poor performers.

I mention these situations as warnings since they are hard to predict. I have learned this the hard way, having had people show up as participants who were so accomplished that they should have been *designing* the product, never mind using it. Such users were able to foresee and work around the most troublesome areas, almost as if they knew they were there. One or at most two of these people during a test is reasonable, but if you see three or four, it plays havoc with your test results. These participants also tend to downplay whatever problems they might encounter, although they may be critical ones.

What makes the situation even worse is when the development team attending the test does not agree that these people are "ringers." The team is more than happy to bask in the glow of receiving unexpected but excellent results. Now, if you could just get all "ringers" to buy the product in sufficient numbers, everyone would be happy.

ACQUIRING PARTICIPANTS

Okay. So far so good. You have analyzed the user profile for your product, received confirmation that indeed you understand who the end user is, and have developed a list or matrix of the people that you would like to test with a description of their characteristics. The next step is to obtain the services of people who fit this description in order to conduct the test. However, before I discuss how and from where to acquire these people, there is one more step. You need to develop a screening questionnaire (more typically known as the *screener*) that will identify and screen for the characteristics you desire. This document is absolutely essential if you will be delegating responsibility for acquiring participants to either a peer or an outside agency. The screener is the means to communicate your requirements to another party. See Chapter 7 for information on how to develop the screener. Once you develop the screener, you are in a position to let others help locate participants by using your screener to qualify the candidates.

Now let's discuss some of the sources from which you can acquire participants. Here are the most common ones.

EMPLOYMENT AGENCIES

Employment agencies are a good source of participants for end users of common software packages and the like. There are temporary employment agencies now for almost every position in the work force, from word processing to programmers to system analysts. If you anticipate that you will be doing usability testing on an ongoing basis, it is best to work out a relationship with at least two temporary agencies. This is important for two reasons. First, because for difficult-to-find participants with uncommon backgrounds, you may need both agencies working to find people in order to meet your quota. Second, having a relationship with two agencies, and letting them know that you are shopping for price, enables you to negotiate the best rate. I recently conducted a usability test that required over 35 participants over a period of three weeks. I needed two agencies to fill out the roster, and was able to use the amount of people required and the fact that I was working with two agencies to negotiate a 20 percent discount.

Pricing varies by location in the country and of course by the skill level of the person you require. Expect to pay for end users at an hourly rate, which includes the agency fee and the person acquired. You may have to pay for a minimum of time, usually four hours. This means if you are using secretarial personnel whose agency rate is priced anywhere from $12 to $18 per hour, you may pay $50 and up for their services, even if you only use them for two hours. The agency usually needs this minimum time to justify its costs of advertising and acquiring people. Once you establish a relationship with a company and use that company on an ongoing basis, you can negotiate both the hourly rate and the minimum time required for people.

When using temporary agencies, there are some important, possibly biasing effects to keep in mind. First, the people who are recruited from agencies share the similar characteristic of being in the market for a job. This may affect their behavior during a test. Participants may be overly acquiescent and hesitant to criticize, thinking that it could hurt their chances to land a job at your company. Sometimes, this assumption is the result of misleading or erroneous information provided by the agency, so be careful not to let agencies imply that the testing process is in any way a tryout or possible entrance to a job with your company. Other times, it is based on the fact that the person has intentionally been given very little information about what he or she will be doing in order to avoid any potential expectations about the test. Suffice it to say, do not be surprised if people show up for a usability test with unclear expectations.

Another factor that makes an agency person different from the nonagency population is his or her availability to test during the day. That should not be the primary reason that you use people from an agency. Expect to do testing during the evening if your user profile requires specialized skills only possessed by people who ordinarily are working during the day, such as lawyers, accountants, chemists, and so on. It simply may require too much compensation to pull them away from their day jobs.

In terms of establishing a sound relationship with the temporary agency, it is very important that you be clear about what you are doing and what your needs are. Do not expect the agency to understand the discipline of usability testing. Having explained usability testing to a number of different agencies, I have had mixed results. I try to keep it very simple; lately describing testing simply as "market research." Simplicity and brevity are also important, so that the agency cannot inadvertently describe the testing procedure to potential candidates. In short, tell agencies only as much as they need to know to acquire the right participants and no more.

In addition to the screening questionnaire that the agencies will use, give them a written description of the exact way in which you would like your study described to potential candidates. Do not simply communicate this information verbally over the phone because something will get lost in the translation. Ask them to read your description verbatim. Keep it simple, keep it short, and, if necessary, keep it vague, such as, "We're conducting market research." Personally, I do not even like to use terms such as, "We'll be looking at ease of use." I prefer to fill in the participant about the exact nature of the research once he or she arrives.

Here are some anecdotes to illustrate the point. I have had people show up for tests, thinking that they were getting a demonstration of a new product which required *no effort* on their part. In the worst cases, people have arrived with preconceived expectations of the ease or difficulty of the tasks they would be performing. In one case, a person came in and explained to me that she was told by the agency that "even a baby could accomplish the tasks" she would be asked to perform. If that isn't biasing, I don't know what is. In trying to convince her to participate, the agency had gone over the line in making it seem as painless and simple as possible.

The best part about using temporary agencies is that as long as they are professional and reliable, they take the workload of acquiring participants completely off your shoulders. This can be a tremendous relief when it is all you can do just to pull the study together. Once you find an agency that serves your needs, hang on to it—it's a valuable resource.

One last point. It may be necessary for you to go through your own personnel department in working with temporary agencies. Some companies prohibit their employees from contacting agencies directly. If that is the case, spend some time to educate your in-house resource on all the potential pitfalls mentioned previously.

MARKET RESEARCH FIRMS

Market research firms recruit people for their client's marketing studies. Consequently, they will know exactly what you are talking about when you tell them that you need particular end users for a research study. They may not understand usability testing per se, but bringing in computer users, scientists, doctors, lawyers, chemists, and so on, for the purpose of gathering opinions and preferences is their business. The larger ones can get any type of person you ask for, for a price, and they usually can do it in a very short time frame. The best ones can literally get you people over the weekend for a study that starts on Monday. Almost all major cities now have at least one market research firm. Since they network with each other in order to conduct studies around the country and internationally, once you find a good one you can usually find another agency in a different city if you need to.

Market research firms therefore are the vehicle to use when it is important that you conduct usability testing in different geographical locations. They can also help with some of the other types of research tasks, such as surveys and focus groups.

Expect to pay a premium for acquiring participants from market research firms, especially if you need people quickly. They may ask anywhere from $50 to $125 and up per person, depending on the difficulty of obtaining the person and the amount of phone calls required. This does not include the actual compensation that you pay to the participant. However, once again, if you use the market research firm on a regular basis, you can negotiate the price down considerably, especially if it is a firm that is not yet established and is looking for business.

Typically, the firm will want to overrecruit by 20 percent in order to ensure that you get the right number of people. If you say you need 10 end users, the firm typically will want to line up 12 people and have 2 of them act as substitutes if another preson cancels or is a "no-show."

There is much less of a concern of a professional marketing firm biasing the participant and saying the wrong thing than there is with a temporary placement agency. However, it is critical that you provide a clear, concise screening questionnaire since the marketing firm still will not understand your product or possibly much about the person that you are looking for. So, be precise and clear in your communication.

Market research firms can also supply the facility for conducting the usability test. They typically are set up with focus group observation rooms complete with microphones, video tape/audio tape, and one-way mirrors. This is definitely the way to go when it is important that you conduct an anonymous study of your product (e.g., the company who made the product is not mentioned) and cannot have participants come to your own location.

EXISTING CUSTOMERS FROM IN-HOUSE LISTS

An excellent source of participant candidates is your own company's list of existing customers. If there is no formal list kept, explore other sources such as warranty card returns, various promotions to which customers have responded, or mailing lists. When contacting such customers, it is imperative, since you are representing your company, that you make clear that there are no "strings" attached and there is no hidden agenda. That is, their participation is not a marketing strategy intended to eke out more sales, but simply a means to gather information about future products and improve them accordingly. You should say this in writing in the recruiting letter, mentioning that this research is *not tied in any way* to a sales promotion.

Customer lists are a great source of participants who are experienced. If you are running a study with both experienced end users and those who have never used your product, then use the customer lists as a means of gathering the experienced people.

EXISTING CUSTOMERS THROUGH SALES REPRESENTATIVES

In larger companies the sales team may have access to the customers you would like to use for testing. However, the same caveats apply here as for temporary agencies. Since the sales reps already have relationships with customers around the country, they may have a different agenda than you do. In their zest to appear "in the know" to their customers about future products, they may say too much about the test. Or, they may simply be unaware of the usability testing process and the need for "average" as well as excellent performers.

Be specific about the types of people you need, as well as the importance of being vague about the subject matter of the test. In one test that I helped design that used existing customers and for which the sales reps served as the recruiters, one participant had obviously been primed by a sales rep. For his "test" of a new release of an existing product, he had diligently *studied the entire 300-page user guide of the current product the night before*. It seems that he took the notion of a usability "test" a mite too far. The key to counteracting these tendencies is to communicate clearly to your recruiters; that way you can nip these problems in the bud.

PERSONNEL DEPARTMENTS

Your company's personnel department may be able to direct you to qualified end users in your own organization. For example, if you are working on a product that requires a certain word processing expertise and you cannot use people who are working on the project directly, the personnel department can direct you to people within the company who would tend to have the appropriate experience, such as a financial group. You then could call them up yourself and make all the arrangements for using them as participants. Now, obviously internal personnel are not your first choice, but may be perfect for preliminary, more exploratory research. The personnel department, as I mentioned, may also want to coordinate your use of outside agencies, both temporary agencies and market research firms. It may have already set up relationships with these companies through other people doing research studies in your company of whom you may not be aware.

COLLEGE CAMPUSES

College students are always looking for extra cash and are delighted to help out by participating in usability tests. If college students are part of your user profile, by all means set up relationships with local colleges. One way to acquire students at colleges is to work directly with the college's outreach department that seeks out relationships with local businesses. In their desire to establish these relationships, these outreach departments will often bend over backwards to help you acquire what you need. In the case where there is no department providing that service, you will need to find a way to contact the students directly. Several ways are through:

- Bulletin boards
- Advertising in the college newspaper
- Word of mouth among college acquaintances
- Contacting the head of the Psychology department (Psychology departments are constantly conducting experiments using the student population as participants.)

Since it is so easy to acquire college students and they love the extra cash, you run the risk of overusing this population. As with any other group, college students have their own specific characteristics which may bias your study if you use them exclusively. For example, college students are probably more willing to try new things than the general population, and they are less apt to purchase products in their more precarious financial state. Therefore, use them judiciously and not as your sole source of participants.

NEWSPAPER ADVERTISEMENTS

Advertise in your local newspaper in the classified ad section for "participants needed for research study." In the advertisement, be vague. (Let me be precise about what I mean by vague. Just refer to market research or product testing without providing precise details about what the person will be doing.) Only state the qualifications necessary and the approximate amount of money you are willing to pay for qualified participants. Depending on your time constraints, you can have interested candidates either communicate to a mailing address or respond by phone. Responding by phone is much more labor intensive on your part, especially if you get many more interested people than you have slots for, but it is faster if you are working against a deadline. If you can, use a phone line with an explanatory message on voice mail or a standard answering machine. That way you can return calls at your leisure. Using a mailing address not only allows you greater control over the process, but controls the amount of responses. People are less likely to respond to a mailing address than to a phone call. Make it clear in your ad that people must qualify to participate.

If you are planning to do extensive testing, you will probably want to develop a database of qualified candidates for your product so that you can move quickly when it is time for a test. Following are the steps for doing so.

1. Advertise in the paper for a certain broad base of characteristics.
2. When interested people call up, send them a comprehensive questionnaire which elicits information about their backgrounds.
3. Once you get the questionnaire back, add the person's information to a database with different fields representing the different skills required.
4. When it is time for a test, you can then search the database by skill level required and call only qualified candidates.
5. Update the database after each test, showing the date of the last test. The advantage of this approach is that you are always ready with a list of potential participants who represent the market breakdown for your product on short notice.

Note: Depending on your needs and how frequently you conduct tests, it may require a full-time administrator to manage the database and manage the participant contact prior to the test.

USER GROUPS

Not many years ago, it was unusual to find more than one or two user groups who met regularly to share information about a particular product or service. Today there are literally hundreds of user groups whose common interest is the improved utility of products such as computers, operating systems, and particular spreadsheets. Typically, these groups are composed of people who range anywhere from novice to the most expert end users of particular software packages, hardware devices, and the like. What makes them an especially valuable resource is the fact that you can contact everyone in the group at once. Here is how.

Contact the chairman or head of the group directly. Ascertain when the next meeting is and prepare a solicitation to be distributed at that meeting. Have all the people who are interested contact you directly as soon as possible after that meeting. The entire process could even be conducted via electronic mail. For example, Compuserve, a prominent on-line service, lists a variety of user groups that you can contact directly.

QUALIFIED FRIENDS

All of us know people who may be qualified to participate in a study. This is especially true of products that are used by the population at large and for whom the characteristic audience is very broad based. You might have friends that share all the characteristics of your internal end users with the exception that they do not work for your company, a real advantage.

If you do end up using friends in your study, make sure that your relationship does not affect your professionalism. When testing, do everything exactly as you normally would including reading the orientation script, being sure not to talk about the study until after it is completed, and not being overly chummy during the test.

Regardless of whom you use to help you acquire participants, control the process as much as possible by being as specific as possible about your needs, anticipating miscommunications, and writing down the exact words you want the procurers to use. It is your study, it is your results, and the whole affair is seriously compromised when the wrong people show up.

SOME THOUGHTS ON PARTICIPANT COMPENSATION

It is customary to compensate those who serve as participants, although it need not always be monetary compensation. Participants acquired "off the street" or via an agency for a study where your company has been kept anonymous would all receive monetary compensation and possibly a small token of appreciation such as a pen or a T-shirt. Expect to pay the going rate on the open market for the skill level you are requesting. If your product will be used by secretarial personnel, expect to pay the hourly rate for secretaries. If you will be testing lawyers or doctors or other professionals, you may need to pay close to the hourly rate for that profession. If you will simply be testing with typical "consumers," with no specific profession required, expect to pay anywhere from $35–$75 for a 1/2 day session. Most times you will need to test in the evening if your user profile indicates end users who are not available during the day. If money is no object, however, you can get people to come in whenever you like.

Participants sent from one of your company's large clients, however, should be compensated differently depending on the relationship of your two companies. If their participation is part of an ongoing research relationship where they benefit from being privy to your company's future product line as much as you benefit from their input, then a token gift alone might suffice.

Even in the case where you have an ongoing research relationship with your customer, your company should offer to foot all the expenses such as travel and meals associated with having the person participate. If no strong relationship exists, you could provide anything from a small honorarium to paying the person's salary for the time he or she participated. Some other compensation choices are: discounted products from your company's sales catalog, gift certificates, or a simple memento, such as a T-shirt or calculator.

While you should always provide *something* of value in appreciation for participation, it is of the utmost importance that you do not imply in any way that compensation is tied to the person's performance. Participants simply get paid for showing up and giving it their best, and that's it. Even joking about this with the person is not a good idea, as it plants a seed in the person's mind that he or she needs to be "positive," which may prevent the person from being critical.

PREPARING

THE TEST

MATERIALS

7

INTRODUCTION

One of the more labor-intensive activities required to conduct a usability test is developing the test materials that will be used to communicate with the participants, collect the data, and satisfy legal requirements. It is important to develop all required test materials well in advance of the time you will need them. Apart from the obvious benefit of not having to scurry around at the last minute, developing materials early on helps to explicitly structure and organize the test. In fact, if you have difficulty developing one particular type of test material, it can be a sign that there are flaws in your test objectives and test design.

While the specific content of the materials will vary from test to test, the general categories required will hardly vary at all. This chapter contains a list of the most common materials you will need to develop a test, as well as examples of the various types of test materials. As you develop them, think of these materials as aids to the testing process. Once they are developed, their natural flow will guide the test for you. Be sure to leave enough time to include the materials in your pilot test. The test materials reviewed in this chapter are as follows:

- Screening questionnaire
- Orientation script
- Background questionnaire
- Data collection instruments (data loggers)
- Nondisclosure agreement and tape consent form
- Pretest questionnaire
- Task scenarios
- Prerequisite training materials
- Posttest questionnaire
- Debriefing topics guide

THE SCREENING QUESTIONNAIRE

DEFINITION AND PURPOSE

The screening questionnaire is the means for qualifying and selecting participants to participate in the test. Its content is typically obtained from your user profile and test plan. The questionnaire is usually presented over the phone, although it can also be given to potential participants in person or through the mail. If you will be using a colleague, an outside consultant, or an agency to help you recruit participants, the screening questionnaire is your primary way of describing the people you need in an unambiguous format. While some agencies will develop their own screeners based on information you provide, *you must review their questionnaires before they begin using them*, to ensure that your instructions have been understood.

A screening questionnaire can be extremely simple or quite involved, depending on the variability and background of the potential participants of the product. Either way, I have found that developing the screening questionnaire exposes any uncertainties and lack of clarity in one's own understanding of the end users. It forces you to express the background of your participants in precise, measurable terms.

DEVELOPMENT AND ADMINISTRATION GUIDELINES

Following are some simple guidelines for developing a screening questionnaire to be administered over the telephone.

1. **Review the end user profile or expected market profile in order to understand the backgrounds of the people you need to test.**

2. **Focus on and pull out those characteristics that are unique to your product and not just general categories of the population.** For example, spreadsheet experience qualifies as a unique prerequisite for an add-on product that makes spreadsheets easier to use. But, since the product will be used by all age groups, you need not screen for a particular age group to include in your test sample. Later, as you are acquiring participants, you can simply make sure that you get a representative sample of different ages.

3. **Once you have isolated the different factors for which you are screening, formulate questions to ascertain whether a person has that expertise.**

4. **Now organize the questions in a specific order.** It usually makes sense to place those questions first that are most likely to disqualify a person, keeping in mind basic telephone etiquette at the same time. For example, if you were testing a desktop publishing product that was designed for seasoned end users with knowledge of color theory, you would not want to ask 20 very general questions only to find out in question 21 that the person you are speaking with does not know saturation from hue. You should establish that background early in the call to limit the phone time. On the other hand, that is not the type of high-level question you can ask first either. You need to work your way into it.

5. **Develop a format that allows easy movement through the questionnaire while on the phone.** Allow the caller to branch from one question to the next without thinking too much about the answers. This is especially important if you use an outside agency and the callers do not have an in-depth understanding of your product.

6. **Test the questionnaire on colleagues and revise.** (Yes, you are right. This *is* a usability test of the screener!) If it is a phone questionnaire, use the phone. You would be surprised, but it makes a difference.

7. **If it is not obvious by your format, develop an "answer sheet" separately or right on the questionnaire that provides the replies that qualify a participant, and how many of each category you need.**

Now that you have the questionnaire developed, here are some guidelines for administering it over the phone or having someone do it for you. (The latter is always advisable if you have the resources.)

1. **Inform the potential participant who you are.** If the usability test is being run as an anonymous one (the name of the sponsoring company remaining confidential), then of course the research firm or person calling should mention this fact and give the reasons for anonymity.

2. **Explain why you are calling.** Briefly explain the nature of the research. By all means, be sure to mention that the job requires the participant to be videotaped, since you want participants to raise any objections to being taped now, and not when they arrive for testing. Ask the potential participant if he or she is interested in hearing more, and, if so, explain how long (worst case) it will take you to ask all the questions on the screening questionnaire. (If it is a really long questionnaire, try to fudge the part about how long it will take. Many professionals simply say that it depends on the answers, which is true I suppose.) If the person is not interested, then express your thanks, mention how much fun he or she will be missing, and, if appropriate, ask for recommendations of other interested parties.

3. **Based on your test plan's end user profile, question the person about his or her qualifications, such as computer experience, job responsibilities, and equipment used.** If you need to gather personal information, such as age or salary, frame your questions in ranges, since people are often reluctant to divulge exact personal details. For example, instead of asking, "How old are you?" ask instead,

   "Into what category does your age fall?"

   __18–29   __30–39   __40–49   __50 +

4. **As you eliminate or accept people, mark them off on your list.** There is nothing more embarrassing than calling the same person and getting them out of the shower two days in a row.

5. **If you are using an outside agency, have the agency try the questionnaire on you as if you were a potential participant.** See how the person who calls you responds to different and/or ambiguous answers to the same question. It is your money and your study. Make sure the agency does it right.

   Figure 7.1 shows an example of a screening questionnaire that was developed for the usability test of an inexpensive personal printer. This questionnaire could be administered by phone or in person. Note how the questions are intended to screen for a very specific market, namely an unsophisticated end user with very simple printing needs. The responses in *italics* represent the experience and printing needs of that desired end user. Answers that differ disqualify a potential participant from participation.

1. Do you work with a computer on a regular basis or plan to purchase one within the next 3 months?
   Yes

2. How many printers have you previously purchased?
   0 or 1

3. Have you ever purchased a laser printer or do you use one on a regular basis?
   No

4. When printing, how many different typefaces do you use at one time?
   3 or less

5. Of your total time spent using a computer, please indicate the percentage of time you spend using each application.

Word Processing	*<80%*
Spreadsheet	*≤80%*
Database	*<10%*
Desk Top Publishing	*<5%*
Other	*<5%*

6. If you currently use a computer and printer, do you require a wide-carriage printer or one that can print multipart forms?
   No

Figure 7.1 Sample Screening Questionnaire

THE ORIENTATION SCRIPT

DEFINITION AND PURPOSE

The orientation script (also known as the test script) is a communications tool meant to be read verbatim to participants. It describes what will happen during a test session, sets the tone for that session in the minds of the participants, and is intended to put them at ease. It achieves this by informing the participants of what they will be doing, and reinforcing the fact that the product and not the participant is being tested. Remember that participants often have only the vaguest idea of what they will be doing, possibly having been presented with only some ambiguous reference to "participation in market research," or the like. For a particularly nervous participant, the orientation script can provide reassurance that he or she is actually the "right" person in the "right" place.

The script may be read to the participants in the testing area or in a "waiting or meeting area" prior to moving to the testing space. My own preference is to read it just before beginning testing activities, which occur in the main testing area.

DEVELOPMENT GUIDELINES

When developing an orientation script, there are three major guidelines to remember.

1. **Keep the tone of the script professional, but friendly.** It should *not* be chummy or overly familiar as if the participants were your buddies. For example, in the food service industry, the waiter who asks for your name and continues to use it ad nauseam during the meal comes to mind as an instance of this lack of professionalism in the guise of improved service.

2. **Unless you have an extremely complex test, limit the orientation script to one or two pages.** Anything longer than that will not be retained by the participants in any case. Any instructions beyond two pages probably means that you are including actual test materials such as task scenarios, as part of your script.

3. **Plan to read the script to each participant verbatim.** Do *not* attempt to memorize the script, paraphrase it, or simply "wing it" from session to session. Here is why this is so important:

   - You want to present the exact same information to each participant so that all the participants are exposed to identical conditions prior to the test. By paraphrasing the script, you may change what you say in very subtle ways.

     Note: If you feel self-conscious reading the script or feel that it sets an overly formal tone, then simply tell the participant why you are reading it. For example, "I'm going to read this script to you now so that I provide the exact instructions to you that I provide to everybody else, and so that I do not forget anything of importance."

   - People are easily influenced by past events. Imagine that you have just tested the first four participants and are about to test the fifth one. Three of the first four have performed miserably. Not only did they have great difficulty with the product, but they hated using it. You may be feeling down and discouraged, and are unknowingly about to project your feeling of frustration to the fifth participant by the manner in which you introduce the session. However, reading the script forces you to use the same language, which in turn makes it easier to control the nonverbal aspects of your communication, such as your mannerisms, expressions, and voice modulation. In short, it is harder to express your own frustration when you read the script.

- More than one test monitor may be conducting the test over a period of time. If that is so, there is a need to minimize the differences in the test monitors as much as possible. Reading the script at the very least accounts for controlling the initial information that is communicated to the participants.

- Those members of the development team not present at the sessions will want to know precisely what was said to the participants. Showing the script to interested parties who were unable to attend the usability test accomplishes this objective. It also communicates professionalism and rigorousness on your part.

- You may forget an important point. There are so many details involved with monitoring a test, why make it hard on yourself? Use the script and cross "what to say" off your list of things to remember and worry about.

TYPICAL CONTENTS

Following is a list of the typical contents of an orientation script. However, do *not* feel that you need to include every category in your own script. If you do, you might end up writing an essay.

1. **Make introductions.** Introduce yourself, of course, and anyone else whom the participant is likely to encounter during the usability test. You need not go into great detail about people's backgrounds; just a passing reference to the function of each person is fine. For example, you might say, "That person over there will be attending to the videotape camera," or "That person over there will be taking some timings." *Never* volunteer the fact that any person associated with the test or observing in the same room has worked on the product that the participants will be testing. Of course, if a participant asks (hardly anyone ever does), then by all means tell that participant the truth, but do not *volunteer* that information. The reason for this is simple; you want the participants to feel absolutely unencumbered about providing any negative feedback. Associating real people with the product only makes being honest that much more difficult.

As test monitor, include yourself in this "nonassociation" guideline if you are affiliated with the product. (Ideally, you will not be affiliated with the product.) Explain your role as the person who will be monitoring the test, observing, and taking notes. If you are not affiliated with the product, then play up the fact that you are a neutral observer. If you will be monitoring the usability test in the test room, then explain exactly what you will be doing during the test.

2. **Offer refreshments.** Being offered refreshments will help the participants to relax and feel at home. They are more apt to indulge if you already have a cup of coffee, soda, or water in your hand. "Breaking bread" together is a wonderful ice-breaker. Do not downplay the fact that your participants may be nervous. It is very common and you need to address it.

3. **Explain why they are here.** You may think that they already know this information, but you would be amazed at what participants are told about their involvement. Provide enough detail and context about the product for them to perform the tasks. Do not feel you need to provide product history, number of participants being tested, and so forth. Express appreciation for their willingness to participate and how much their input helps produce a better product, *regardless of how they perform*. In no way, shape, or form should the performance of the participants be tied to their compensation for participating, *even as a joke*. You can be sure that the thought crossed their mind. No need to reinforce it.

4. **Describe the lay of the land.** Point out and describe the equipment. Let the participants know whether they will be staying where they are, moving to another room, and so on. Locate the restrooms. Let them know if:

   • People are watching from behind a one-way mirror or from another room via cameras.

   Note: Do not get cute here and say, "Oh that old thing. It's just so we can see all sides of the equipment."

   • The session is being videotaped. It is *never* a good idea to lie to participants about being observed or taped in order *not* to make them nervous. First of all, it is not ethical. Second, once the test starts, almost all participants forget their concerns about being watched and taped, depending on the testing environment.

5. **Explain what is expected of the participants.** Describe how the usability test will proceed without providing every last detail. Broach the subject of nondisclosure, if you have not already done so, and how that will be handled. Encourage them to perform as they normally would (e.g., same speed and attention to detail, given the fact that it is an artificial situation). Encourage the participants to ask questions and to take breaks if they need to.

Avoid any reference whatsoever to your expectations of their behavior or performance. Remain absolutely neutral in terms of their expected performance.

For example, do not say any of the following in order to make them less nervous:

- "Most people find this extremely easy."
- "We brought you in for an extremely simple test."
- "I'm sure you'll have no difficulty with this product, so don't be nervous."

While well intentioned, these are exactly the *wrong* things to say. By making those references, you have essentially put the participants on the defensive if things *do* get difficult. At the slightest hint of adversity, they may begin to hurry and try harder in order to fulfill your expectations. After all, if it is simple and they are having a hard time, then by definition they must be slow. No one likes to think of himself or herself that way.

6. **Assure the participants that they are not being tested.** This is probably the most familiar adage of testing, and you should certainly say this. However, do not hold out hope that they will necessarily believe you just because you say it. This slogan has become the "it's for your own good" slogan of our youth. It is often repeated but never believed. Only the manner in which the test is conducted, and the way in which you react to the person's behavior, will cause the truth of this adage to sink in. Your manner, body language, and voice modulation during difficulties all communicate much more than just the words. In sum, do not be surprised if at the first sign of difficulty, you hear the participant mutter that familiar refrain, "Oh, I'm an idiot. That wasn't the program's fault."

7. **Explain any unusual requirements or testing conventions, such as "thinking aloud" protocol.** Demonstrate how these special situations work, and reassure the participant that you will be available to remind him or her how to do it, if need be.

8. **Mention that it is okay to ask questions at any time.** Of course, explain that you may not answer those questions in order to simulate the situation of their being alone and having to rely on their own resources and materials at hand. Make that aspect of your role very clear. You are not there to solve problems participants encounter.

9. **Ask for any questions.** Before you begin, be absolutely sure that the participants understood your instructions. Due to being nervous and/or poor acoustics in the room, the participants may not have fully heard or understood your

"Hi, my name is John Doe. I'll be working with you in today's session. Let me explain why we've asked you to come in today.

We're here to test how easy it is to use a new product, a turbocharged widget, and we'd like your help. In order to ensure that the name of the company does not influence you in any way, I'll keep the identity of the sponsoring company anonymous until the very end.

You will be performing some typical tasks with the widget today, and I'd like you to perform as you normally would. For example, try to work at the same speed and with the same attention to detail that you normally do. Do your best, but don't be all that concerned with results. This is a test of the widget, still in prototype form, and it may not work as you expect. You may ask questions at any time, but I may not answer them, since this is a study of the product and its written support materials, and we need to see how they work with a person such as yourself working independently.

During today's session, I'll also be asking you to complete some forms and answer some questions. It's important that you answer truthfully. My only role here today is to discover both the flaws and advantages of this product from your perspective. (Alternately if an outside consultant: I'm an independent researcher hired by the sponsoring company, and I have no affiliation with the product whatsoever.) So don't answer questions based on what you think I may want to hear. I need to know exactly what you think.

While you are working, I'll be sitting nearby taking some notes and timings. In addition, you and I will be in a room which others may be watching via cameras. Also, the session will be videotaped for the benefit of those who could not be here today.

Do you have any questions?

If not, then let's begin by having you sign the nondisclosure agreement and consent to tape form."

Figure 7.2 Sample Orientation Script

instructions. If you are not sure, ask them to parrot back a particular point by inquiring, for example, "Do you remember how to use the thinking aloud protocol?"

10. **Refer to any forms that need be completed and pass them out.** This includes background questionnaires, pretest questionnaires, permissions, and so on.

See Figure 7.2 for an example of an orientation script.

THE BACKGROUND QUESTIONNAIRE

DEFINITION AND PURPOSE

The background questionnaire provides historical information about the participants that will help you to understand their behavior and performance during a test. It is composed of questions that reveal their experience, attitudes, and preferences in all areas that might affect how they perform. For example, if you are testing a database management system (DBMS), it will be helpful to know if the participants have used a DBMS before, and, if so, which one(s) and for how long. While you will not know if that experience will affect their performance negatively or positively, you almost certainly know that it *will* affect their performance differently than a person without DBMS experience.

The background questionnaire is typically filled out just prior to the test. Sometimes, particularly if it is lengthy, you might mail it to the participant ahead of time.

The information to be included in the background questionnaire is initially culled from the participant profile in your test plan. The background questionnaire is similar to a phone screener, although more detailed. The phone screen need only determine if a potential participant falls into a broad category, such as 3 + years of experience with word processors. That is enough information to include the person as a participant in the "experienced word processing user group" or to screen them out. The background questionnaire, however, goes further by exploring which word processing packages the participant used, for how long, and how the packages were learned. This more specific information can help explain a participant's behavior during the test. Perhaps the participant is choosing buttons or menu selections based on expectations formed from using a competitive product that no other participant used.

In addition to the previously stated reasons for acquiring the correct cross section of participants and providing insight about each person's performance from a historical perspective, there are two more purposes for the background questionnaire. Both come into play on the day of the test, just prior to its beginning.

1. **To confirm that the "right" people show up.** It is amazing how often mix-ups occur when there are so many details to manage. If you did not make the phone calls or write the letters yourself to screen and acquire participants, it is important to verify that the people who show up actually possess the skills and knowledge you expected. It is not that unusual for temporary agencies to misunderstand what you are doing and to send unqualified people. If you do get the wrong people showing up, you will need to decide on the spot whether to use them or release them. You will also need to communicate to the person or organization supplying your participants that they need to do a better job of qualifying the participants.

2. **To provide a synopsis of each participant for the test monitor and for product developers who observe the test.** If you anticipate that the usability tests will be observed by a development team or other interested parties, it is important that they know the background of each person *as they observe the test*. It is both confusing and misleading to observe a test without a sense of the skills, knowledge, and experience of the specific participant. There is no basis on which to judge how participants are doing or why they are performing as they are. To avoid this potential misunderstanding, make the background question- naire available to the observers immediately after the participant fills it out. The observers can reference it while the test proceeds.

DEVELOPMENT GUIDELINES

1. **Ascertain all background information that you feel may affect the performance of the participants.** Figure 7.3 is composed of categories of personal characteris- tics and experience of participants typically gathered when testing a software product.

2. **Design the questionnaire for the ease of both yourself (in analyzing the responses) and the participants (in having to remember their history), by avoiding open-ended questions.** Have the participants check off boxes or circle answers. This will also minimize their time to fill out the questionnaire (im- portant if they will be filling it out the day of the test) and will decrease the number of unintelligible answers.

3. **Try the questionnaire out on someone who fits the end user profile or even on a colleague.** It is amazing how easy it is for ambiguity to sneak in.

4. **If the questionnaire is brief (a page or two), then let the participants fill it out just prior to the test.** You might even conduct an interview to collect the information, or ask them to expand their answers, which also allows you to establish a rapport with each of the participants. If the questionnaire is lengthy,

Category	Characteristics/Experience
Demographics	Age (use a range) Sex Highest grade completed Subjects studied Major Left or right handed (could affect mouse usage for example)
Computer experience	Total time using Frequency of use Types of equipment used Types of software used Frequency of software used Operating systems used Types of screen interaction used (e.g., a graphical interface vs. a DOS-based interface)
Application/product experience (e.g., accounting and/or word processing)	Total time using Frequency of use Types of tasks performed Frequency of tasks Types/brands (in house vs. vendor supplied)
Preferences	Attitude toward computers Attitude toward your type of product Attitude toward using documentation Learning style preference (e.g., read then do, try then read, learn by doing)
Other	Typing skill

Figure 7.3 Personal Characteristics and Experience List

consider sending it to the participants prior to the test. They can either bring it with them to the test or mail it back as long as there is sufficient time before the test.

Figure 7.4 shows a sample background questionnaire associated with the test of a company's latest widget analyzer, a product that runs on a PC.

SAMPLE BACKGROUND QUESTIONNAIRE

Name:_____   Company:_____
Job Title:_____

Please answer the questions below in order to help us understand your background and experience.

EDUCATION (Please circle the highest grade level achieved below.)

Grade School   High School   College: 1 2 3 4

Graduate: 1 2 3 4   Post Graduate

If you graduated from college, please list your major area of study.

_____

COMPUTER EXPERIENCE

1. What is the total length of time you have been using personal computers.
    _____

2. On a typical day, how often do you use a computer to perform your job?
    _____

3. Please circle the types of computer applications you have used before,
    followed by the approximate months of experience with each one used.

    Application   **Months of Experience**

    Database   _____
    Spreadsheet   _____
    Word Processing   _____
    Desk Top Publishing   _____
    Design (e.g., CAD/CAM)   _____
    Manufacturing   _____
    Engineering   _____
    Other: _____

    _____   _____
    _____   _____
    _____   _____

Figure 7.4 Sample Background Questionnaire

PRODUCT EXPERIENCE

1. How long have you worked with widget analyzers?

   _____

2. Have you ever worked with the XYZ widget analyzer? ___Yes ___No

3. Have you used other widget analyzers as well? ___Yes ___No

   If yes, please specify the type and brand name.

   _____

4. What type(s) of widget analyses do you typically perform on the job?

   _____

5. Please describe the widget analysis configuration on which you typically work, for example the number of widgets analyzed at once and the type of analysis performed.

   _____
   _____
   _____

6. Do you ever develop new analysis techniques as part of your job?
   ___Yes ___No

   If yes, about how many hours per week do you spend developing new techniques?

   _____

7. If you have used a PC-based program to control your widget analyzer, what type is it?

   _____

   How long have you used it? _____

Figure 7.4 (*Continued*)

THE DATA COLLECTION INSTRUMENTS (DATA LOGGERS)

DEFINITION AND PURPOSE

The purpose of the data collection instruments (data loggers) is to expedite the collection of all data pertinent to the test objectives. The intent is to collect data during the test as simply, concisely, and reliably as possible.

There are a myriad of data types from which to choose. For simplicity's sake, data collected during a test falls into two major categories:

1. Performance data
2. Preference data

Performance data consists of objective measures of *behavior*, such as error rates, time measures, and counts of observed behavior elements. This type of data comes from observation of either the live test or review of the videotape after the test has been completed. The time required to complete a task is an example of a performance measure.

Preference data consists of the more subjective data that measures a participant's *feelings or opinions* of the product. This data is typically collected via written, oral, or even on-line questionnaires or through the debriefing session after the test. A rating scale that measures how a participant feels about the product is an example of a preference measure.

Both performance and preference data can be analyzed quantitatively or qualitatively. For example, on the performance side, errors can be analyzed quantitatively by simply counting the number of errors made on a task. Errors could also be analyzed qualitatively to expose places where the user does not understand the product's conceptual model.

On the preference side, a quantitative measure would be the number of unsolicited negative comments made by a participant. Or, qualitatively, each negative comment could be analyzed to discover what aspect of the product's design the comment refers to.

In terms of the product development life cycle, exploratory tests usually favor qualitative research, due to the emphasis on the user's understanding of high-level concepts. Validation tests favor quantitative research, due to the emphasis on adherence to standards. Assessment tests usually gather both types of measures.

Following are examples of performance data.

TIME DURATIONS

- Time to complete a task
- Time to achieve a criterion level of competence
- Training time to achieve benchmark performance
- Time to recover from an error
- Time spent reading vs. working

COUNTS AND RATES

- Number of errors
- Percentage of tasks completed successfully
- Frequency of assessing on-line help
- Number of omitted steps or procedures
- Scores on a comprehension test

Following are examples of preference data.

PARTICIPANT COMMENTS AND OPINIONS

- Preference of Version A vs. Version B
- Suggestions for improving the product
- Number of *negative* references to the product
- Rationales for performance
- Ratings or rankings of the product

Let us not get ahead of ourselves though. Before simply collecting data, you need to consider the following basic questions:

1. What data will address the problem statement(s) in your test plan?
2. How will you collect the data?
3. How will you record the data?
4. How do you plan to reduce and analyze the data?
5. How and to whom will you report the data?
6. What resources are available to help with the entire process?

The answers to these questions will drive the development of the instruments, tools, and even the number of people required to collect the data. Data collection should never just be a hunting expedition, where you collect information first, and worry about what to do with it later. This holds true even for the most preliminary type of exploratory testing. If you take that approach, you run the risk of matching the data to hoped-for results.

Also, an imprecise shotgun approach typically results in an unwieldy amount of data to reduce and analyze, and tends to confuse more than enlighten. The type of data you collect should be as clear in your mind as possible prior to the test and should be tied directly to the questions and issues you are trying to resolve.

GUIDELINES AND STRATEGY

Following is a systematic strategy for developing the collection instruments that takes into consideration the six critical questions discussed previously.

1. **Review the problem statement(s) outlined in your test plan.** If after reviewing these, you have a difficult time ascertaining what data to collect, *regard that as an important message*. More often than not, it means that you need to clarify the problem statement(s) to make them more specific. This may require reinterviewing the developers and educating them as well.

2. **Decide what type of information to collect.** Match the type of data collected to the problem statement of the test plan. Figure 7.5 shows several matchups of problem statement with data collected.

   Please be aware that there are numerous ways to collect data that address these problem statements. The ones shown in Figure 7.5 are only examples.

   If you are unsure where to begin, start simply. For a typical test, it is common to collect at least the following information for each participant observed:

   • Whether each task was completed successfully
   • Whether prompting or assistance was required
   • Time required to perform each task
   • Major problems/obstacles associated with each task
   • Observations/comments concerning each participant's actions

3. **Select a data collection method.** Once you are clear about the type of data you want to collect and how it will help you to achieve the test objectives, the next challenge is to develop the means for collecting that data. In terms of data collection instruments, you are limited only by your imagination, resources, and

Problem Statement	Data Collected
How effective is a tutorial in teaching a specific task?	Time expired between accessing the tutorial and successful completion of the task. - OR - Comparison of error rates of participants using and not using the tutorial.
How easy is it to perform a specific task using a new hardware-based product?	Error rate among all participants. - OR - Number of steps required to perform the task.
Do novice participants access our new hypertext help system?	Number of unsolicited accesses of the help system prior to task completion. - AND - Explanations of why participants did not avail themselves of the help.
How accessible is information in the user's guide?	Time expired between searching for a specific piece of information and locating the correct page.

Figure 7.5   Problem Statement/Data Collection Table

the time required to develop them. Will you have help with the collection? Will you have help reducing and analyzing the data once it is collected? It makes no sense at all to design a data collection method that requires extensive analysis of 20 hours of videotape if you only have two weeks after the test in which to provide a test report.

Let me suggest an approach that I have used successfully. Envision yourself creating the test report and even making a presentation to members of the team. Visualize the *type* of findings you will want to report, if not the actual content. Then, given the amount of time and resources at your disposal, plan how you will get to that point once the test has ended. Your data collection effort should be bounded by that constraint, unless you realistically feel that you or someone else will be able to analyze additional data at a later date.

Data can be collected by yourself, other observers, the participants themselves, or through automated tools known as data loggers or data recorders. Let's look at some of these methods to understand the options available.

FULLY AUTOMATED DATA LOGGERS

Fully automated data loggers are tools for collecting data by using a computer, with no intervention required by the test monitor or the participant. Typically, they are keystroke-capture recorders used as part of a usability test of computer software. The software keeps a record of every keystroke made by a participant and when it occurred. It compiles this data for review after the test. Some loggers will not only count the number and type of keystrokes made, but will ascertain where in the program a participant ventured when trying to complete a specific task. These loggers will note which screens were accessed and the total time spent on each. One could tell, for example, how many times a participant accessed help or on-line documentation, or even if and when a participant accidentally logged off the program. Please note, however, that it is extremely time consuming to analyze the results of a keystroke capture session. There are many more efficient ways to expose usability problems.

ON-LINE DATA COLLECTION

Data collection by the test monitor can take the form of collection forms on a computer screen. The computer screen is used by the test monitor to record participant actions and to enter observations and comments directly into a computer. Rather than noting the actions and events on a paper form, the test monitor enters events as they occur simply by choosing from predetermined choices on the screen. The computer program automatically time stamps the event and creates a log. By simplifying the data entry down to the selection of a radio button or check box or code, the test monitor or an observer can more easily keep up with a participant's performance during the test. The test monitor or the observer can also enter free-form text into the program as well, rather than having to do it manually.

Figure 7.6 shows an example of one screen of a test log created using TestLogr, a commercial data logger.

This product allows you to enter quick codes which represent specific events that happen during the test. It allows you to forego pencil and paper, and

		Date: 08/29/93	
		Current Log: DEMO	

TAPE TIME	MEANING	DESCRIPTION	WALL TIME
00.00.00	Start Test	Sample Test	08:07:19
00:00:07	Start Task	Task 1 - Set up the digitizer.	08:07:26
00:00:37	Error	Opens wrong manual.	08:07:56
00:01:02	Document	Finds mistake. Opens Quick Setup Guide.	08:08:21
00:01:42	Critical	Does not follow sequence in guide.	08:09:01
00:02:02	Help Needed	Had to intervene. Placing cable in backwards.	08:09:21
00:02:37	Comment (User)	This is really really hard.	08:09:56
00:02:59	Comment (Observer)	She's right. This is really really hard.	08:10:18
00:05:02	Inter Question	Ask later: Why did you start on page 10?	08:12:21
00:05:31	Comment (User)	I want to go home.	08:12:50
00:06:15	Finish Task	Task 1 - Set up the digitizer.	08:13:34
00:06:15	===TASK===	Total Time: 00:06:15	08:13:34
00:06:51	End Test	End of Test	08:14:10
00:06:51	===TEST===	Total Time: 00:06:51	08:14:10

F1=Help   F3=Exit   F7=Finding   F8=Add   F9=Edit   Del=Delete   PgDn/PgUp

Figure 7.6   Sample Test Log Using TestLogr

makes for a simple summary of the test later. In addition, since the program can be synchronized with your video recorder, it allows you to move to the exact spot on tape to review an event later. There are also statistics routines available for summarizing the data that has been logged.

You could also develop your own data logger as shown in Figures 7.7a and 7b. This version was developed using Visual Basic for Windows.

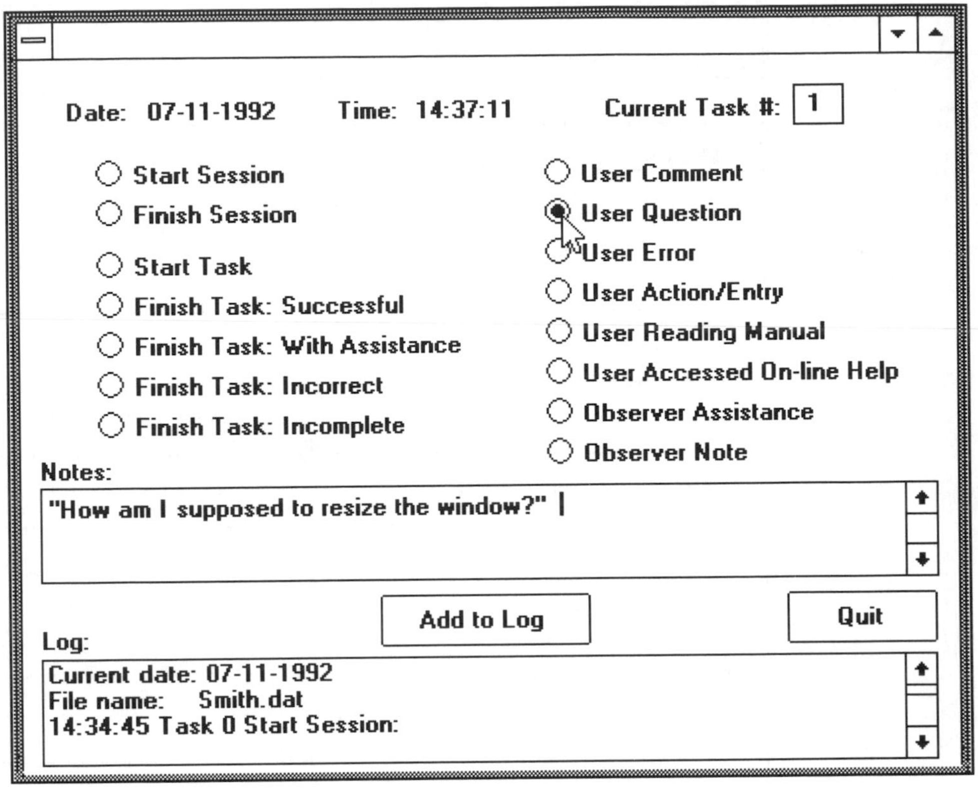

Figure 7.7a   Ad Hoc Data Logger Entry Screen (Courtesy of T. Tullis, Canon Information Systems)

In the examples given in Figures 7.7a and b, start and completion times as well as the completion status are logged by clicking the appropriate radio buttons on the screen. Then participant actions and events are entered by choosing the corresponding radio button. Comments are typed directly into the "Comments" text entry field.

Following the test, a second program reads each participant's file and derives summary statistics, such as average completion times, percentage of tasks completed successfully, and so forth. The comments are also written to a file for inclusion in the test report.

Data loggers such as these can move you from data collection to data reporting faster than most manual collection, since much of the data is already entered. The downside is that the amount of concentration required to use the program at first may limit the amount of test monitor interaction with the participants. Of course, if one is conducting an unobtrusive test, with little interaction, the

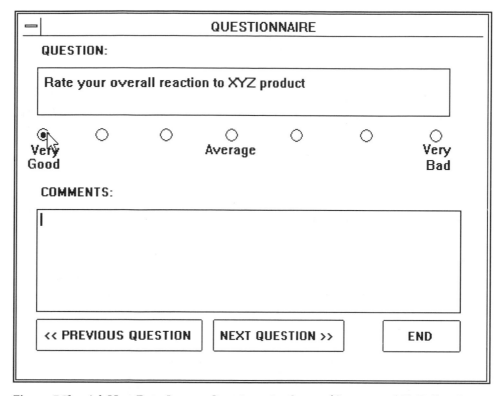

Figure 7.7b Ad Hoc Data Logger Questionnaire Screen (Courtesy of T. Tullis, Canon Information Systems)

point is moot. Or, you could simply have another observer log the events on this program while you, the test monitor, give your full attention to the more subtle aspects of behavior. When pen-based computers with handwriting recognition software become perfected, that will provide an even more promising alternative to the entry of written comments.

USER-GENERATED DATA COLLECTION (SELF-REPORTING)

Another form of data collection is one initiated by the participants themselves, and is especially helpful to organizations with few internal resources. User-generated data collection can take one of two formats, either on-line or manual collection. In the on-line format, the participant accesses a data collection form on the same computer that is being used for the test. The form, usually a questionnaire or checklist, interrogates the participant about a task just completed. The screen can be fetched by the participant (more intrusive) or can be displayed automatically by the software upon completion of a task or upon reaching a time benchmark (less intrusive). In the latter case, participants may even perceive that the data collection is a seamless part of their task. The questionnaire will typically cover such items as participant rankings of ease of use, preferences for one type of interface over another, frequency of using an index, and so on.

In the second format, manual collection, each participant fills out a written questionnaire after completing a specific task, section of a manual, or type of interface. Filling out the questionnaire represents a pause in the test, so the questionnaire needs to be structured to make it as unobtrusive as possible. In designing these questionnaires and checklists, one needs to be wary of the following two potential pitfalls [103] [107]:

1. Wording the questions in a biased way
2. Using terms unfamiliar to the participants

The user-generated/self-reporting technique naturally lends itself to the collection of comparative data (e.g., two different interfaces, two different manual styles, etc.) and to the type of test where subjective data (preference data) is the main focus.

MANUAL DATA COLLECTION

Manual data collection is performed by one or more human observers of the test either during or after the test, using customized paper data collection forms. This is the format you are most likely to use if you are just beginning to test. Data collected could be in the form of notes, observations, counts, or time durations. The forms employed can vary from the elaborate (custom-designed multipage forms) to the simple (drafts of the screens or pages of the documentation being tested). The form can be used for collecting quantitative data, such as the number of times a manual was accessed, or qualitative data, such as specific comments made by a participant. It can also be used to collect interpretations of a participant's behavior by the observer. For example, you might note that a particular participant seems very confused while reading page 5. There are several examples of data collection forms to support manual data collection at the end of this section.

OTHER DATA COLLECTION METHODS

As previously mentioned, data collection is limited only by your imagination. Several years ago, when a colleague and I were conducting a test of the documentation of a mainframe telecommunications system at Bell Laboratories, we came upon a simple way of determining what sections of the manual were being completely ignored. We glued together every page of the manual with a special glue that provided very slight resistance when a page was turned. The participants noticed nothing unusual during the test, attributing any stickiness of the pages to the fact that the book was new. At the end of the test, we had a foolproof method for establishing which sections of the manual were never used. Wherever the glue was still in place, we knew that a particular participant had never even glanced at that page, and we discovered whole sections that were still glued together. I have to admit that this method resulted less from our zeal to break new ground in scientific methods than it did from simple laziness. Neither of us wanted to focus on the pages that were avoided during the test, nor review hours of videotape to establish what each participant was and was not reading.

When designing a data collection form to be used by yourself and other observers, design for efficiency and ease of use. The idea is to anticipate the events that will happen during the test and to design the form or screen to limit the amount of data entry required as much as possible. Do *not* require a handwritten entry when a check-off box will suffice. By anticipating the type of data and the actions of the participants you will be observing and noting, your

Code	Event
B	Begin a task.
E	End a task.
P	Prompted by test monitor.
M	Exceeded time benchmark.
X	Incorrect action.
" "	Quotations represent a verbatim user comment.
R	Reading the manual.
H	Accessing help screen.
?	Probe user about this activity during the debriefing session.
O	Observation by test monitor.
**	Very important action.

Figure 7.8 Simple Coding Scheme

form can significantly reduce the time required to collect data. This frees you to pay attention to the subtleties of the test and to probe each participant's behavior as needed.

Once you have minimized the amount of writing you will need to do during the test as much as possible, there are two methods still available for reducing further the amount of writing required by human observers. One way is to write notes using shorthand or your own version of shorthand. Make sure that you have a translation of your shorthand available if someone else needs to read your notes.

The second method is to develop one- or two-letter codes or number codes to represent each critical event that might occur during the test. The test monitor will jot the code down every time the critical behavior is witnessed. Figure 7.8 shows a simple coding scheme for data collection.

Name:		Participant #:
Date: Time:		Pg ___ of ___

Task Name	Elapsed Time	Observations Comments & Notes

Figure 7.9   Generic Data Collection Form

Customize your own codes to your specific needs. The coding schemes can get quite elaborate, so make sure that you can at least remember them without having to look them up, as that defeats one purpose of having them. The other purpose is for quick evaluation of the data collection sheets during analysis. Make sure that the codes are easy to spot, especially if someone else will be helping you analyze the data.

XYZ GETTING STARTED TUTORIAL

Start: _____   End: _____

Directions to Test Monitor:

Please observe the participant using the entire tutorial from beginning to end. Write down the page number and a short description of all *unexpected* events.

Page No.   Observations/Remarks

Figure 7.10 Data Collection Form for a Written Tutorial

SBDCF.A11   **Data Collection Screen**   **9/30/93**

Task: Move the information in columns C1–C4 to columns E5–E8.

A	B	C	D	E
		Widgets		
		Baskets		
		Doohickeys		
		Bootstraps		

Performs correctly?   y/n _____

Incorrect commands accessed?   _____
                                             _____
                                             _____

Uses Manual?   y/n _____
T of C?   y/n _____
Index?   y/n _____
Other manuals?   _____
                                             _____
                                             _____

Uses help?   y/n _____
Term sought?   _____
                                             _____
                                             _____

Other Observations/Comments

Note: A = Assistance required.

F1=Help F3=Exit F7=Finding F8=Add F9=Edit Del=Delete PgDn/PgUp

Figure 7.11   Screen-Based Data Collection Form

If you will be using more than one observer to collect different types of data, consider using different data collection forms. One person's form might be specifically designed for noting times, while another's might be designed for capturing participant comments and observations. The video camera operator, for example, is a good candidate for noting start and completion times and may only require a form containing a listing of the tasks.

There are examples of three types of data collection instruments for manual collection. The first example (Figure 7.9) *see page 166* is a generic form that can be used for any type of product, be it hardware, software, or documentation.

The second example (Figure 7.10) *see page 167* is a form for collecting all user actions/events that occurred when using a written tutorial.

The third example (Figure 7.11) *see page 168* is a collection form for monitoring the use of a screen-based product, a spreadsheet. In this case each screen-based task performed by the participant is represented on a single form with questions following.

THE NONDISCLOSURE AGREEMENT AND TAPE CONSENT FORM

DEFINITION AND PURPOSE

The purpose of the nondisclosure agreement is to prevent the unauthorized disclosure of proprietary product information that participants may encounter during the test. This document is almost always required for those products developed for the external marketplace prior to release.

The purpose of the videotape and/or audiotape consent form is to get written permission from the participants to tape them during the usability test. Typically, this form also establishes how you may or may not use their image or voice.

This permission should not be abused. Protect the confidentiality of your participants as much as possible, by not showing or using their full name on the tape and by limiting the use of the tapes to those with a "need to know."

Most likely you will want to have the legal department of your company review both documents to ensure that the language is correct and protects both your company and the participants. It is very important to inform the participants *before* they arrive that they will be required to avoid disclosing what they

Thank you for participating in our product research program. Please be aware that information will be disclosed to you that XYZ Company does not wish to be disclosed outside of the company. It is imperative that you do not reveal information that you may learn in the course of your participation. In addition, we will be videotaping your session to allow those XYZ staff members who cannot be present to observe your session and benefit from your feedback. Please read the statements below and sign where indicated. Thank you.

I agree that I will disclose no information to any person, firm, or corporation about the product research conducted by XYZ Company, or about the specifications, drawings, models or operations of any machine or devices encountered.

I understand that videotape and audiotape recordings will be made of my session. I grant XYZ Company permission to use these recordings for the purposes mentioned above, and waive my right to review or inspect the tapes prior to their dissemination and distribution.

Please print name: _____

Signature: _____

Date: _____

Figure 7.12   Sample of Simple Combined Nondisclosure and Tape Consent Form

learn, but more importantly that they will be videotaped or audiotaped. While it is rare, some people will refuse to let you tape them or will want to know precisely how your company will use their image.

If, in spite of precautions, you are faced with someone who refuses to be taped and insists that he or she was never informed, you can either use them without taping them or release and compensate them.

Figure 7.12 shows a simple combined nondisclosure and tape consent form. Many organizations use much more elaborate ones than shown here. Should you decide to use this one verbatim, please ensure that your own legal department reviews it first.

THE PRETEST QUESTIONNAIRE

DEFINITION AND PURPOSE

Unlike the background questionnaire, also given before the test and whose purpose is primarily informational, the purpose of a pretest questionnaire is to address specific test objectives, such as a participant's first impressions of a product, to qualify the placement of participants into a specific group, or to establish their level of expertise. As such, the pretest questionnaire is considered an integral part of the test design. It is worthwhile to discuss each of these purposes in detail.

1. **To ascertain participant attitudes and first impressions about a product's ease of use *prior* to using it.** One of the prime elements of usability testing is the initial impression of a product by the participant. For example:

   - Does the product *look* easy to use?

   - Does the participant understand the terminology?

   - Is the product similar or very different from previous products, or even from previous releases of the same product?

   - Is the method of organizing information in the manual obvious and seemingly intuitive?

These initial impressions set the stage for the actual usage of the product, and it is often very helpful to understand the participant's feelings and expectations *before* that usage occurs. If a product *appears difficult* to use, then it already has an obstacle to overcome. Conversely, if it *appears simple* or *intuitive* to use, then it has an advantage, and an end user might expend more time trying the product before calling a hotline or abandoning it altogether. Therefore, gathering "pre-usage" information can help you to understand the participant's behavior later.

In terms of conducting this research, the test monitor might show the participant a screen, or a control panel, or the table of contents of a manual, and ask the participant to rank how easy the item in question will be to use. This first ranking will be based solely on first impression prior to performing any tasks. You might also ask the basis for the participant's ranking to understand the cause of any initial confusion or trepidation.

The research can also be expanded to explore how actual usage affected those initial impressions. This is accomplished by providing the exact same pretest questionnaire after the usability test. (Guess what? This makes it a posttest questionnaire.) The intent is to investigate whether product usage increases or decreases rankings of initial impressions. If the rankings decrease, you know that the product's usage did not live up to its initial appearance. If the rankings increase, then you know that the participant's image of the product improves with usage—an excellent result indeed. This type of research can help one to understand just how much of an effect an intimidating or overly complex design is having on performance.

A variation of this theme goes beyond simply asking the participant to state his or her first impression of a product. You can also inquire about the participant's very specific understanding of those elements of a product that you expect to be self-evident without prior usage of the product. For example, the terminology of the control panel on a printer should be self-evident to a novice user, as should the initial screens of a software interface. If not, it is very helpful to know that, and it is also helpful to see if a participant learns the terminology by using the product.

The research is identical to that stated previously. *Prior to any use of the product*, provide the participants with a knowledge-based test that asks them to define terms with which they are expected to be familiar. After the performance test portion of the usability test, have them fill out identical questionnaires to see if using the product increased, decreased, or had no effect on their understanding. Their performance can help drive the decision to retain or change terminology, always a political football at best.

Figure 7.13 shows an example of a terminology test used to determine the self-evidence of the terminology on a printer. Prior to filling it out, let the participants view the product in question or let them fill out the questionnaire while looking at the product. This provides any context that would help to understand the terms. However, do not allow them to *try* the product. A terminology questionnaire could be used for evaluating screens, manuals, or other hardware products.

2. **To ascertain the opinions of the participants about the *utility* or value of the product prior to using it.** This is different from the previous category in that here you are looking at the opinions of the participants about the value or utility of the product's raw functionality. While the former concern was a first impression of usability, here you simply want to know the inherent value of such a product *before even considering usability as a factor*. This is especially important research for cutting-edge products that are new to the marketplace or new to your target market. It is helpful to know if certain types of users harbor an inherent bias for or against a particular product or technology, and how using the product affects that bias.

For example, if you were testing a PC-based appointment calendar/organizer, you might want to know if your target population initially harbored a fear or

Name: _____

In a sentence or two, write a definition for each term that appears on the following representation of the printer's keypad. Describe the term's meaning or intended usage as it applies to this printer. If unsure, please guess.

Status:

Courier:

Ready:

Letter Gothic:

Pause:

CG Times:

Busy:

Courier Compress:

Paper:

Load/Eject:

Quality:

Advance:

Letter Quality:

Fast Draft:

Font:

Figure 7.13 Example of a Terminology Questionnaire

resistance to using such a product. Perhaps this group is composed of staunch users of manual organizers who have no desire to use an on-line equivalent. You could ask them questions about the value of appointment calendars, and then ask them the same questions after they used the product. By giving similar or identical questionnaires to the participants before and after the usability test session, you can see if their opinions change for the better or the worse. This type of research is not only helpful in evaluating overall usability, but can provide valuable insights to your marketing team that can help to sell the product to different types of customers or offer it to different internal customers. In addition, it is always gratifying to see if your product can convert die-hard skeptics into customers.

The other very important issue here relates to the relative value of usability compared to other product factors. If you *just* consider the usability of performing relevant tasks and not the inherent value or desire to perform these tasks, you are doing yourself and the product a great disservice. You are missing an important piece of information if the question of functionality is not examined. If end users value the benefits of a particular product, then they will put up with more problems than if their interest is minimal. Knowing this information can help you to prioritize your test results and eventual recommendations. Unfortunately, I have seen usability tests conducted in just this fashion, that is, with little attention paid to the inherent value of the particular product or technology. This usually happens when testing occurs late in the development cycle.

Figure 7.14 shows an example of a questionnaire that explores the participant's opinions about the utility of an on-line time planner prior to trying it.

3. **To qualify participants for inclusion into one test group or another.** The next two categories are entirely different reasons for the pretest questionnaire, having to do with qualifying your participants. Suppose your test design calls for both experienced and inexperienced participants along a certain dimension. Your screening questionnaire, given orally over the phone, may have initially placed potential participants into either experienced or inexperienced groups based on their answers to some general questions. Your background questionnaire collected information about their breadth of experience. Now suppose you needed to go the extra mile to more precisely establish a potential participant's background. A more detailed questionnaire given prior to the test can be used to ascertain the potential participant's experience level more accurately and to place him or her into the appropriate group. (Technically, what I am about to describe could be an add-on to the background questionnaire, even though the type of questions are different.)

For example, suppose your test design calls for participants with varying levels of spreadsheet expertise. A common means to establish a person's expertise is to

Name:_____

Before having you actually try out the XYZ Time Planner, we would like to understand the value you place on this type of a product. Please answer the questions below to the best of your ability.

1. I would find an automated time planner and scheduler helpful.

    Yes___ No___

    If yes, how would it be helpful?

    If no, why would it not be helpful?

2. I currently use the following aids to schedule my time. (list all)

3. If the price was right, it is very likely I would buy such a product.

    __*Strongly Disagree* __*Disagree* __*Neither Agree nor Disagree*

    __*Agree* __ *Strongly Agree*

4. In general, I enjoy using high-tech products.

    __*Strongly Disagree* __*Disagree* __*Neither Agree nor Disagree*

    __*Agree* __*Strongly Agree*

5. Usability is a very important factor in my decision to purchase a new product.

    __*Strongly Disagree* __*Disagree* __*Neither Agree nor Disagree*

    __*Agree* __*Strongly Agree*

Figure 7.14 Example of a Product Value Questionnaire

simply have that person rate himself or herself, either by degree of expertise or by confidence level. Although this is better than guessing, it is not all that reliable. I have seen the most competent participants rate themselves as barely novice on a rating scale, and vice versa. There are two other ways to perform this rating that are more reliable.

The first way is to develop a chart, similar to the one shown in Figure 7.15, composed of the major functions of the product or application with a place for the participants to estimate the frequency with which they perform those functions.

The participants simply check off a frequency of usage for each of the major functions of the product. Since you can assume that more frequent usage is associated with a higher degree of competence, you can assign the participants who have more frequent usage to the more experienced category.

The second way is a variation of the self-rating method, but with more precision and less subjectivity. Unlike the single overall ranking that is unreliable, this version asks participants to rate their expertise on a variety of functions. An example of this technique is shown in Figure 7.16.

The interesting feature of this technique is that it results in an overall score, for example 12, when all seven responses are tallied. Then, based on your understanding of the application, you provide arbitrary cutoff points in which novice, intermediate, and advanced participants reside. In this case novice participants are those who reside in the 0 to 10 range, intermediate participants reside in the 11 to 18 range, and advanced participants reside in the 19+ range. Both types of questionnaires attempt to quantify the rating rather than just having people assign labels to themselves.

4. **To establish the participant's prerequisite knowledge prior to using the product.** Suppose you had a product that was intended for end users who were mathematicians. Without this very specific critical knowledge, in this case mathematics, the end user will be unable to use your product effectively. In order to ascertain the person's knowledge in this area, give him or her a questionnaire (or in some cases an actual test) that establishes how knowledgeable he or she is. This is not at all unlike a screening questionnaire (see the screening questionnaire section presented earlier in this chapter) or the criterion test used in conjunction with the development of prerequisite training materials (see the prerequisite training materials section presented later in this chapter). The only difference from the screening questionnaire is that you are not using this information to weed people out of your study. You are simply verifying the degree of their expertise in order to help evaluate their results. Very often the person will already have filled out a simpler version of this

Name: _____

During a typical spreadsheet session, how often do you perform the following functions?

Function	Frequency				
	Almost Always (90-100 %)	Mostly (65-89%)	Sometimes (36-64%)	Rarely (11-35%)	Almost Never (0-10%)
Using Function Macros					
Using Command Macros					
Creating a Database					
Using a Data Form					
Sorting Data					
Creating a Criteria Range					
Finding Specific Records					
Creating a Chart					
Changing Chart Types and Formats					
Adding Borders					
Changing Patterns					
Changing Axes					
Creating Arrays					
Linking Spread-Sheets					
Splitting Windows					
Adding a Legend					

Figure 7.15   Sample User Experience Questionnaire

Name: _____

Please rate your expertise on each of the following spreadsheet activities:

USING MULTIPLE WINDOWS
never done   expert
0   1   2   3   4   5

SETTING UP A WORK SHEET
never done   expert
0   1   2   3   4   5

SETTING UP AND REVISING A FORMULA
never done   expert
0   1   2   3   4   5

CUTTING AND PASTING CELLS
never done   expert
0   1   2   3   4   5

CREATING MACROS
never done   expert
0   1   2   3   4   5

MODIFYING FONTS
never done   expert
0   1   2   3   4   5

FORMATTING A CELL
never done   expert
0   1   2   3   4   5

Figure 7.16   Sample User Experience Questionnaire

pretest questionnaire as a screener because it was not possible to provide such an in-depth questionnaire beforehand.

The only difference from the criterion test used with prerequisite training is that you have no intention of training the person if he or she performed "poorly" on the questionnaire. If you discover that a particular person was really not qualified, you could choose to release that person or run the test differently.

Of course, there *is* one more reason for having your participants fill out this type of questionnaire, and it is a political reason—namely, to have the expertise of the participants as a matter of record in case a member of the development team challenges the test results by saying a participant was not qualified.

THE TASK SCENARIOS

DEFINITION AND PURPOSE

Task scenarios are representations of actual work that the participants would conceivably perform using your product. Task scenarios are expanded versions of the original task list (previously developed as part of the test plan), adding context and the participant's rationale and motivation to perform those original tasks. In many cases one task scenario will comprise several tasks from the task list grouped together, since that is the way that people perform their work on the job.

Task scenarios should describe:

- The end results that the participant will strive to achieve
- Motives for performing the work
- Actual data and names rather than generalities
- The state of the system when a task is initiated
- Readouts of displays and printouts that the participants will see while performing the task

Task scenarios may either be distributed to or read to the participants. If written, use jargon-free language (from their viewpoint; if they know a term, it is not jargon). You could develop the task scenarios at the same time as the task list, but doing it sequentially and in phases simplifies the process.

DEVELOPMENT GUIDELINES

Following are five key guidelines for the development of task scenarios.

1. **Provide realistic scenarios, complete with motivations to perform.** The motivations can be explicit or implicit. Use actual case studies, task analyses, customer phone calls, and customer visits as the basis for your scenarios. The closer that the scenarios represent reality, the more reliable the test results. In addition, the participants will find it easier to "stay in role" and overcome any latent hesitation and self-consciousness if the scenarios reflect familiar situations, with realistic reasons for performing the tasks. For example, rather than simply asking the participants to print a document from a database system, tell them what the file will be used for, how it was created, and for whom it is intended.

The context of the scenarios will also help them to evaluate elements in your product's design that simply do not jibe with reality.

2. **Sequence the task scenarios in the order in which they are most likely to be performed.** This helps to:

   - Retain the illusion of authenticity.

   - Guide the participants in approximately the same way they would learn on the job.

   - Expose the snowballing effects of errors and misconceptions. For example, if a participant misnames a file in an early task, that is not all that serious. However, when in a later related task that same participant uses that file name as the basis for naming 20 subordinate files, the problem's ramifications become serious indeed, and may escalate to a higher priority when you view the overall results. This is just what you want to see happen in the lab.

   If sequential order is not crucial to performance, then consider varying the order of presentation of scenarios to different participants. This approach, known as *counterbalancing*, enables you to avoid potential biasing effects, such as when a scenario that is always presented last benefits from a participant's experience with previous tasks. For an example of counterbalancing, see the within-subjects design section presented in Chapter 5.

3. **Match the task scenarios to the experience of the participants.** Not all participants should exercise identical aspects of your product. Some system features, screens, and/or sections of a manual should never be accessed by a novice participant during the usability test because these features, screens, and/or sections of the manual are too advanced for a novice. For example, if you have a section in your manual on advanced features, you would not include task scenarios that accessed that section for first-time users. Conversely, more experienced participants may simply skip over basic features, screens, and/or sections of a manual. Therefore, if you will be utilizing participants of varying experience levels, then make sure that the degree of difficulty of a scenario is congruent with the experience level of the participant.

4. **Avoid using jargon and cues.** Avoid product jargon or cues that serve as giveaways of the correct results. Avoid wording that includes actual buttons, menu items, and screen titles. If you must use those terms to describe a task, it probably indicates a flaw in the product's design. It is crucial that you do *not* provide unintentional cues to the participants that they would not ordinarily experience outside of the testing environment.

   For example, even asking a novice participant to *save a file* is a giveaway if there is a "Save" command on the product. It points the participant in the right direction. Instead, say something like, "Ensure that your document is retained in the computer with the changes you've just made." (I know this sounds ridiculous, and the participant may look at you funny and say, "Do you want me to save the file?" If the participant does, just say yes, and realize that sometimes it is necessary to make a fool of yourself in the interest of science.) Of course, in very early exploratory testing, you may intentionally ask the participants to find a particular "save" screen or command, but that is a different kettle of fish entirely.

5. **Try to provide a substantial amount of work in each scenario.** Do *not* guide the participants through the product piecemeal, unless your product is in such a primitive state that you must work that way. Rather, provide a goal, clearly stated in simple language, and let participants do the rest. For example, if you were testing a word processing system, an appropriate task would be:

"In the document entitled 'Jones.R,' edit the current address so that the letter will be sent to your boss instead of the current recipient."

To accomplish this task, it is implied that the participants must either learn or exhibit the following skills:

- Locate a particular file.

- Access and display that file.

- Edit that file.

- Save that file.

Whether the participants can perform or figure out these intermediate steps in order to complete the goal of the scenario is precisely what you want to learn from the usability test. If you simply ask them to locate, access, edit, and save a file, you never see whether the participants can put it all together, as they must on the job. Your tasks should force the participants to exhibit their conceptual understanding of the product, and should expose their misunderstandings about how to use the product. A simplistic navigation of pages in a document, or screens, or other hardware components is simply not a challenging test.

Remember, from the participant's viewpoint, the product, whether it be hardware, software, documentation, or training, *is always* considered a means to an end. The participant's central focus is the work and the procedures required to perform that work. The product being tested is incidental to that, not central. Not only is this an important principle for effective testing, it is also the basis for user-centered design per se.

Now that you have reviewed the five key guidelines for the development of task scenarios, you may be asking yourself whether you should read the task scenarios to the participants or simply hand them out for the participants to read. This question is valid and is accompanied by two schools of thought. One supports reading the scenarios to the participants, while the other supports distributing them and letting the participants read them. Following is some additional information to clarify this choice.

READING THE SCENARIOS TO THE PARTICIPANTS

An advantage to reading the scenarios, especially if they are complex, is that you can interact with the participants and make sure they understand what to do. You certainly do not want to watch them flounder for 10 minutes or go completely down a wrong path simply because they misunderstood what to do. Reading the scenarios to the participants also enables you to control the pace of the usability test. This control is important if your test is very interactive, say during an exploratory test, and you will be probing the participants at the conclusion of each major scenario.

LETTING THE PARTICIPANTS READ THE SCENARIOS THEMSELVES

Let the participants read the scenarios themselves if you are testing from another room or if you want to minimize contact with the participants, as you would during a validation test. Use your pilot test(s) to ensure that the scenarios are clear and unambiguous. Even with that safeguard, you still may want the participants to read the scenarios out loud and ask questions before beginning a task.

Decide if you want the participants to see only one scenario at a time. If there are many scenarios or if the scenarios are very complex, viewing them all at one time could be intimidating and distracting. Participants may try to get ahead of themselves even subconsciously, or they may perform in a different way if they know information from the current task will be needed later. They may also look ahead in the documentation which could affect timing.

One way to control the flow of information and also help with timing a task is to have the participant access and read the tasks from a computer. A task clock begins to time the task as soon as the participant leaves the screen from which it is displayed. Upon completion, the participant accesses the same file which shows the next task on the list. Or, you may ask the participant to check it off. That stops the clock on the first task. Using this method, you can set the program to display one scenario at a time, which effectively solves the problem of looking ahead.

TASK NO.	TASK DESCRIPTION	TASK DETAIL	
1	Unpack the printer.	Req's:	Unopened box, QSG.
		SCC:	Printer removed from box and ready for further preparation.
		MTC:	5.0 min.
2	Install the on-board manual.	Req's:	On-board manual, QSG.
		SCC:	On-board manual placed in its slot.
		MTC:	2.0 min.
3	Connect power cord.	Req's:	Power cord, QSG, printer.
		SCC:	Power cord placed in its socket correctly.
		MTC:	3.0 min.
4	Choose appropriate interface cable.	Req's:	Four (4) cables clearly marked on the table (include serial cable as one choice), QSG (cable table).
		SCC:	Correct cable chosen from the four and subject indicates it is the correct one.
		MTC:	2.5 min.
5	Connect interface cable.	Req's:	Interface cable, QSG, printer, PC.
		SCC:	One end of cable placed firmly in its seat in the printer, and the other end seated firmly in computer's port.
		MTC:	6.0 min.
6	Install the print cartridge.	Req's:	Cartridge pack (instructions removed), QSG, printer. Note: Cartridge should be stripped of any company markings to ensure anonymity of company.
		SCC:	Cartridge placed firmly in its housing directly against the green dot. (Also self-test will serve as dual SCC.)
		MTC:	5.0 min.
7	Load the paper.	Req's:	Box of paper, printer paper tray, QSG.
		SCC:	Paper placed correctly in paper tray underneath two corners. Note: Could ask P to form feed to test if paper is placed correctly.
		MTC:	3.0 min.
8	Turn the printer on.	Req's:	Printer with all connections, paper, cartridge, etc., QSG.
		SCC:	P slides switch to on position. Printer powers on.
		MTC:	1.0 min.

Figure 7.17   Example of a Task List for Setting Up a Printer out of the Box

Task List Legend

MTC = Maximum time to complete
OBM = On-board manual
QSG = Quick setup guide
Req's = Requirements to perform the task
P   = Participant
SCC = Successful completion criteria
TM   = Test monitor

Figure 7.17   (*Continued*)

> You have recently ordered a brand new printer over the phone and are waiting to receive it via courier at any time. Momentarily, the courier from Federal Express will arrive, drop off the product, and have you sign for it. Once you sign for it, we will begin our session. Please set up the printer in the same manner as you normally would at home. If you normally use instructions, please do so today. If you normally do not use instructions until you get stuck, then work that way today. Signal me when you reach the point at which you feel ready to print your first document. Any questions before we begin?

Figure 7.18   Sample Task Scenario for Setting Up a Printer

Figures 7.17 and 7.18 show how a task list becomes a task scenario. Figure 7.17 includes the first eight tasks of the task list from Chapter 5. (Note that the original list was in a form for developers to see.)

Now in Figure 7.18 the tasks from the task list are subsumed under a single-task scenario designed for the participants to read during the test. The scenario encompasses all eight tasks because these represent the first activities for setting up a printer. It provides a realistic scenario to place the participant within a familiar context. Note that the choice to use the documentation is left to the participant. Because of this, you may see participants attempting to work on their own, then using the document. Be aware that you may not see tasks occurring in the same order as shown on your data collection form. Of course, you do not have to go to all the trouble of having the package delivered by a phony courier, but that extra bit does help the participant relax, get into the role, and not be fearful about appearing foolish. Also be aware that with a different test design, one whose objective was to establish the efficacy of the documentation once it was accessed, you could have just as easily *insisted* that the participants use the documentation.

THE PREREQUISITE TRAINING MATERIALS (OPTIONAL)

DEFINITION AND PURPOSE

Prerequisite training refers to any training provided to participants prior to the actual usability test that raises their skill level to some preestablished criterion or allows them to be tested further along their learning curve. It could range from a simple 10-minute description of the product to a comprehensive two-day workshop. Following are several situations that warrant prerequisite training and, as such, suggest when this type of training should be provided.

1. **You want to make sure that the participants you are testing possess some prescribed minimum level of expertise deemed necessary to use the product effectively.** The expertise in question could range from the ability to use a graphical user interface (GUI) to expertise in accounting. In either case a projected end user of the product is expected to be proficient in some area, and you want to make sure that each participant is qualified. For example, suppose you are testing a graphics package that presupposes a certain level of desktop publishing expertise. If your participants are unqualified, it will reflect poorly and unfairly on the product, since the projected end user will have more expertise. By checking each participant's expertise prior to the test and providing some specific desktop publishing training in the cases where participants fall short, you provide a fairer test of the product.

   Or, in a common situation today, your product requires knowledge of how to manipulate a GUI, including controlling a mouse or track ball and managing pull-down menus. If you use a participant who has all the other appropriate characteristics of your user profile but who is a GUI novice, you will spend the first hour or two of your test watching the participant struggle to master the intricacies of using a GUI, and very little time on the behaviors that will affect the product's success. Instead, why not provide prerequisite training on using a GUI and begin the usability test *after* the participant has shown GUI proficiency.

2. **You would like to evaluate usage of your product further along the participant's learning curve.** Developers sometimes feel, and rightfully so, that the usability testing process is biased toward the testing of novices, and that they are unable to see experienced participants try out their products. Another way of stating the problem is that too often usability tests evaluate "ease of learning" (the ability to grasp the fundamental concepts and simple features of a product), and do not adequately evaluate "ease of use" (those behaviors that follow mastery of the early concepts and basic features). In other words, usability tests measure how well a beginner uses the product, but not someone who is more likely to put the product through its paces. This is a legitimate criticism, since it is hard to refute the logic that a novice participant and one who has used the

product for even a week will expose very different problems with a product and will use it quite differently.

One way to address this issue and at the same time make for a more comprehensive test is to test some participants who are further along the learning curve before beginning the usability test. However, if your product is new, participants with even a week of experience simply do not exist, and it is impractical to allow participants a week to get their bearings.

A solution to this dilemma is to artificially move the participants along the learning curve through intensive, structured, prerequisite training. The training should simulate a week (or two weeks, or a month if you prefer) of typical use. You accomplish this by first establishing the level of expertise for a week-old user (the skills and knowledge he or she would possess). Then you develop a data collection instrument to measure that expertise. Finally, you develop a training package that reaches those skills and knowledge. The training media could be self-paced, instructor led, on line, or a combination.

For those participants who take the training, the usability test begins after they have achieved this criterion level of performance. If you approach the problem systematically, you probably can achieve criterion for a week-old user with two or three hours of training, practice, and questions. The important point is that you establish that the participants have met criterion before they are tested, so everyone begins from at least some minimum expertise.

As an added benefit, take advantage of these training sessions to study how the participants learn the product, almost as an informal exploratory session. But the "official" reason for the prerequisite training is to see how experienced participants perform on the product during the usability test.

3. **Your product has a section devoted to advanced features strictly for experienced end users that you would like to test extensively.**

-OR-

You have previously tested and established the usability of the simpler features of your product and do not want to retest those during your current test. This is similar to the last case, but instead of focusing on the experience of the participants, the focus is on a particular aspect of the product. The easiest way to explain is by example. Following are two examples of the preceding situation.

EXAMPLE 1. Suppose that, due to time constraints, you want to start the test immediately with the advanced features of the product for some participants, but the simpler features or functions are a prerequisite for using the advanced features. You have not been able to locate or simply do not care to locate experienced end users of your product. Therefore, you provide prerequisite training that systematically teaches the simpler features, and begin the usability test immediately with the advanced features.

EXAMPLE 2. Perhaps the control panel on your hardware product consists of two sets of discrete functions. One set of functions is simple, familiar, and originates from a previous release of the product. You expect the end user to be able to use these right out of the box with little confusion, and previous testing has determined that documentation is not required. However, another set of functions is brand new and represents an advanced feature set. Everyone on the team agrees these features are non-intuitive and will require documentation to master. In this case you are able to find experienced end users as participants, but want to make sure that they all share some minimum skill level.

The safest way to approach this situation is to provide a criterion test (a proficiency check) to the experienced participants prior to the usability test that essentially qualifies them. If they pass the criterion test, they may immediately begin the usability test of the advanced features. If they do not pass the criterion test, then they first receive prerequisite training on *those features that they missed on the criterion test*, until they reach criterion. Then they begin the usability test of advanced features.

This conservative approach ensures that you are testing apples and apples, and not apples and oranges. You operationally define what you mean by "experienced skills," check for the presence of those skills, and correct when necessary.

HOW TO DEVELOP AND ADMINISTER PREREQUISITE TRAINING

Developing a training package is not a trivial task, and a comprehensive discussion of the topic is beyond the scope of this book. However, it is worthwhile to review the basic steps required to develop prerequisite training. Following is a step-by-step procedure for developing prerequisite training using the example of a situation where the participants must possess some predetermined expertise (such as GUI skills) prior to usability testing.

1. **Develop learning objectives.** The learning objectives should be specific and measurable. Using the example of prerequisite training that teaches how to use a GUI, one of your objectives must certainly revolve around using a mouse. A specific measurable objective for mouse navigation would be:

The participant will be able (on the first try) to move an object from one side of the screen to the other within 7 seconds, 95 percent of the time.

Similarly, a measurable objective for manipulating a pull-down menu would be:

The participant will be able to correctly select a specified menu option within 5 seconds, 95 percent of the time.

2. **Develop a criterion test that measures the skills and knowledge the qualified participant is expected to exhibit.** Once you have developed the learning objectives, many would immediately begin to develop the training materials. Actually, that step is premature. Your next step is to develop the criterion test items that will measure success or failure of the objectives.

   An example of a test item for our hypothetical GUI training would be:

   Using the mouse, move the file entitled "John Doe" into the folder entitled "Customer Accounts."

3. **Develop training materials that teach the participants to pass your criterion test.** Now it is time to build the training materials around the objectives and test items, the idea being to get your participants to pass the criterion test before beginning the usability test. The training should provide specific, structured educational materials that include plenty of organized practice exercises and feedback. A technical expert providing a few tips and pointers is not a structured training package. The training may be self-paced written materials, self-paced computer-based materials, instructor led, a video, or various combinations. It could even be an "off-the-shelf" package, as long as it achieves the learning objectives. In the case of GUI training, you would almost certainly provide specified periods of practice, since manipulating a mouse requires sharpened hand–eye coordination. In the case of teaching participants to master a more cognitive discipline such as using a spreadsheet, you would require more conceptual training.

4. **Give the *criterion* test to each participant who represents himself or herself as being qualified on the particular subject matter.** Once the materials are prepared, and you have had a chance to pilot test and refine them on some internal participants, you are ready to use them as part of the usability test. Prior to the beginning of the actual performance portion of the usability test, give the criterion test to each participant who has ranked himself or herself as "experienced" or who has been identified as being "experienced." If these participants pass the criterion test, then they may begin the usability test. If they do not pass, provide them with the training package or, if they were very close to passing, simply provide remediation on the points they missed.

5. **Give the training to each participant whom you know is unqualified or who represents himself or herself as unqualified.** Provide the training to all those who are ranked as "novices." Then upon completion of the training, give each

of these participants the criterion test. If they pass, then they may begin the usability test. If they do not pass, then provide remediation for the points they missed. Since it is important that each qualified participant possess at least the minimum expertise, do not leave off the step of providing the criterion test. Else you run the risk of biasing your usability test unnecessarily.

6. **Before beginning the usability test, remove the prerequisite training materials, unless you intend to supply them with the product.** This is an important caveat, since the training represents a very pointed, structured, and condensed document/package users often do *not* receive. (Obviously, this is a telling statement about product usability. Such training *should* be included as needed.) The training materials are usually much more focused than any other document on very specific objectives, and represent a week's worth of trial and error. The reason you need to remove them is because, under real conditions, the end user would not normally have access to them. However, if you do normally supply such materials with the product (possibly as a tutorial), then by all means let the participants have access to these training materials during the usability test if they desire.

Speaking from my own experience, the prerequisite training is often far superior to other materials the participants receive, since it is so pointed toward getting them started. Often the standard documentation and training materials they receive are much more generic and supportive of both simple and advanced features.

Following is an example of prerequisite training that was developed as part of a usability test I conducted for a client. I was responsible for developing and monitoring the test, but I worked with an in-house task force who took responsibility for much of the test preparation. The prerequisite training was developed by one of the members of the task force possessing instructional technology expertise.

To set the stage, the product being tested was a gas chromatography workstation, a sophisticated chemical analysis system. As participants, I used actual customers of an earlier version of the product. The new product was a software product running on a PC workstation from which a user controlled up to four gas chromatographs (GCs). The GCs are used in a variety of industries, such as petroleum, environmental, and pharmaceutical, to analyze chemical compounds. The new product, unlike its predecessor, used a graphical user interface (GUI), so the prerequisite training consisted of Windows training and the basics of navigating the product's interface, complete with exercises. Following is an excerpt from the prerequisite training for this usability test.

SAMPLE PREREQUISITE

TRAINING COURSE[1]:

INTEGRATING DATA FILES

In the previous exercise, you analyzed a "canned" chromatogram called Testplot as a way of learning about methods. In this section, you will use a data file called "EXAMPLE.D" to learn more about integration.

You will be performing the following tasks:

1. Load a data file called "EXAMPLE.D."
2. Integrate the data file with the default integrator events in "DEFAULT.MTH."
3. Edit the method's integrator events.
4. Reintegrate the data file using the revised method.

[1]Excerpt from a prerequisite training course developed for a usability test. (Courtesy of Hewlett Packard, Inc.)

5. Review the results.

6. Save the method as "OPTIMETH."

Before you start, be sure that:

- You have reloaded the default method.
- You have your instrument's Data Analysis Main Screen displayed (select Main Screen in Data Analysis).

SETTING THE SCENE FOR THIS EXERCISE

Imagine that you have already made several trial runs with a new sample to optimize the chromatography. You are satisfied with the separation and the analytical data is in a file called "EXAMPLE.D," where the ".D" extension identifies this file as containing run data. Your goal now is to optimize the integration.

HOW TO SIMULATE AN ANALYSIS USING THE EXAMPLE.D DATA FILE

During a run, the ChemStation automatically performs all of the following operations:

1. Collects the raw analytical data in a data file.

2. Loads the data file into the X-register.

3. Integrates the raw data.

4. Stores the processed data in the data file.

5. Identifies the peaks.

6. Allocates the baseline.

7. Clears the Data-Analysis draw window.

8. Redraws the chromatogram.

9. Draws in the retention times, the baseline, and the integration marks to show how each peak was integrated.

10. Prints the report.

Step 1 is the Data Acquisition operation and Steps 2 through 10 are Data Analysis operations.

In this exercise, you will manually perform the same steps that the ChemStation performs automatically during a run.

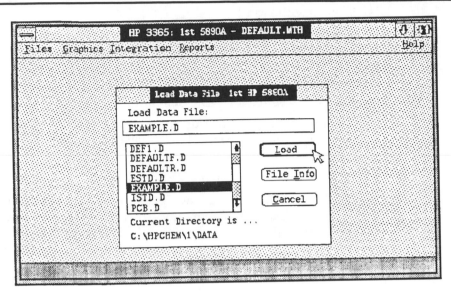

Figure 7.19   Load Data File Window

For example:

- By starting with the raw data file EXAMPLE.D, Step 1 is already done for you.
- You manually load and integrate the data file (Steps 2 through 9).

  The peaks are integrated and identified, the baseline is allocated, the draw windows are cleared, and the chromatogram is drawn with baselines and retention times.

- When the integration is complete, you manually print the report (Step 10).

LOADING THE EXAMPLE.D DATA FILE

To load the EXAMPLE.D data file:

1. Select Main Screen from the Data Analysis menu.
2. Select Load Data File from the Files menu.
3. Select EXAMPLE.D from the scrolling table in the Load Data File window as shown in Figure 7.19.
4. Select the Load pushbutton.

An hourglass icon appears warning you to wait while the data file is being loaded. When the loading process is complete, the chromatogram that represents the EXAMPLE.D data file is drawn in one of the Data Analysis windows.

INTEGRATING WITH THE DEFAULT INTEGRATOR EVENTS

At this point, you have loaded the raw data that represents the 11 peaks of EXAMPLE.D but have not yet integrated it.

1. Select Integrate from the Integration menu.
2. Watch as the ChemStation:

    • Integrates the raw data.

    • Identifies the peaks.

    • Allocates the baseline.

    • Clears the Data Analysis draw window.

    • Redraws the chromatogram.

    • Draws in the retention times, the baseline, and the integration marks to show how each peak was integrated.

The message line at the bottom of the screen tells you the status (done) of the integration process. See Figure 7.20.

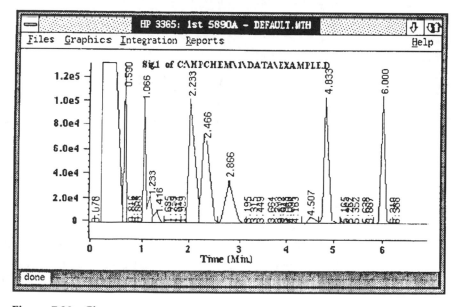

Figure 7.20 Chromatogram

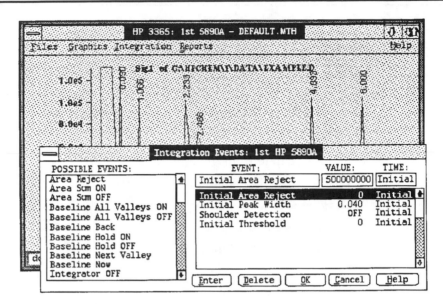

Figure 7.21   Integration Events Menu

EDIT THE INTEGRATOR EVENTS

You can optimize this integration by editing the default integrator events. To start the editing process, select Integration Events from the Integration Events menu as shown in Figure 7.21.

ENTER AN INITIAL THRESHOLD

Use the initial threshold to reject the integration of unwanted peaks and areas produced by baseline noise. A high value (up to 25) rejects more peaks than a small value (down to −12).

Change the Initial Threshold value to 0 to reject the integration of small unwanted peaks and the baseline noise.

1. Select Initial Threshold in the Events table.

2. Move the cursor to the Value Text Box and enter 0.

3. Select the Enter pushbutton to enter this change into the Events table.

4. Select the OK pushbutton.

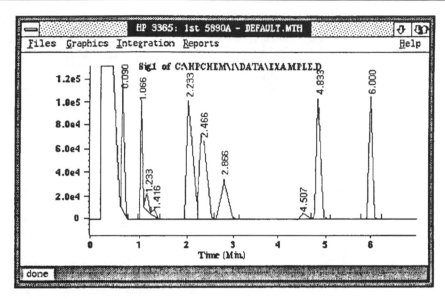

Figure 7.22 Revised Chromatogram

REINTEGRATING WITH THE NEW EVENTS

1. Open the Integration drop-down menu and select Integrate.

Note: *The ChemStation integrates the EXAMPLE.D data file with the new integration events and redraws the chromatogram with new baseline and peak separations.*

2. Look at the revised integration in Figure 7.22 and note how the chromatogram has improved.

Note: *Only the peaks of interest have been integrated.*

REVIEW THE RESULTS

1. Select Print Report from the Report menu to display the results of your analysis in a Percent report. See Figure 7.23.

Note: *The report contains the areas for only 11 of the peaks.*

2. Close the report by selecting Close from the report window's Tabulate menu.

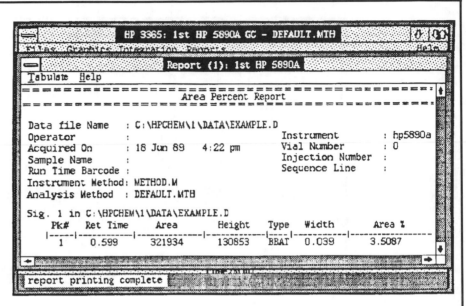

Figure 7.23   Report Window

Note: *This was a fairly simple chromatogram. A more complex chromatogram may require additional integration events to optimize the integration.*

3. Select Return To from the Files menu to return to the instrument's top-level screen.

CHECK YOURSELF

Here is a series of tasks for you to try. All are discussed in the previous chapters.

- Set the GC Injector B pressure to 12 psi.
- Set the GC Injector B temperature to follow the oven temperature.
- From the ChemStation, load the default method and change the oven program to start at 80 degrees and ramp at 5 degrees/min to 105.
- Now change the integration parameters to turn on shoulder detection.
- Create a two-vial sequence by modifying the Sample Log Table you created in the Sequence Section.

Take note of the real examples used and the criterion test (e.g., "check yourself") at the end of the excerpt. If users did not "pass" the test, they received remediation until they were proficient. At that point, the actual usability test began.

Interestingly enough, this training was an example of the phenomenon that I previously described, in that it was superior to the previous training and documentation these customers had received. After completing the test, one participant, who would be responsible for teaching the new product to others in her company, insisted on taking copies of the prerequisite training back with her on the job. She had never seen any other materials that spoke so directly to novice users just getting started. Other participants voiced similar refrains which were taken to heart by my client. As a result, a tutorial similar to the prerequisite training is now included as part of the documentation set.

WHAT ARE THE BENEFITS OF PREREQUISITE TRAINING?

Having discussed the purpose and the "how-to" of prerequisite training, I feel it is worthwhile to pause and discuss the advantages of this underused element of the usability test, because it offers some important benefits.

1. **It allows you to provide a more comprehensive challenging usability test.** Since prerequisite training allows you to work with experienced end users (even if you cannot find any initially), you can exercise more sophisticated functionality of the product than you otherwise could when only testing beginners. For example, when testing a software interface, you can design tasks that require a grounding in the basics of navigation, error handling, and so on. Or, when testing documentation, you can observe participant behaviors *after* they have already understood the organization and layout of the document. You can watch people exercise the more subtle aspects of the design which normally are not used by beginners. Looking at it another way, you are testing ease of use more than ease of learning.

2. **Prerequisite training allows you to test the more obscure functionality of the product that might normally get overlooked during a test.** Normally, during a usability test there is not enough time to exercise the more advanced features, to see if they are intuitive or to see if the documentation's explanations are lucid enough to guide the participants successfully. With a test designed around prerequisite training, the tasks can begin with the more difficult and less obvious features. *This may be the only opportunity to see these functions utilized prior to release of the product.*

Remember, with this technique, you can witness behaviors that normally would not occur until after a week or two of using the product. This is unusual and very advantageous. Rather than having someone call in a problem on the company hotline after product release, you get to see it occur in the lab. It also lets developers and writers work on functionality that ordinarily gets overlooked.

3. **Developing such training forces you to understand how someone learns to use your product.** A very real by-product of developing the prerequisite training is that it forces everyone on the development team to relate to how end users learn to use the product. Normally, the only people concerned with such information are the training developers and/or technical writers. The software and hardware developers often come to appreciate the level of a novice using the product, and the obstacles they face in learning the product.

SOME COMMON QUESTIONS ABOUT PREREQUISITE TRAINING

1. **In the case where you want to test the more advanced features of a product, is it not inherently biasing to teach participants how to use your product prior to a usability test? Will anyone actually make errors during the test?** These questions are often voiced as a concern. The answer to both is yes, participants still make many errors, especially on complex products. Once the actual training is removed, *if the product is poorly designed and nonintuitive*, participants stumble even on the tasks they have just learned. It seems that poor design always wins out. However, this technique probably will *not* work if your product is extremely simple, because participants can remember confusing points and inconsistencies. In that case, you may need to introduce a period of "forgetting" (a few days to a week) between the training and the testing to eliminate that tendency.

Also keep in mind that, since the participants have received training in the basics, your test design should include more difficult, more challenging tasks than you normally would provide to novice users.

2. **Doesn't prerequisite training increase the total time required to run the test?** Yes, it does. The downside of testing advanced participants is the time factor. You will need to build in time for your participants to take the training as well as the usability test. It is not unusual to spend an entire day or more with one participant for sophisticated products with complete documentation sets.

However, to mitigate that aspect, remember that the entire team, who may normally want to view the test, need not be there for the prerequisite training. In fact, the training could occur at an entirely different time. Nor must the test monitor be there, although it is better if the test monitor is present. If need be, the prerequisite training can be handled by someone else entirely. In that case, using the criterion test is doubly important in order to ensure consistency among training sessions conducted by different trainers.

THE WRITTEN POSTTEST QUESTIONNAIRE

DEFINITION AND PURPOSE

The main purpose of the written posttest questionnaire(s) is to gather preference information from the participants in order to clarify and deepen your understanding of the product's strengths and weaknesses. The information you gather typically would include their opinions and feelings about the product's ease of use and ease of learning. Written questionnaires are used to collect general information across the entire population of participants. The same questions are asked of each individual in exactly the same way, and precision is extremely important.

Conversely, oral questions (discussed in Chapter 9) can be adjusted for a single individual in order to better understand what happened during that *particular* session. Those questions are not standardized; there is a general subject but variation from session to session.

There are two major considerations when developing a questionnaire, content and format. Content has to do with the subject matter about which you choose to inquire. Format has to do with the design and wording of each question and the arrangement of the overall questionnaire.

Developing an effective, unambiguous questionnaire takes time and effort. No matter how clearly you feel you have stated a question, someone is liable to misinterpret it. Do not think you will simply throw together a few questions just prior to the test. If you do not have time to develop the questionnaire properly, including several revisions and a pilot test, you are better off presenting the questions orally. With an oral format you can interact with the participants and clear up ambiguities and misunderstandings on the spot. If you have never developed a questionnaire before, seek out some help from someone with more experience. For more in-depth study, see [6] [26] [73] [99] [132] [134].

DESIGN GUIDELINES

In this section I will focus on guidelines for establishing the content of questionnaires followed by a listing of the most common question formats and how they are used.

1. **Use the problem statement(s) from the test plan as the basis for your content.** Be concise and precise in what you choose to ask. Keep your questions to the point, and avoid digressing into abstract areas. A good test of the relevance of a question is to ask yourself how the answer will move you closer to a design decision. If it is unclear how the answer to a question will move you toward a

design decision, you might want to strike the question or reword it. Especially if you will be debriefing and questioning each participant orally, it is not necessary to include every last item on paper. A 20-page questionnaire (yes, I have seen them that long) following a two-hour test is no one's idea of a good time. Instead, make sure that the written questionnaire includes only those items that *each* participant needs to answer. These include:

- Major items directly related to a specific problem statement(s).
- Items related to specific trends or patterns among participants or those where you will be measuring statistical significance.
- Controversial items on which the design team has not been able to agree. (You will want a written record of those responses.)

2. **Develop questionnaires that will be distributed either during or after a session.** Depending on your test design, you may want the participants to fill out the questionnaire either during or immediately following the test session, or at both times. For longer test sessions (2+ hours), it often pays to separate the usability test into discrete phases comprised of several tasks each and provide questionnaires to the participants after each phase is completed. This will help the participants to recall their reactions and feelings more easily, since they will have just completed the tasks about which they are being questioned. Also varying the flow of the test during a long session can help to relieve boredom and fatigue.

3. **Ask questions related to that which you cannot directly observe, such as feelings, opinions, and suggestions for improvement.** Stick to questions that have to do with subject preferences. Do *not* ask performance-related questions that can be more accurately answered through direct observation.

For example, if one of your test objectives is to evaluate how often the participants access the index in a manual, that is best assessed by direct observation during the test. It is a waste of time and damages your credibility to ask participants to estimate the number of times they referenced the index. The exception to this would be if you were unable to directly observe the test. In that case, though, you would still be better off having the participants note each time they accessed the index during the test. Relying on their memory after the fact is not nearly as effective.

However, using the same example of the index, what you *cannot* observe is:

- Whether the user thought the index was well designed
- How the index compares to others that they have used
- Whether it was organized the way they preferred

These are the types of issues that can only be implied and not definitively answered by observations, and should form the basis of your questioning.

4. **Develop the basic areas and topics you would like to cover.** Here are some suggested topics for tests of screens, documentation, and control panels.

General Software Screen Issues

- Organization of screen matches real-world tasks?
- Amount of information adequate?
- Appropriate use of color?
- Similar information consistently placed?
- Problems with navigation?
- Problems with losing your place in the system?
- Computer jargon?
- Too much or too little information on screens?

General Documentation Issues

Accessibility:

- Organization explicit and obvious?
- Directive and supportive information visually separated?
- More important information highlighted in some way?
- Index helpful?
- Necessary to read long passages to determine correct locations?
- Cross-referencing adequate?
- Both experienced and novice users accommodated?

Clarity:

- Terminology confusing?
- Limited use of paragraphs?
- Adequate feedback after completing actions?
- Sentences appropriate length?
- Conversational tone appropriate?

Graphics:

- Adequate use of examples?
- Pictures of equipment, screens accurate?
- Combined text and illustrations integrated?
- Decision tables rather than dense text presentation?

Organization:

- Organized by user's job and tasks?
- Adequate white space?
- Consistent patterns and chunking of information?
- Headings self-explanatory?
- Consistent layout on a page of similar elements, such as notes, summaries and page numbers?

Technical Accuracy:

- Task descriptions and procedures correct?
- Examples provided technically accurate?

General Hardware Control Panel Issues

- Terminology of buttons self-evident?
- Placement of control panel appropriate?
- Display messages easy to see?
- Display messages easy to understand and free of jargon?
- Meaning of icons self-evident?
- Consistency of operation for all controls?
- Additional controls desired?

5. **Design the questions and responses for simplicity and brevity. Minimize complicated instructions.** Minimize responses that require extensive writing, such as open-ended questions. Instead, use close-ended questions, such as check boxes, scales, true–false statements, and short fill-ins. Close-ended questions eliminate any advantage participants with good writing skills might have over those participants with poor writing skills.

There are a variety of common types of formats of close-ended questions. Following are some tried-and-true formats (including examples of each) that you can use.

LIKERT SCALES

Likert scales are scales on which the participants register their agreement or disagreement with a statement. The judgments depicted in Figure 7.24 are quantified on a five-point scale.

Overall, I found the widget easy to use. (Check one).

__ Strongly Disagree   __ Disagree   __ Neither Agree nor Disagree

__ Agree   __Strongly Agree

Figure 7.24 Likert Scale

SEMANTIC DIFFERENTIALS

Semantic differentials are scales (usually seven point) on which the participants are asked to register the degree to which they favor one of two adjective pairs. They can be used to gather usability as well as aesthetic preferences. The judgments are quantified on a 1–7 scale, but you will notice that, in order to prevent any bias associated with higher vs. lower numbers, both ends of the scale read from 1–3, with 0 being a no-preference choice.

Using the rating scale shown in Figure 7.25, the participant would circle the number nearest the term that most closely matches his or her feelings about the product.

FILL-IN QUESTIONS

Fill-in questions provide more latitude to the participants, since they are free to say whatever they like rather than choosing from a predetermined list. Usually,

Modern	3	2	1	0	1	2	3	Traditional
Simple	3	2	1	0	1	2	3	Complex
High tech	3	2	1	0	1	2	3	Low tech
Reliable	3	2	1	0	1	2	3	Unreliable
Easy to use	3	2	1	0	1	2	3	Complex to use
Familiar	3	2	1	0	1	2	3	Unfamiliar
Professional	3	2	1	0	1	2	3	Unprofessional
Safe	3	2	1	0	1	2	3	Unsafe
Durable	3	2	1	0	1	2	3	Fragile
Attractive	3	2	1	0	1	2	3	Unattractive
Interesting	3	2	1	0	1	2	3	Boring
Small	3	2	1	0	1	2	3	Large
High quality	3	2	1	0	1	2	3	Low quality
Expensive	3	2	1	0	1	2	3	Inexpensive

Figure 7.25   Semantic Differentials

you will limit the amount of room for the answer with the provision that the participants can expand their answers during the debriefing session. Figure 7.26 shows an example of a fill-in question. Notice the limitation of three points and then on to the next question. This limitation forces the participants to prioritize their points and to place only the most important ones on paper.

CHECK-BOX QUESTIONS

Check-box questions allow the participants to choose from a preselected list of options as shown in Figure 7.27.

I found the following aspects of the manual particularly easy to use. (Please list from 0–3 aspects.)

_____

_____

_____

Figure 7.26 Fill-in Question

Please check the statement that most closely approximates your feelings about documentation.

___ I always use documentation.
___ I use documentation only when I must.
___ I never use documentation.

Figure 7.27 Check-Box Questions

BRANCHING QUESTIONS

Branching questions allow you to control the path of the participants through the questionnaire and address certain questions only to those whose experience or preference warrants it. In the example shown in Figure 7.28, you are interested in seeing the value of a design change to the participants. In this case, for those who would rather use the software to configure the product, you would like to know just how much they are willing to spend.

6. **Use the pilot test to flesh out and refine the questionnaire.** Since it is difficult to produce an unambiguous and unbiased questionnaire (especially if you are very familiar with the subject matter), it is imperative that you conduct a pilot test of the questionnaire. The pilot questionnaire test, which should coincide with the pilot usability test, will give you a sense of whether or not the questions are eliciting the right information. Ask the participants specific questions about the questionnaire itself, such as "Were the questions confusing?" Also, look for biased questions and questions that "lead the witness" to the correct answer. Remember, it is very easy to inadvertently design questions that imply the answer you would like to see.

A. Would you rather set the configuration switches from the software instead of from the hardware?

___ NO (skip to question C)
___ YES (continue)

B. If you answered "YES," what is the maximum you would be willing to pay for the ability to set the configuration switches from the software? (Assume the widget's base price is $650.00.)

I would be willing to pay (check only one):

___ $0
___ $1–$50
___ $51–$100
___ over $100   (Please fill in the highest price you would be willing to pay. $ _____)
___ I don't know enough about configuration switches to answer.

Figure 7.28   Branching Questions

In addition to evaluating your questions, the pilot can also provide:

• Ideas for further questions
• Identification of questions that are superfluous
• A sense of how long it takes to fill out the questionnaire

Following is a sample posttest questionnaire for a digitizer, a hypothetical product consisting of hardware, software, and documentation.

ABC Digitizer
Name: _____   Usability Survey

Please answer the following questions based on your experience using the Digitizer. Where appropriate, we would appreciate if you would explain your answers in the space provided below the questions.

1. Overall, I found the ABC Digitizer easy to use. (Check one.)

_____ *Strongly Disagree*

_____ *Disagree*

_____ *Neither Agree nor Disagree*

_____ *Agree*

_____ *Strongly Agree*

2. I found the Blue key (shift key) an easy-to-use method for accessing additional functions on the keypad.

_____ *Strongly Disagree*

_____ *Disagree*

_____ *Neither Agree nor Disagree*

_____ *Agree*

_____ *Strongly Agree*

3. I found the following aspects of the ABC Digitizer particularly easy to use. (Please list from 0–3 aspects.)

A. _____

B. _____

C. _____

4. I found the following aspects of the ABC Digitizer particularly difficult to use. (Please list from 0–3 aspects.)

A. _____

B. _____

C. _____

5. I found the Digitizer's interface (mouse, pull-down menus, and dialogue boxes) an easy method for performing digitizing functions.

_____ *Strongly Disagree*

_____ *Disagree*

_____ *Neither Agree nor Disagree*

_____ *Agree*

_____ *Strongly Agree*

6. Using the following rating sheet, please circle the number nearest the term that most closely matches your feeling about the ABC Digitizer.

Simple.......... 3... 2... 1... 0... 1... 2... 3... Complex

High tech...... 3... 2... 1... 0... 1... 2... 3... Low tech

Reliable......... 3... 2... 1... 0... 1... 2... 3... Unreliable

Easy to use..... 3... 2... 1... 0... 1... 2... 3... Complex to use

Friendly .... 3... 2... 1... 0... 1... 2... 3... Unfriendly

Professional.... 3... 2... 1... 0... 1... 2... 3... Unprofessional

Safe............. 3... 2... 1... 0... 1... 2... 3... Unsafe

Durable......... 3... 2... 1... 0... 1... 2... 3... Fragile

Attractive...... 3... 2... 1... 0... 1... 2... 3... Unattractive

High quality.... 3... 2... 1... 0... 1... 2... 3... Low quality

I like .... 3... 2... 1... 0... 1... 2... 3... I dislike

7. Please rate the documentation by checking off the term that most closely reflects your opinion.

A. Information was easy to find.

_____ *Strongly Disagree*

_____ *Disagree*

_____ *Neither Agree nor Disagree*

_____ *Agree*

_____ *Strongly Agree*

B. I would have organized the material differently.

_____ *Strongly Disagree*

_____ *Disagree*

_____ *Neither Agree nor Disagree*

_____ *Agree*

_____ *Strongly Agree*

C. The amount of graphics was appropriate.

_____ *Strongly Disagree*

_____ *Disagree*

_____ *Neither Agree nor Disagree*

_____ *Agree*

_____ *Strongly Agree*

D. Terminology was clear and precise.

_____ *Strongly Disagree*

_____ *Disagree*

_____ *Neither Agree nor Disagree*

_____ *Agree*

_____ *Strongly Agree*

E. I always knew when to access the documentation.

_____ *Strongly Disagree*

_____ *Disagree*

_____ *Neither Agree nor Disagree*

_____ *Agree*

_____ *Strongly Agree*

F. The amount of screen explanation was adequate for performing the tasks.

_____   *Strongly Disagree*

_____   *Disagree*

_____   *Neither Agree nor Disagree*

_____   *Agree*

_____   *Strongly Agree*

8. Please add any comments in the space provided that you feel will help us to evaluate the ABC Digitizer. We would especially appreciate your input on the following topics:

   • Functions that are essential and/or superfluous for your work
   • Aspects of the product that are either better or worse than competing products
   • Features you'd like to see on future products

THE DEBRIEFING TOPICS GUIDE

DEFINITION AND PURPOSE

The purpose of the debriefing topics guide is to provide the structure from which to conduct the debriefing session. Unlike a questionnaire, which lists the specific questions that each participant will be asked, the debriefing topics guide lists the general topics that you would like to discuss. It suggests a line of questioning, the exact nature of which depends on the circumstances during each test session. It is similar to a moderator's guide developed for a focus group in that not every topic will be discussed. For example, you may ask a question about a section of the document of only those participants that actually reference that section during the test. If the participants do not reference it, they will not be asked that question or they may be asked why they did *not* reference it. Or, you may ask experienced participants certain questions and novice participants other questions.

Keep in mind that, in addition to the guide, you will also be making notes during the test on the specific items that you need to probe during the debriefing session. So, there may be two sets of notes from which you are drawing the content of your debriefing session.

Figure 7.29 shows a sample debriefing topics guide.

Topics Guide for Post-test Debriefing

If not covered during the test itself, make certain to address the following issues during the debriefing.

Hardware:

Appropriate functions?
Other functions desired?
Notice place for extra cartridge?
Cabling locations intuitive?
Footprint reasonable for their lab?
Compatible with present products in lab?
Networking easy to implement?
Keypad layout and feel?
Stackable?
Since product can be controlled from two places, why did they choose the controller they did?

Software:

GUI meets their needs?
Explore exit message if they lose their data
Explore specific navigation errors made during test
Able to move between applications easily?
TSR help or hindrance?
Did they pick up on color coding?
Error handling improvement from Release 1.5?

Documentation:

Accessibility, accessibility, accessibility (our biggest weakness).
Use index as main entrance? If not, why not?
Graphics detailed enough? Want more?
Scanning improved from previous?
Any confusion about searching in Help or User Guide?
Quick reference used? If not, why not? Appropriate level of detail?

Figure 7.29   Sample Debriefing Topics Guide

CONDUCTING

THE TEST

8

INTRODUCTION

Having completed the basic groundwork and preparation for your usability test, you are almost ready to begin testing. While there exists an almost endless variety of sophisticated and esoteric tests one might conduct (from a test comprising a single participant and lasting several days to a fully automated test with 200 or more participants), in this chapter I will focus on the guidelines and activities for conducting the classic "one-on-one" test. This "typical" test consists of four to ten participants, each of whom is observed and questioned individually by a test monitor seated in the same room. This method will work for any of the four types of tests mentioned: exploratory, assessment, validation, or comparison. The main difference is the types of objectives pursued, that is, more conceptual for an exploratory test, more behavior oriented for assessment and validation tests. The other major difference is the amount of interaction between participant and test monitor. The early exploratory tests will have much interaction. The later validation test will have much less interaction, since the objective is measurement against a standard.

For "first-time" testers I recommend beginning with an assessment test as it is probably the most straightforward to conduct. At the end of this chapter, I will review several variations and enhancements to the basic testing technique that you can employ as you gain confidence.

In terms of *what* to test, I would like to raise an issue previously mentioned in Chapter 2, because it is so crucial. That is, the importance of testing the whole integrated product and not just separate components. Testing a component, such as documentation, separately, *without ever testing it with the rest of the product*, does nothing to ensure ultimate product usability. Rather it reinforces the lack of product integration. In short, you eventually would like to test all components together, with enough lead time to make revisions as required. However, that being said, there is absolutely nothing wrong with testing separate components as they are developed throughout the life cycle, *as long as you eventually test them all together*.

There is one exception to this rule. If you believe that the only way to begin any kind of testing program within your organization is to test a component separately as your only test, then by all means do so. However, you should explain to management the limited nature of those results.

GUIDELINES FOR MONITORING THE TEST

INTRODUCTION

Before describing, via a series of checklists, the step-by-step testing activities of this stage, I would first like to cover the basic guidelines for monitoring a test. These include guidelines on probing and assisting the participant, implementing a "thinking aloud" technique, and some general recommendations on how to work with those you will be testing. For me personally, these guidelines are among the most important in this book for two reasons. First, this is the point in the testing process when you cannot only misunderstand what you are seeing, but you can very easily *affect* what is happening to the detriment of the participant or the product. Human perception is enormously affected by and predicated upon *preconception*. What we *think* we see is not necessarily what *is* happening. As proof of this phenomenon, after you monitor a test that is also being viewed by other observers, note the lack of agreement among yourselves about particular situations that were observed by all.

Second, these guidelines represent skills that are the hardest of all to teach via a book. As with any skill that has a strong flavor and grounding in interpersonal communication, test monitoring skills have a strong element of learning by doing and by practicing, rather than intellectual mastery. It takes many tests before one is really comfortable in monitoring a test, and the best way to learn initially is to watch someone who knows how to do it.

Having now fulfilled my professional obligation to warn you to temper your expectations in mastering these skills and to proceed cautiously, let's discuss some of the basic guidelines for monitoring a test.

MONITOR THE SESSION IMPARTIALLY

Take the attitude that you have no vested interest in the results one way or the other. Present the product neutrally (this does not mean you need to be solemn), so that the participants cannot ascertain any preference on your part. Never indicate through your speech or mannerisms that you strongly approve or disapprove of any actions or comments offered by a particular participant.

React to "mistakes" in exactly the same way as you do to correct behavior. Never make participants feel stupid or inadequate (even inadvertently), by how you respond to their actions. If a participant is having problems, remember that it is the fault of the product. Period. Otherwise, you have the wrong people as participants. Even if you say and do all the right things, participants will still blame themselves. If that happens, remind them of the value of their difficulties to you in understanding how the product actually works. Encourage them to freely explore areas without concern for "looking good."

Encourage participants to focus on their own experiences and not to be concerned with what other people of similar characteristics might hypothetically think or need. However, if a participant has insight about how some other category of end users might react to some portion of the product, then hear him or her out. For example, if a manager has information about how his or her subordinates might fare during the test, by all means encourage that input. This can help you to refine later tests for the category of end users that was mentioned.

BE AWARE OF THE EFFECTS OF YOUR VOICE AND BODY LANGUAGE

It is very easy to unintentionally influence someone by the way in which you react to that person's statements, both verbally and through body language. For example, moving closer to someone indicates acceptance of what that person is saying, moving further away indicates rejection. Raising the pitch of your voice usually signals agreement, while lowering it communicates the opposite. To prevent these biasing effects, make a special effort to be mindful of your voice and body language. The best way to improve your awareness of how you are affecting a session is to review the tapes of your session, noting how and when you inadvertently provided cues to a participant. Do not be too hard on yourself. Even the most experienced test monitor slips up occasionally.

TREAT EACH NEW PARTICIPANT AS AN INDIVIDUAL

While you know intellectually that each participant is unique, there is a very human tendency to be unduly affected by the performance and comments of the last person you observed. To compensate, make an effort to "clear the slate" psychologically prior to beginning a session. Remember to treat each participant as a completely new case, regardless of what previous results and sessions have shown. Try to simply collect behaviors without undue interpretation.

Leave time in the schedule for you as the test monitor to take a break between sessions. If time is very tight, line up fewer participants rather than rushing many through in "assembly line" fashion. Remember, if you are testing five to ten participants, each participant represents a precious opportunity for your product. So favor quality over quantity, especially as it pertains to understanding cause and effect. If you do not understand why errors are being made, it is hard to come up with a solution.

DON'T ''RESCUE'' PARTICIPANTS WHEN THEY STRUGGLE

There is a tendency to jump in and help participants too quickly when they become confused or lost. I have noticed this especially of inexperienced test monitors. The tendency to rescue is due to our natural empathy and even embarrassment when watching someone struggle. Instead, at those times especially, encourage participants to verbalize their feelings.

By not letting the participants struggle, you lose the opportunity to understand what happens when people get lost and how they recover. Very often participants will venture into unexplored areas and open up entirely different issues. If you are using a "thinking aloud" technique, remind the participants to keep talking. If you have not set up such a technique beforehand, then probe the individual participants who are having difficulty to find out what caused the difficulty.

To counteract your tendency to rescue, remind yourself why you are there and why you are testing. It is better to watch the participants struggle now than to receive calls on the company's "hotline" later. Also, there is absolutely no replacement for a struggling participant to convince a skeptical developer that there actually *are* problems with his or her beloved product.

IF YOU MAKE A MISTAKE, CONTINUE ON

Do not panic if you inadvertently reveal information or in some other way bias the session. Just continue on as if nothing happened. At worst, you will invalidate only a small portion of the test. At best, your comment or action will not even be observed by that participant.

MAKE SURE THAT THE PARTICIPANTS ARE REALLY FINISHED WITH A TASK BEFORE GOING ON TO THE NEXT ONE

If you are verbally presenting tasks to a participant one at a time, wait a few moments after you see the current task completed before moving on to the next one. Very often, especially if a participant is unsure of a task, there is a moment of indecision after completing the task when a participant is not sure if he or she has performed correctly. If you jump in too soon, because you notice the participant is finished, you are confirming that he or she has performed correctly and undercutting that moment of indecision. If you pause for a moment, the participant may actually redo the task incorrectly.

Be especially careful if you are sitting close to the participants, because if they notice you making a mark on your data collection sheet, that can signal them that they have completed a task, even if they are not sure. The best way to prevent this problem altogether is to have the participants signal when they are finished, as part of the test protocol. This will help you to resist "rooting them home."

USE HUMOR TO KEEP THE SESSION RELAXED, AND INDICATE TO THE PARTICIPANTS THAT THERE IS NO RIGHT OR WRONG RESPONSE

Unfortunately, seriousness of purpose is often equated with taking oneself seriously. Too much solemnity in the interest of being serious inhibits people and limits the amount and quality of information that you gather. Remember that you are dealing with people who are performing with two or three sets of eyes (or more) on their every move. Humor can counteract their self-consciousness and help them to relax. If they are having fun, they are more apt to let their defenses down and tell you what is really on their minds.

Humor in this instance is the type that keeps things "light" and on an even keel. It is perfectly appropriate to laugh along with the participants when they find something humorous about the product, or to be nondefensive about the product's flaws. Of course, be sure to laugh *with* and not *at* your participants.

IF APPROPRIATE, USE THE "THINKING ALOUD" TECHNIQUE

The "thinking aloud" technique is a simple technique intended to capture what the participants are thinking while working. To implement this technique, have the participants provide a running commentary of their thought process by thinking aloud while performing the tasks of the test. Have them express their confusion, frustration, and perhaps even their delight. When done well, the technique assists you to "read their minds." It is especially effective for conducting early exploratory research (such as evaluating the participant's conceptual model of a product), because it exposes the participant's preconceptions and expectations about how the product works. While the technique has its share of advantages and seems to be an ideal means to capture all the implicit information of a usability test, it is not without some disadvantages. Therefore, do not use it indiscriminately. Following is a list of advantages and disadvantages of the "thinking aloud" technique.

ADVANTAGES OF THE "THINKING ALOUD" TECHNIQUE

- You are able to capture preference and performance information simultaneously, rather than having to remember to ask questions about preferences later.

- The technique can help some participants to focus and concentrate. They fall into a rhythm of working and speaking to you throughout the test.

- You are constantly receiving early clues about misconceptions and confusion before they manifest as incorrect behaviors. These early clues help you to anticipate and trace the source of problems more easily.

DISADVANTAGES OF THE "THINKING ALOUD" TECHNIQUE

- Some participants find the technique unnatural and distracting, since thinking aloud is very different from their own learning style. If a participant is not an "analytical" learner, he or she may feel severely inhibited.

- Thinking aloud slows the thought process, thus increasing mindfulness. Normally, this is a good effect, but in this case it can prevent errors that otherwise might have occurred in the actual workplace. Ideally, you would like your participants to pay neither more nor less attention to the task at hand than they normally would.

- Regardless of learning styles, preferences, and other considerations, it is just plain exhausting to verbalize one's thought process for two to three hours.

HOW TO ENHANCE THE "THINKING ALOUD" TECHNIQUE. If you decide to use this technique, following are some ways to improve its effectiveness.

- **Avoid using it for very short or pointed tests where the uniqueness of the technique does not have time to wear off.** For example, I was once testing whether or not participants noticed and understood one specific label on a hardware product. That objective comprised the entire test, and each session lasted for all of 10 minutes. I found that thinking aloud heightened the participant's awareness of a task that was usually performed on "autopilot." The very act of saying, "Now I'm loading the paper. Now I'm pulling out the tray," made the process unusually deliberate. Consequently, I stopped using this method after the second participant, since it was simply too artificial in this case.

Fortunately, for most people thinking aloud becomes rote over time, and the participant's awareness returns to the less heightened, more customary state after a short period of time.

- **Demonstrate the technique first, so that participants feel less self-conscious.** Demonstrate a few seconds of thinking aloud while performing some nonrelated task to make sure that the participants get the hang of it. Then let them try it and ask you any questions if they need to.

- **Do not force the technique if you encounter strong resistance.** If the participants resist adopting the technique by ignoring your cajoling and prodding to think aloud, or simply saying it is too distracting to them, take the hint. Do not push the technique, but instead probe as needed.

- **Acknowledge that you are listening to your participant's comments by periodically repeating comments back and following up.** Reinforcing a behavior causes it to reoccur. Therefore, let the participants know you hear them and are writing down their comments.

- **Consider a different technique entirely.** Test two participants together and encourage them to think aloud to each other. For more on this technique, see the variations on the basic technique section presented later in this chapter.

PROBE AND INTERACT WITH THE PARTICIPANT AS APPROPRIATE

If you are conducting a true experiment or even a validation test, your interaction with the participant will be very minimal. On the other hand, interaction, especially for a test occurring early or midrange in the development cycle, is mandatory in order to fully understand the "why" behind performance and preference. Interacting with the participant appropriately is a difficult skill to master and should not be undertaken lightly. In fact, it is one of the more advanced skills that a usability professional should possess. Even a sigh at the wrong time can influence results and render all or a portion of the results useless.

On a project with a tight schedule, where many design decisions hinge upon the test results, it is important to explore all ambiguous actions and situations. You haven't the luxury of letting things unfold without intervention.

If this is your first test, then proceed cautiously. Feel your way gradually and learn from your mistakes. Err on the side of interacting too little. If you accidentally divulge information, simply keep going, noting the point in the test where this occured.

Following are general guidelines that present the basics of probing and interacting. Keep in mind that there is no substitute for sensitivity and practice.

When probing:

- **Don't show surprise.** Keep in mind that you are creating an atmosphere in which it is perfectly acceptable and in fact expected to make mistakes. Therefore, reacting with incredulity may destroy that atmosphere because it puts a participant on the defensive. For example, suppose a participant accidentally destroys the file on which he or she is working. Rather than saying anything, let the consequences speak for themselves. If the participant becomes unduly alarmed, simply say something like, "Was this unexpected?" and give the participant a chance to recover.

  Of course, your calm interjection of, "Is there some problem?" while the participant is inadvertently destroying an hour of work often makes for humorous, incongruous situations, but it is usually best to play this situation "straight." Do not immediately let on that you are aware of what has happened. Even comments in jest, such as, "I'm sure there are more files where those came from" are liable to have a negative effect. (As an aside, set up the test so that files are never really deleted, and can easily be restored. You might need to begin again at the point where the file destruction occurred.)

- **Focus on what the participants expected to happen [69].** When the participants have obviously done something different from what was expected or are lost or confused, ask them what they expected to happen in order to understand the root cause of the situation. Do not feel the need to describe in any way what *you* expected to happen. Simply describe the events that occurred as if they were everyday occurrences and leave off any indication of expectation. Do not imply that anything is wrong necessarily. Do not imply "correct" results.

- **Act as a mirror to reflect back what the participants are saying and help them to express their thoughts in a useful way.** Do not say too much and do not volunteer information unless it is an administrative issue or logistical point. If someone is hopelessly stuck and needs a hint, then it is fine to offer assistance. Otherwise, you should not say anything. Do not imply to the participants that there is any right or wrong answer, or that their statement is similar or different from other participants. Most people do not want to seem different from others, so your comments could affect what they say.

- **Do not always ask direct questions.** The real challenge with probing is the subtletly required. You simply cannot always ask direct questions, especially if the participants sense that you are affiliated with the product in any way. Direct questioning of the type, "How did you get all the way over to that screen?" will tend to make the participants extremely defensive as if they were being grilled. A better approach is to ask, "Is everything moving along as expected?"

Ask neutral questions rather than "loaded" ones that imply an answer. An example of a loaded question is, "Most people find this feature easy to use. How about you?" A more neutral phrasing would be, "Is this feature easy or difficult to use?" or "What were you thinking when you used that feature?"

Ask questions that do not imply right or wrong answers. Focus on the participants' preferences and the value they place on features and functions. Some additional examples of neutral questions are:

- What are you thinking right now?
- You seemed surprised/puzzled/frustrated, were you?
- Exactly how did that differ from what you expected to happen?
- Would you expect that information to be provided?

- **During the session, limit your interruptions to short discussions.** Save longer issues for the debriefing session. Too many and too lengthy interruptions will disrupt the thought process of the participants and affect their performance. Jot down topics on your data collection form about which you want to ask questions. Then ask them during the debriefing session. This method is preferable to constantly interrupting the participants while they are working. Keep your probes short, sweet, and to the point.

- **Probe in response to both verbal and nonverbal cues from the participants.** A good test monitor pays attention to the reactions of the participants at all times. Very often, participants will make very subtle responses to what they are seeing or doing. A raised eyebrow, a biting of the lower lip, all can indicate a reaction to the product. The test monitor can take advantage of those moments as an opening to the thought process or feelings of the participants. For example, if a participant starts frowning or sighing while performing a task, you might want to probe with the following question, "This seem problematic to you, is it?" or "What are you thinking right now?" So, read the body language of the participants. Personally, this is one of the main reasons I favor being in the same room as the participants. *There is so much non-verbal implicit information that the participants express that is hard to read from another room.*

- **Look for opportunities to understand the rationale for a particular behavior or preference.** If someone expresses that a particular aspect is interesting or valuable or problematic, however casually, probe to find out why. If a participant mentions other ways of performing or designing a function, ask for examples of what he or she means.

- **Handle one issue at a time.** It is very easy for participants to become sidetracked on tangential issues. Focus on the task at hand. Avoid venturing off into several issues at once or revealing information that is yet to be covered. It is simply too distracting. Make a note to cover the other issues later.

- **Don't problem solve.** Do not use the testing time to fix problems that are discovered. The vast majority of problem resolution should wait until after the participants leave for the day. This is not to say that you cannot ask the participants how they *would* have designed a feature. Obviously, that in itself can be revealing and sometimes helpful.

  But, more often than not, participants are neither qualified as technical writers or software/hardware engineers, nor are they aware of the constraints of the project. So their suggestions may be highly impractical and distract you from what they are more qualified to do than anyone else— reveal what they can and cannot do and what they like and do not like.

  If the participants offer design suggestions, do not discourage them. Write down the suggestions whether they have merit or not. But, if they are clearly impractical, do not waste valuable time exploring the ideas at length.

ASSIST THE PARTICIPANTS ONLY AS A LAST RESORT

Whereas probing is the act of soliciting information from the participants and is often an integral part of the test design, assisting the participants to complete a task is invasive and should only be done when absolutely necessary. Let's be very clear about this. *As soon as you assist, you are affecting the test results in a major way.* If you are tracking the number of tasks performed correctly, you need to differentiate between those that required assistance and those that did not. Never lump both of those categories together. As much as you want to avoid assisting the participants, there are times when it is unavoidable. Following are some suggestions for when and how to assist the participants during a test.

WHEN TO ASSIST

- **When a participant is very lost or very confused.** Obviously, assistance at the first sign of difficulty is not advised. If you can, wait until the participant has gone beyond the time benchmark for the current task before providing assistance or offering a hint. At that point, you have already scored the task as "unsuccessful" anyway, and your assistance can no longer affect that compilation.

- **When performing a required task makes a participant feel uncomfortable.** For example, the test may require the participants to perform an action that they ordinarily cannot bring themselves to do, such as deleting a file without having a backup system in place. (I'm serious. Certain actions are so deeply ingrained that people refuse to do them even if they know it's a test.) Or, participants may feel that the task they are performing is just not realistic and requires some additional background information or context. In such cases you may have to provide a more in-depth explanation.

- **When a participant is exceptionally frustrated and may give up.** People have their own thresholds of frustration, after which they will simply stop working. On the other hand, periods of frustration are often gold mines of information about the product's weaknesses, and much can be learned from letting a participant struggle. It is up to the test monitor to gauge a particular participant's frustration level before jumping in. The key here, in terms of getting the most information, is identifying the frustration level at which the participant will give up and not exceeding it. Knowing when to jump in comes through experience. Letting a participant know you empathize with him or her and encouraging the participant to hang in there can help extend the time the participant will stay with a task before giving up.

- **When the product is in a "before-final" state and you need to provide missing information to the participants.** Almost always, usability testing occurs before an interface or document is complete. This will require the test monitor to fill in missing information that ordinarily would be there. For example, an error message should have appeared on the screen but did not. As test monitor, you should provide the appropriate message and continue on.

- **When a bug occurs or a participant's actions cause a malfunction that requires repairs.** Very often, making repairs to a product in the middle of a test will involve actions that the participant should not see, since the repairs could reveal crucial information or procedures that the participant is not yet privy to. If a repair is needed, the test monitor must not only intervene, *but must remove the participant from the test room.* Have someone else take the participant to a predetermined waiting area, if you need to help with repairs. Be sure to tell the participant that he or she has done nothing wrong, and that it is the tenuous nature of the product at this stage of development that caused the problem. Conveying the information is important since participants may become tentative if it appears that they have caused damage.

HOW TO ASSIST

Having identified those times when it is appropriate to assist, the next order of business is discussing *how* to assist. There are some important considerations that will minimize the effect you will have on the overall test results.

- **NEVER, EVER blame the participants, even indirectly, for a problem.** The fastest way to lose and/or bias a participant is to blame the participant for problems during a test. Just as the "customer is always right," so is the adage, "mistakes are always the fault of the product." Do not lose your cool and react negatively even in the most trying of circumstances (e.g., when a participant's actions crashed the machine or caused alarms to sound).

- **Clarify the concerns of the participants.** Ask leading questions that let the participants express what is happening and what, if anything, they are finding confusing. If they say that they are stuck, do not immediately take that as permission to show them what to do. You *want* to see what the participants do when they reach this point, not discover how quickly you can help them. Often, they make horrific detours (from the viewpoint of the consequences) and it is invaluable to see that take place. Do everything you can to avoid telling them *how* to do something.

- **Provide gradually more revealing hints to get the participants past an obstacle, rather than revealing everything all at once.** If the participants are lost or confused, provide them with hints, rather than "spilling the beans" all at once. Providing hints lets you ascertain the minimum amount of information required for error recovery and will help the development team design solutions later. Perhaps telling the participants to reread an instruction is all they need.

- **Be aware of the tasks to come and the effect your comments could have on the performance of the participants.** In the course of helping the participants when they become confused and cannot continue, it is very easy to inadvertently reveal information that helps them to perform tasks that appear later in the test. Therefore, keep the rest of the test in mind when assisting on the current task. When in doubt about how much to reveal, the best thing is to err on the side of saying too little.

USING CHECKLISTS

Having completed a review of the basics of monitoring, you are now ready to begin the actual process of testing. Because of the myriad details to remember and coordinate when testing, it will help immensely if you develop a series of checklists to guide this process. The lists will prevent you from forgetting any important points. I have included three generic lists to get you started [17].

- **Checklist 1,** to be used about two weeks before the test.
- **Checklist 2,** to be used about one day before the test.
- **Checklist 3,** to be used during the day of the test.

These checklists begin after all the preparation work has been accomplished. Use them as a starting point from which to create your own customized lists that include the specifics of your own testing situation. Your customized checklists should include those places in the test where you need to be especially observant or where you may even interact with each participant in some way. For example, one of your checklists might include:

- Places in the test where you need to mimic a realistic function that does not yet work on the software. You might have to press a hot key for a certain screen to appear.
- Particular problematic sections of a manual where you want to ask questions while a participant is working.
- A reminder to count the number of references to a specific help screen.

Now let's move through the generic checklists one at a time and discuss each item.

CHECKLIST 1: ABOUT TWO WEEKS BEFORE THE TEST

√ Take the test yourself.
√ Conduct a pilot test.
√ Revise the product.
√ Check out all the equipment and the testing environment.

1. **Take the test yourself.** Take your own usability test and look for design flaws. Try to assume the mind set of your prospective users. Take timings to ensure that the test is achievable in the time allotted. Make sure to use your own questionnaires and read them carefully. Revise the test before continuing.

2. **Conduct a pilot test.** After you have made revisions based on taking the test yourself, conduct a pilot test using internal participants (employees of your company) whose background is similar to your end users. Conduct the entire test, including reading the orientation script and providing the test scenarios. Practice the various data collection techniques you will be using. Instruct the participants to fill out all questionnaires that are part of the test.

   The importance of conducting one or more pilot tests cannot be overstated. Do not cut this step short, or you will find that your first one or two real participants will be used "to get the bugs out" of your testing process, essentially acting as the pilot test. Not only does pilot testing allow you to practice, it enables you to refine your test plan as a result of having discovered that certain tasks were not applicable, that questionnaires were misunderstood, and that other areas or sections you had not thought to explore could benefit from testing.

3. **Revise the product.** Yes, revise the product. Do not be surprised when you identify areas of the product that obviously require fixing, based on the pilot

results, without the need for further confirmation by the real test. After all, why waste valuable time testing those features and functions that you know are broken? Uncovering product problems is one of the reasons why conducting a pilot test well in advance of the usability test makes so much sense. If you should discover problems, you have time to correct them before the usability test.

A note of caution is in order though. Be careful about making too many product changes just prior to the start of the usability test, especially software or firmware changes. Too many changes too quickly may cause the product to "crash" unexpectedly, and you run the risk of jeopardizing the usability test altogether. I speak from experience having learned this the hard way. Against my better judgement, I once allowed a programmer to make changes to the product right up to the day before the usability test. When test time arrived, the product was "buggy" and would not work longer than five minutes without "crashing." Needless to say, the test had to be canceled and rescheduled for a later date, and the team lost a window of opportunity in a tight schedule.

Having learned my lesson, I now take a much more conservative approach to allowing product changes before the usability test. I make sure to leave adequate time to debug and test the changes so that the chances of a product crashing during the test are minimized.

4. **Check out all the equipment and the testing environment.** If you will not be using an area dedicated solely to testing, check that the room you will be using is available for the entire time. Also make sure that the equipment you have reserved, leased, or borrowed is available and in working order. This includes everything from cameras to recorders to computers.

CHECKLIST 2: ONE DAY BEFORE THE TEST

√ Check that the video equipment is set up and ready.

√ Check that the product, if software or hardware, is working.

√ Assemble all written test materials.

√ Check on the status of your participants.

√ Double-check the test environment and equipment.

1. **Check that the video equipment is set up and ready.** If your camera does not provide written titles, acquire an erasable white board or slate to hold up in front of the camera to record the participant number and date. In addition, check that you have enough videotape.

2. **Check that the product, if software or hardware, is working.** Remember Murphy's law here. It never fails. Also check that any monitoring equipment, such as data logging programs and stopwatches, is working correctly.

3. **Assemble all written test materials.** Assemble all written test materials, including scripts, test scenarios, questionnaires, and data collection forms. Be as organized as possible, since you will be shuffling large amounts of paper during the test. Consolidate each participant's forms into an individual packet that you simply distribute prior to that person's session. Remember, the less you have to think about logistics, the more you can concentrate on watching the test with undivided attention.

4. **Check on the status of your participants.** If you are handling arrangements for the participants yourself, call the first wave of participants to verify that they will be participating. Continue to do so each day as the test progresses. If an agency or a colleague is handling the participant arrangements, then verify that everything is set up and a fallback procedure is in place in case someone does not show up.

5. **Double-check the test environment and equipment.** Murphy's law returns.

CHECKLIST 3: THE DAY OF THE TEST

√ Scan your customized checklist.
√ Prepare yourself mentally.
√ Greet the participant.
√ Have the participant fill out and sign any preliminary documents.
√ Read the orientation script and set the stage.
√ Have the participant fill out any pretest questionnaires.
√ Move to the testing area and prepare to test.
√ Establish protocol for observers in the room.
√ Provide any prerequisite training if your test plan includes it.
√ Either distribute or read the written task scenario(s) to the participant.
√ Record the start time, observe the participant, and collect all critical data.
√ Have the participant complete all posttest questionnaires.
√ Debrief the participant.
√ Thank the participant, provide any remuneration, and show the participant out.
√ Organize data collection and observation sheets.

√ Using a tape recorder, summarize your main thoughts about the test results.

√ Provide adequate time between test sessions.

√ Prepare for the next participant.

1. **Scan your customized checklist.** Remember, the lists here are generic. Your own list should be specific and guide you through an entire session. Scan the list to refresh your memory about the sequence of events.

2. **Prepare yourself mentally.**

   - **Review the problem statements and overall test objectives, which may have become obscured amidst all the details you have been handling.** Mental preparation sets the stage for how you will handle the test; how open, how alert, how unbiased. Remind yourself of the main issues you will be covering and on which you will focus during the usability test.
   - **Once all preparation is complete, prepare yourself and your attitude.** Let go of any expectations about test results. Remain as open as possible. The best analogy I have seen for the appropriate attitude when conducting a test comes from the Zen tradition, which speaks of "Beginner's Mind" [130].

   "Beginner's Mind," in that tradition, refers to the discipline of always remaining in the present moment and not taking on the "all-knowing" attitude of an expert. In the context of testing, it describes the attitude of someone who knows very little about the product and has very few preconceptions. This is especially important in the case where it is necessary (but not recommended of course) for you to test your own materials.

   Have confidence in the ability of the testing process to expose the product's deficiencies. Rather than embracing all the predictions of the "experts" on the development team, take the attitude that reactions of participants are closer to how the product will fare when released. Keep that in mind throughout the entire process to guard against becoming defensive when results are not what you expected.

   - **Create an open, nonjudgmental environment.** This guideline is listed under mental preparation because it is less tangible than the physical environment that you create. However, it is every bit as important. It has to do with creating an environment in which participants feel completely at ease, even if they make mistakes. If the importance of creating an open, nonjudgmental environment is not immediately obvious, then recall how you personally have felt in the past when performing even familiar tasks in front of an audience. Participants should not feel the slightest sense of being judged or of having to obtain any particular types of results. Once they do, it affects their behavior and introduces a bias.

- **Be curious about what participants do and why.** Curiosity is simply the natural result of "Beginner's Mind" Do not be defensive about their actions.
- **Expect the unexpected.** *Every* test will result in the unexpected. If this were not the case, there really would not be much reason to conduct a usability test. Remember that it may be necessary for you to deviate from the original test plan should a participant uncover important issues that no one had previously considered and that require exploration.

3. **Greet the participant.** Meet the participant or have the participant met outside the testing room in an area that is private, accommodating, and, if possible, stocked with refreshments. Relax, introduce yourself, make small talk, and help the participant feel at ease. Acknowledge and try to understand any nervousness the participant may feel. Perhaps there is something the participant was told that was upsetting and that you will be able to address. Especially if the usability test revolves around new or unfamiliar technology, the participant is very likely to feel in awe and intimidated.

Treat the participant with respect. Show appreciation for his or her willingness to come in and provide this research for you. It is important to guard against projecting an "ivory tower" or "think tank" mentality where this "poor little participant" is being allowed to enter.

Always begin by asking the participant to "parrot" back what he or she was told about today's session by the recruiting person or agency. Often, you will find that the participant has been given information that is biasing and can seriously affect the test session. You need to know that in order to rectify it.

For example, not long ago, for a test I conducted, I used a temporary agency to recruit the participants. I discovered that when the participants expressed concern about the nature of their assignment, the agency's standard reply was, "Don't worry, even a baby can do it." Talk about getting off on the wrong foot! This answer is a serious problem because it sets a false expectation about the ease of a product's use. During the test, encountering the slightest difficulty will confirm (in the participant's mind) that he or she is an absolute moron. As a result, the participant tries too hard and performs unnaturally and under extra pressure. If you find that your participants are being prepped in an unprofessional manner by an agency, you need to contact the offending party before the next test session and instruct them about what to say. Do not simply ignore the situation.

4. **Have the participant fill out and sign any preliminary documents.** These documents include:

- Background questionnaire
- Permission to tape form
- Nondisclosure document

5. **Read the orientation script and set the stage.** Yes, make sure to read the orientation script aloud to the participant each time you start a session. Explain and demonstrate any special techniques you will be using, such as "thinking aloud." Once again, relate to any nervousness on the part of the participant, and if it is excessive do not just jump into the test, but see if there is a tangible cause. Clear up any misconceptions that may still exist about what is expected of the participant. Emphasize that it is *impossible* to really make a mistake.

6. **Have the participant fill out any pretest questionnaires.** The pretest questionnaires I am referring to are the ones intended to gather product-related information and not just demographic data about the participant. Unless there is a need for the participant to view the product first (possibly to give first impressions), the questionnaire can be filled out in the waiting area.

7. **Move to the testing area and prepare to test.** If observers are present in the room, make brief introductions. Explain the setup of the room to the participant, and let him or her see the equipment if you feel it is appropriate. Never avoid the fact that the participant will be observed, *even if he or she is very nervous*. It is not ethical, and it will make things worse if the participant finds out later. (*Note*: you may also tour the testing area while reviewing the orientation script, whichever seems more natural to you.)

Position yourself and the participant according to the environment you have previously set up. Assuming that you are going to be working adjacent to the participant, following are some basic positioning guidelines.

- **Never set up in front of or directly behind a participant unless you are well beyond the range where the person will feel your presence without being able to see you.** Those locations, front and directly behind, create a sense of anxiety in most test participants and tend to accentuate a sense of self-consciousness. Your best bet is to be slightly behind and to the side, where the participant can just see you out of the corner of his or her eye. If you are too close, the participant will be concerned with what you are doing and may be distracted from the tasks at hand. The same holds true generally for additional observers—keep them away from the front and directly behind unless they are at a considerable distance. Since I strongly encourage you to have observers view the test sessions, more explicit guidelines for managing observers during a test follow.

8. **Establish protocol for observers in the room.** It is best if observers can watch the test through electronic observation from another room or through a one-way mirror. However, since some readers will not have the luxury of either option, yet will want to encourage direct observation, it is important to plan ahead how observers will behave. You want to reap the benefits (observers are more likely to abide by the test results if they have seen the test in person) and avoid the negative aspects (biasing the participant). The test monitor must feel comfortable and capable of controlling the proceedings.

   - **Introduce everyone to the participant.** Even if the observers will be well away from the participant during the test, but in the same room, it is still common courtesy to introduce everyone to the participant. This will help to make the participant feel less self-conscious, less like a guinea pig. First names are fine, titles are unnecessary, as are project assignments. Do not, for example, introduce an observer as, "Joe Schmidt, who wrote the user manual for the software you'll be working with today." It is an unusual participant who can openly criticize a user manual while the author watches from the other side of the room. An introduction of "This is Joe Schmidt" is sufficient.

   - **During the testing session, the observers should be as inconspicuous as possible, completely out of the sightline of the participant.** The observers should be well away from the testing station, at least 10 to 15 feet. (If the room is not big enough to allow this much of a buffer, then it probably will just not work.) While this may interfere with their ability to see exactly what is happening, anything closer runs the risk of a group of people hovering over the participant like mother hens. If it is a very large room, have the observers watch the proceedings from a television monitor that is displaying the video camera feed, as shown in Figure 8.1. In that way they can remain in the room without crowding the participant or affecting the test.

   - **During the session, the observers should not make any comments or ask questions.** The test monitor should control the session with no interruptions from the observers. The only exception would be if there are technical problems and the test needs to be interrupted or revised. Observers should jot down important topics and wait for the debriefing session to discuss them, not bring them up during the test.

   - **During the debriefing, observers can be asked to join in the discussion.** The decision to have observers participate in the debriefing is the call of the test monitor based on his or her confidence at being able to control the process. Especially where observers can provide an added dimension to the test monitor's questioning (e.g., when products are targeted toward an

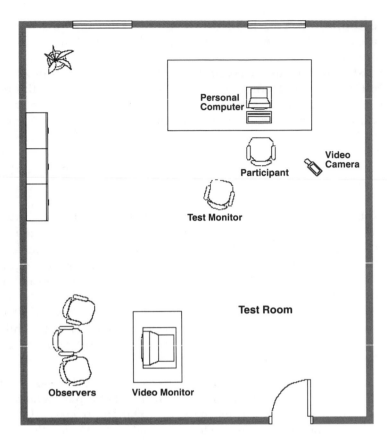

Figure 8.1   Monitoring Configuration with In-Room Observers

extremely specialized audience), it is valuable to bring them into the process. Also, observers may raise concerns specifically related to their own component (e.g., the person who is responsible for the paper handling aspect of a printer may have very specific questions about the paper tray).

Structure the debriefing session beforehand to minimize confusion to all concerned. Have the test monitor begin the debriefing and complete his or her line of questioning completely. At that point, have the observers join in and ask whatever questions they like, or ask the participant to expand upon subject matter already discussed. Be sure to prevent a sense of "shooting" questions at the participant from every direction, and when necessary intervene to stop that from happening.

• **The test monitor has final say on observers in the room.** Try it out with the express agreement that the test monitor will ask the observers to leave if the participant is being affected by their presence.

One final word here on observers. If the observers will only be attending a limited number of sessions, it is important to remind them to withhold final judgements until the test report is complete or at least until a preliminary presentation is made to them by the test monitor who has viewed *all* the test sessions. Rushing to judgment is one of the most common tendencies of observers who view a limited number of test sessions.

9. **Provide any prerequisite training if your test plan includes it.** Prerequisite training may be required to acclimate the participant to your product prior to the test or to bring the participant's expertise to a predetermined criterion. Prerequisite training might involve anything from a simple "20 minute tour" of the product to a full-day, in-depth session. In either case the appropriate time to administer prerequisite training is after introductions and just prior to the actual test.

10. **Either distribute or read the written task scenario(s) to the participant.** If this is a test with little or no interaction required between the participant and the test monitor, then provide written task scenarios for the participant. Since a very long list of tasks can be intimidating, you may want to present the scenarios in phases. After the participant completes one phase, simply present the next one. If the test is more exploratory in nature and there will be much interaction with the participant, then consider reading the scenarios one at a time to the participant. This method provides better control of the pace of the test.

11. **Record the start time, observe the participant, and collect all critical data.** Finally, you are ready to begin collecting information. Your helpers should be briefed and ready to go. Using your data collection instruments, begin to monitor and write down test events.

12. **Have the participant complete all posttest questionnaires.** Once the main testing has been completed, take a short break if it is appropriate. Then, without further discussion of the test, have the participant fill out all written questionnaires. It is important to do this prior to any discussions with the test monitor or other observers to minimize any biasing effects.

13. **Debrief the participant.** Take a moment to peruse the questionnaires that the participant has just completed in order to ascertain if there are additional issues to raise during the debriefing. A more in-depth discussion of debriefing can be found in Chapter 9.

14. **Thank the participant, provide any remuneration, and show the participant out.** If the participant is not being paid, it is always appropriate to give a token gift at the very least. Leave the door open for contacting the participant at a later time to clarify any questions that may arise about the session.

15. **Organize data collection and observation sheets.** Collect any data collection forms, comments, and so on, from other observers. Place all the information from the just-completed session into one file folder. If you are using an automated data collector, make sure the data is backed up and secured on disk.

16. **Using a tape recorder, summarize your main thoughts about the test results.** I have found this taped summary to be an invaluable aid for jogging my memory when I am analyzing the results later, especially if I have been testing many participants. It is faster and simpler than writing a summary, and it is a welcome relief to use the recorder if you have been taking notes for several hours. Simply verbalize your main impressions of the test. This technique works best if you can have your comments transcribed for ease of reference.

17. **Provide adequate time between test sessions.** Do not rush yourself. Make sure you have some time to clear your mind between sessions. Monitoring a test requires immense concentration. Pace yourself, especially if you will be testing for three, four, five days, or even longer. Clear your mind so you will be able to treat the next participant with a fresh start. It is best if you can get completely away from the test area, if only briefly. Testing is mentally demanding on the test monitor, so take it easy on yourself.

18. **Prepare for the next participant.** Onward, ever onward.

SOME FREQUENTLY ASKED QUESTIONS

When testing, you will encounter many situations that simply cannot be covered by a guideline. Following are some frequently asked questions regarding two situations that occur quite often. I have also included some comments, often found at the tip of a test monitor's tongue during a usability test, but which are better left unsaid for obvious reasons.

1. **When is it appropriate to deviate from the test plan?** This is one of the most difficult decisions for the novice test monitor. Obviously, experimental rigor requires you to retain the same conditions from session to session. However, it is of little benefit to stick with a test design that is not meeting your test objectives. Since testing is a rare and often expensive undertaking, it is a waste of time and money to continue with something that is not providing you with the data you require.

   Following are some of the more common reasons for deviating from the initial test design. Keep in mind that if you are conducting the type of rigorous research that requires you to hold all conditions constant, your data and findings will be seriously affected by major changes to the test design. With that said, you should consider changing the test plan under the following circumstances:

- **If the participants either do not understand or are not able to identify with your task scenarios.** Consider revising the tasks to more accurately reflect reality. It is not unusual for the development team to lack a clear understanding of the end user and usage for a product, and you may not discover this until the actual test.

- **If you uncover additional areas that need to be investigated, but were not originally included in your test plan.** If there is an aspect of your product that is unexpectedly problematic, it is important that you not stand on ceremony but explore it. For example, you may find that participants are having difficulty simply installing your software package and are taking three times as long as expected. Even though nothing indicated a problem with that module and you had not planned to devote much energy to probing it, you need to explore why it is taking so long.

- **If your questionnaires are asking the wrong questions.** If the questions do not jibe with the problems or issues raised during the test sessions, change them. Ask questions that go directly to the heart of any problems uncovered.

- **If the participant(s) you expected does not show up.** If the wrong person(s) shows up, with different experience and background than expected, consider changing the test design on the spot. For example, if you are expecting a participant who is experienced with a graphical user interface (GUI) and a complete novice shows up, you have two choices. You can ask the person to leave (but pay him or her first), or you can make the best of the situation. The ultimate decision depends on your schedule and whether you have time to reacquire a different participant.

The preceding examples are all legitimate reasons for changing a test in midstream. However, in the beginning, when you are first learning how to monitor a test, err on the side of sticking to the test plan as much as possible.

2. **How long do I let participants continue when they have exceeded the maximum time allotted to a task?** If you have developed benchmark times representing the maximum allotted duration of a task, you need to decide what you will do when the participants take longer than the benchmark. You could stop them as soon as they reach the benchmark, of course, but not being allowed to complete a task can often be discouraging. What I usually do depends on how close the participants are to completing the task.

If the participants are close to completion, I will let them continue, even though *that task will be graded as "incorrect"* After a few more minutes on the task, if they still are not able to complete it, I will ask them to move on to the next task.

If they are not at all close to completing the task, I will usually give them a hint to see if I can get them past whatever aspect is causing difficulty. I will provide the minimum information that will get them moving toward a solution, and no more. Of course, as with the previous example, once a participant receives a hint, the task is graded as either "unsuccessful" or "required prompting." If need be, I will continue to provide hints in the interest of learning the precise information that does the trick. This can help in redesigning the product.

WHAT *NOT* TO SAY TO PARTICIPANTS

I have discussed what you *should* do or say during a test. What you do not say is equally important. With all due respect to David Letterman, here then is my:

"TOP TEN LIST" OF THINGS <u>*NOT*</u> TO SAY TO **PARTICIPANTS**

10.   Saying, "Remember, we're not testing you," more than three times.

9.   Are you familiar with the term "outlier"?

8.   No one's ever done *that* before.

7.   HA! HA! HA!

6.   That's impossible! I didn't know it could go in upside down!

5.   Could we stop for awhile-watching you struggle like this is making me tired.

4.   I didn't really mean you could press *any* button.

3.   Yes, it's very natural for observers to cry during a test.

2.   Don't feel bad, many people take 15 or 16 tries.

1.   Are you *sure* you've used computers before?

VARIATIONS ON THE BASIC TESTING METHOD

Having previously described the basic method for conducting a test, with one participant and one test monitor, I would like to describe some variations of that technique. Here are some of the more common variations, with an explanation of why, when, and how you would implement each one. Ultimately, your testing methodology is only limited by your imagination and the types of questions you need to have answered by testing.

TESTING WITH GRADUAL DISCLOSURE

WHY?

- You want to conduct a test that requires explanatory or written material, but no material has yet been developed.
- You would like to ascertain the amount of support material, either training, documentation, help, and so on, that is required to support a product. For example, you might want to ascertain the content and level of detail required for a written procedure.
- You want to ascertain the degree to which a user interface is self-evident.

WHEN?   Gradual disclosure is usually used early in the development cycle, before support materials have been created.

HOW?   There are two ways to work this technique; with someone helping the test monitor and with the test monitor alone. I have done it both ways and prefer "with assistance," since it eases the burden on the test monitor. During a test without written materials, let the participant attempt to perform tasks without any assistance, relying only upon his or her own abilities and the self-evidence of the product. If the participant becomes stuck and is at a point where he or she would normally access documentation, you provide information orally to get the participant started again.

Either yourself as test monitor or a previously designated subject matter expert (SME) provides only enough information to get the participant working again and not one word more.

In essence, you "gradually disclose" the required information, in lieu of written materials, so that you can ascertain exactly what a user needs to know in order to perform. The information provided could be either product related, such as which key to press, or application related, such as the relationship of the pressure of a gas to its velocity through a column.

Most of the time, when I am testing a product, I am most definitely *not* a subject matter expert (SME) of the application, so I *must* seek help when using this technique. But, even if I were completely fluent on a subject, I would still prefer that someone other than myself disclose the information. By so doing, it enables me as the test monitor to take notes on what occurred, what piece of information was required, and to stay aware of the other aspects of the test.

The tricky part is controlling what the SME says to the participant, since the SME is usually as pleased as punch to talk about the product or his or her area of expertise, and may not be sensitive to the potential biasing effects of what is revealed. After all, if we simply tell the participant explicitly what to do, we've learned nothing.

Therefore, when using this technique, I spend adequate time briefing the SME on how this technique works and making sure that we practice working together during the pilot test. I like to tell the SME that he or she will be acting as the first human user guide in history, and must be sensitive to the fact that the participants are only going to "read" what we tell them. During the test, I may call "time out" when a participant asks a question and then huddle with the SME to discuss how he or she will answer the question. The participant of course has been briefed about the nature of the test methodology and is aware of what is transpiring. In all honesty, some of the most enjoyable and humorous tests have resulted from this interaction, as well as some of the most fruitful.

Gradual disclosure is most valuable when the test is observed by the people who will be responsible for creating the documentation, help, training, and so forth. They can see and hear for themselves what was said and what was most valuable to the user. The technique is an excellent one for establishing the raw content requirements of user support and in keeping a "lean and mean" approach. Only necessary information is documented, and the product's weak points which need extra help are exposed. Of course, an added benefit is that the interface designers can also see how intuitive and self-evident their product really is or is not, since the user must always try to work without support first.

Keep in mind that you need not run an entire test in this fashion. Perhaps you are unsure of only the more advanced functions of a product, and want to see just how little or how much needs to be said to support them. Or, maybe you need to understand how much prerequisite information a user is required to know in order to perform without any help. Simply change the rules of the test at that point, remove any documentation that has been used, and tell the participant to ask questions when he or she is stuck or confused and ordinarily would access some type of user support.

A slight variation of this technique is to supply some very minimal written instructions to the participant and then note where and what type of *additional* information is required. It's a wonderful way to get started on the documentation and fill in the details later.

TESTING WITH A FAVORED CLIENT

WHY? This technique or program is used to employ a user-centered design approach by working closely with an actual customer to help develop your product. Existing customers, or even potential customers you are wooing, provide their expertise throughout your product development life cycle. A secondary benefit of this technique is to cement your relationship with your largest customer(s).

WHEN? The technique is used at key points throughout the product life cycle, the earlier points being the most beneficial.

HOW? Set up relationships with one or more customers who either exemplify your typical customer or who represent a large portion of your revenue base. Call on them at key points to get both input and feedback on your product. For example, show them preliminary concepts, have them meet with the design team, or have them act as participants for usability tests. The possibilities for gathering information are limitless.

Some companies go so far as to make the client part of their development team and practice participatory design [48]. Others, depending on the type of product, bring the customer(s) in to try out the product for a week or two at a time to perform real-world functions, similar to a "residency" program. The best customers to use are often ones who also use your competitor's product, since their feedback is more well rounded and helpful in ascertaining where the advantages and disadvantages lie.

The advantage to your client is the ability to be on the cutting edge of product development in his or her field. The advantage to your company *in addition to the obvious usability benefits* lies in establishing a strong relationship with your best customers. By paying such close attention to them, you keep them away from your competitors.

There are, however, some things to watch out for. Be careful about letting the customer get *too* close to the team, so close that he or she begins to think like a developer. Chumminess breeds a lack of critical intelligence, and the last thing you need is a cheerleader instead of a critic. Also do not completely ignore the rest of your customer base who may work for a smaller company, be less skilled, and so forth.

In recruiting participants, look for customer representatives who are outspoken, knowledgeable, yet fair. Make sure that you have them sign a very binding nondisclosure agreement in which you stipulate that they may not serve in a similar capacity for your competition.

TESTING TWO PARTICIPANTS AT A TIME

WHY?

- To benefit from the communication between two participants jointly working with the product. Their dialogue becomes a focal point for understanding how users attack problems using your product.
- As an alternative to a "thinking aloud" technique.

WHEN?

- During early to midrange development, when it is important to capture the conceptual model and thought process of users.
- When a product is normally used in the field by a team of people rather than an individual.

HOW?   This technique uses two participants simultaneously during a usability test instead of a single participant. Both participants are encouraged to communicate with each other during the test, and it is this communication that is the key difference during a test. Rather than using the "thinking aloud" technique or test monitor interrogation to explore thought process, the exchange between participants serves that purpose. Participants can be allowed to work together in any way they see fit, but usually one person will work on the product, while the other offers advice.

This is a natural for those types of applications where different users normally work together as a team. For one test that I conducted for a client, I used this technique with two participants who normally work together to perform chemical analyses. One person usually develops the analytical technique, while the other uses the software product to run the technique. Interestingly, when solicited for the usability test, these customers *insisted* on appearing as a team, and they worked well together during the test.

Because the dialogue is so meaningful, you will probably want to audiotape and transcribe the communication between the two participants. You may also need to encourage them to talk to each other if there is little communication occurring. The technique is most valuable for early prototypes of products where there is still time to change the basic design.

SELF-REPORTING METHODOLOGY

WHY?

- To collect preference data from a group of participants without the need for a test monitor

- To collect data quickly when resources are extremely limited.

WHEN?

- You want to compare two versions or prototypes of a product with each other on such variables as ease of access, organization, intuitiveness, and so on.

- You want to conduct field studies of a product when an in-lab study is either not appropriate or not possible.

HOW? This technique involves gathering preference information from the participant via a questionnaire delivered either in phases as the participant completes a series of tasks using the product or at the very end of completing all tasks. The former approach makes it easier for the participant to remember his or her perceptions and feelings about using the product. The tricky part of designing the test is to make filling out the questionnaire as unobtrusive as possible so it does not overly distract the participant from performing the tasks.

Consequently, it is critical that the questionnaire be short and designed for ease of use. Fill-in questions, ranking questions, Likert scales, and list-choice questions are preferred over essay type or similar questions that require much thought to complete. It is imperative that the test be piloted to ferret out and eliminate leading and confusing questions.

Alternately, the participant can be asked to simply write down confusing terms or processes to jog his or her memory for a posttest debriefing session, although obviously this would require more time and effort by a test monitor. See [103] for a description of this methodology applied to a specific project.

ANONYMOUS TESTING

WHY?

- To mitigate the effects of a company's name and reputation on the user's perceptions of a product.

WHEN?

- You are gathering critical preference information and are concerned that knowledge of the manufacturer/developer of the product will adversely affect the user's perceptions and opinion of quality, ease of use, and so on. Perceptions can be affected either positively or negatively depending on the company's reputation.

HOW?   This type of test works exactly as any other usability test that you might conduct with one exception. You must take precautions all through the six stages of testing to ensure that the company name is hidden from your participants. This implies, for example, that testing take place off site, that recruiting be handled by an outside source, and that all company markings and/or trademark design features (if possible and reasonable) are removed from the product. Typically, you would use an external test monitor to conduct the test as well.

Having conducted many of these types of tests at different stages of the life cycle, I can vouch for the fact that users are often swayed more by reputation than by empirical evidence. I have seen users, when faced with a hard-to-use anonymous product, initially rate their probability of purchasing the product very low. Later, when the product's manufacturer is revealed during the debriefing, they want to change their rankings dramatically. Therefore, the anonymous test can provide a more honest snapshot of users' perceptions of problems, which might otherwise be masked or minimized.

As usability engineering becomes more prominent and as more research on testing is conducted, we will see many creative variations and improvements to the testing techniques in use today. The preceding list merely scratches the surface.

DEBRIEFING

THE PARTICIPANT

9

INTRODUCTION

Debriefing refers to the interrogation and review with the participant of his or her actions during the performance portion of a usability test. When first sitting down to organize this book, I was not sure whether to assign debriefing to its own stage of testing or to combine it with the previous stage of conducting the test. After all, one could argue that debriefing is really an extension of the testing process. Participants perform some tasks, and you interrogate them either in phases or after the entire test.

But the more I thought about how much I had learned during the debriefing portions of tests, the more I felt that debriefing warranted its own separate treatment, or stage of testing. More often than not, the debriefing session is the key to understanding *how* to fix the problems uncovered during the performance portion of the test. While the performance of the usability test uncovers and exposes problems, it is often the debriefing session that sheds light on why these problems have occurred. Quite often, it is not until the debriefing session that one understands motive, rationale, and very subtle points of confusion. If you think of usability testing as a mystery to be solved, it is not until the debriefing session that all the pieces come together.

PURPOSE

Ideally, for every test that you conduct, your goal should be to understand why every error, difficulty, and omission occurred *for every participant for every session*. The debriefing session is your final opportunity to fulfill this goal before you let the participant walk out the door. It allows you to resolve any residual questions still resonating after a session. The debriefing session gets the participants to explain things that you could not see, such as what they were thinking when they accidentally deleted a file, or to communicate their personal preferences, such as where in a manual to place a specific piece of information. The debriefing session is intended to expose the thought process and rationale behind each participant's actions, especially for those actions about which the test monitor is unclear. If the task-oriented portion of a test indicates or exposes the "what" of performance, then the debriefing portion exposes or indicates the "why" of performance.

SOME GENERAL INTERROGATION GUIDELINES

In a moment I will discuss the steps involved in conducting a posttest debriefing. But first I would like to review a couple of guidelines on questioning participants.

- **Never make participants feel at all defensive about their actions or their opinions.** The debriefing session should have the flavor of a discussion among peers. By no means should it take on the flavor of a defendant on the witness stand being interrogated by a prosecutor or a defense attorney.

- **While questioning a participant, do not react to the participant's answers one way or another.** This is very hard to do if you have a close affiliation with the product, because there is such a strong tendency to want the product to succeed. Consequently, it is very easy to lead the witness by communicating through body language and other nonverbal means that a particular answer is inherently better than another answer. The debriefing session is one aspect of the test session where a skilled and experienced test monitor and interrogator can make all the difference. Once a participant becomes defensive about any of his or her answers, or starts to get a sense of what you are looking for, that person's answers become suspect.

WHERE TO HOLD THE DEBRIEFING SESSION

Debriefing sessions can be held in the same area as the test, or they can be held in a different room entirely. If you feel that you will be referring to the product during the debriefing, then you will want to conduct the session in the same location as the test. However, there may be times when you want to conduct the debriefing sessions away from the test location if the participant is extremely shy. There the participant is more likely to open up than in the test location. This is especially true if your test location happens to be a very large room that is being observed by others either through a one-way mirror or through an electronic observation room. But since it is important for observers to view the debriefing, only move if there is no choice.

BASIC DEBRIEFING GUIDELINES

Following is a step-by-step methodology for conducting a debriefing session after the main performance test. I have tried to consider the needs of both the test monitor and participant.

1. **Gather your thoughts while the participant fills out any posttest questionnaires.** After the test, have the participant immediately fill out any posttest questionnaire(s). Assure the participant that a full-fledged break will be provided as soon as he or she completes the questionnaire. Take advantage of this time when the participant is filling out the questionnaire to gather your thoughts and think about how the test went. Decide which issues are resolved and which are still fuzzy to you.

   For example:

   - Is it apparent why the participant never read an entire section of the user manual which was integral to performing an entire task?
   - Do you understand why the participant got lost in the help system and was unable to exit for five minutes?
   - Why didn't the participant notice the icon that communicated to place the cable "right side up"?

   Review your debriefing topics guide, circling those issues that need to be moved to the forefront since the conclusion of the test. Cross off those topics that are no longer relevant, or a concern.

2. **Review the posttest questionnaire.** Now reverse roles. Let the participant break while you review his or her just completed questionnaire. The questionnaire can also be used as "food for thought" for the debriefing session. Quickly

glance over some of the participant's answers and ratings. Look for unexpected answers that could benefit from exploration. For example, suppose you monitored a test session where the participant obviously had great difficulty and seemed to exhibit quite a bit of frustration while performing. When you quickly scan this participant's posttest questionnaire, you notice that the participant rated the product extremely high. That is a discrepancy worth investigating during the debriefing session. I know I would certainly like to understand why the participant is rating the product so highly. Was the participant aware of the difficulty and just reluctant to give the product bad marks? Did the participant have an "easy" time compared to using a competitive product? Sometimes you might find that as difficult as the test session seemed, the participant's current product is five times worse.

3. **Begin by letting the participant say whatever is on his or her mind.** I like to begin by allowing the participant to say whatever is on his or her mind. Start with a very general open-ended question such as, "So, what did you think?" This does two things. First, it allows the participant to vent, if he or she is feeling really frustrated. Second, because the question is open ended, it means *that the topic the participant chooses to speak of is usually the most prominent one to that person*. That in itself is an important piece of information.

4. **Begin your questions from general high-level issues.** Use your debriefing topics guide, if need be, to help you remember your main concerns coming into the test. Focus on fundamental product questions. For a software interface, focus on questions of navigation, orienting oneself in the program, and overall layout and design. For a user manual, focus on organization, appropriateness of the format, and general accessibility. For hardware, focus on the control panel and appropriateness of functionality.

5. **Move to the specific issues.** Now you are ready to cover the specifics. Move down your data collection form to places where you have made a notation to probe. Figure 9.1 shows an excerpt from a data collection form with "(?)" indicating a probe point.

   The "(?)" indicates some action or comment by the participant that bears further exploration in the debriefing session, yet did not warrant stopping the test to pursue it at that point in time. I will use such a notation to indicate to myself that I have no idea why a participant behaved as he or she did, and to probe later.

6. **Review those places in the participant's posttest questionnaire that you previously marked as areas to explore.** Take your time. Give yourself enough leeway to think about the issues that you need to explore. It is not at all unusual to take as much time for the debriefing session as you did for the

Task	Elapsed Time	Notes
A	4:25	Opened the wrong file. Found his mistake. Opened the wrong file again. Self-corrected due to error message.
B	:30	Perfect. YES!
C	1:25	Very long hesitation. Then correct performance. (?)
D	2:30	Entered the wrong filename. Very lost. "I hate when that happens." Totally missed note after Step 8.

Figure 9.1 Data Collection Form Showing Probe Location

performance section of the test. You might spend 30 to 40 minutes debriefing someone for a 45-minute test, especially if you are testing during the early stages of product or documentation development when your product is not yet set in concrete. By taking your time, you also help the participant to relax a bit and not necessarily answer with the first thought that comes to mind. Give the participant a chance to contemplate his or her answers, to really think through some of the issues and how these issues relate to the person's eventual use of the product on the job or at home.

Stay with one point until you feel confident that you clearly understand the basis for the problem, difficulty, and so forth. To be sure, ask yourself if you could explain a problem's cause to someone else who did not view the test.

7. **Focus on understanding problems and difficulties, *not* on problem solving.** A very common misuse of the debriefing time is to view it as

   • A time to solve the problems uncovered by the test
   • A time to solicit design ideas from the participant

Let's begin by considering the first item. You do not need to understand how to *fix* the problem. In fact, focusing on resolution at this stage often undermines a more creative solution later when you have more time to think about the issue.

Moving on to the second item, participants who are not experts in such disciplines as interface design and technical writing should not necessarily be solicited for ideas about redesign. I have found that most of the time suggestions from the participants are well meaning but impractical. The participants are not able to take into consideration the constraints of the development team, especially time constraints. An exception to this would be when you want to show some specific design ideas in development to the participant.

You might say this is a rather elitist and closed-minded attitude, but think about it. As end users of products, what participants know *best* is whether a product meets their needs or not. However, designing a product to meet those needs is an entirely different skill. That is why companies hire professional designers, engineers, writers, and training personnel. It's the job of these professionals to take the end user needs into consideration and build the product. Please do not misunderstand me. If a participant offers suggestions that make sense, of course you should note them. However, do not make the solicitation of ideas the main thrust of your debriefing session.

8. **Finish your entire line of questioning before opening up the floor to discussion by observers.** I'm a big advocate for letting observers with a vested interest have the opportunity to ask questions of the participant. *But it must be done in a structured fashion that allows you to maintain control of the process.* I *do not* advocate different people firing questions at the participant in random fashion. The two ways I would suggest accommodating observers depend on your physical setup.

   1. If observers are located outside the testing area, then it is best if they write down their questions on a piece of paper and have the test monitor ask the questions. Even though you have told the participants they are being watched, it can still be a bit awkward when they meet the observers in person.

   2. If observers are located in the test room during the test, it is okay for them to ask questions. However, have them do so after the test monitor has completed his or her line of questioning. You can bring them over and even have a round-table discussion if you feel that such a discussion will not intimidate the participant.

9. **If appropriate, leave the door open to further contact.** Once you have completed the session, you might want to suggest the possibility of contacting the participant to clarify any issues that might come up. Be sure to thank the participant for participating in the usability test, and then present the participant with any remuneration before sending him or her home.

Essentially, these nine steps represent the basic debriefing session. However, once you have mastered the basics, there are other advanced guidelines and techniques that are worth learning and practicing. Let's look at a few of them.

ADVANCED DEBRIEFING GUIDELINES AND TECHNIQUES

"REPLAY THE TEST" TECHNIQUE

Replaying the test is an excellent technique for jogging the participant's memory and helping the participant to remember important points he or she would otherwise forget to tell you. By actively recalling events that occurred, the participant re-experiences his or her thoughts and feelings at the time of the usability test.

There are two methods associated with the "replay the test" technique, the manual method and the video method. Let's first look at the manual method.

MANUAL METHOD. After the test session, go back to your data collection form on which you should have taken cryptic but descriptive notes of the participant's actions for each major scenario. An example might be "Opened the wrong file." For those tasks for which you still have questions, describe to the participant his or her actions with enough detail and embellishment so that the participant is able to visualize what he or she was experiencing at the time. Once you have succeeded in "returning to the scene of the crime," so to speak, ask whatever question you have about the particular circumstances.

I have found this technique very helpful in getting the participants to reexperience what was happening at the time, to reconnect with their emotions and reactions at the time that events occurred. There are some caveats though. You really need to pay attention during the test, take excellent notes, and have a good memory. The test should also be of moderate length, else you will not be able to remember what happened during the early tasks and it will be a stretch for the participant as well.

VIDEO METHOD. An even better variation of the manual replay method is simply using technology to replace notes and memory. In the video method, rather than simply describe past events, you and the participant watch a video of the relevant portions of the test session that was just recorded. When participants see themselves and their own expressions, they are better able to recall their own feelings at that moment [30].

Using the video method provides little reason to interrupt the participant to probe during the test portion. You should still make notes about potential problems, so you know which portions of the tape to access. The downside of this method is the inordinate amount of time to cue up and view the tapes. In addition, the test session is literally experienced twice, which is also time consuming.

AUDIOTAPE THE DEBRIEFING SESSION

Another way to enhance the productivity of your data collection is to audiotape the debriefing session and have it transcribed later. This enables you to give the participant your full attention since you need not take comprehensive notes. It's also much easier to pull important remarks out of the transcript than from the audiotape itself.

REVIEWING ALTERNATE DESIGNS

During the early stages of development, use the debriefing session to review alternate versions of the product and collect information about participant preferences. You might show two or three working prototypes of an applications's screen, or alternate high-level designs of a user manual, and solicit opinions from the participant. This is a much more practical and effective way to solicit design preference information from a participant rather than asking the participant to come up with his or her own ideas from scratch.

"WHAT DID YOU REMEMBER?" TECHNIQUE

Very often, one of the objectives of your test is to ascertain whether specific design elements are contributing or inhibiting or even having no effect at all on end user performance. Perhaps a label on a machine, a key note in a user manual, or an important error message on a screen represents an area of concern. For example, did the participant notice a note in the user manual while performing a task? Since you cannot really question a participant about such items during the test itself (Q: "Excuse me, you didn't happen to notice that note over there, did you?" A: "Oh, you mean this one over here. Why no I hadn't until you just mentioned it.Thanks."), because you will bring his or her attention to the object, you need a more subtle approach.

The way the technique works is as follows. During debriefing, show the participant the screen, or section of the user manual, or machine part with the particular element in question either removed or covered up. Then ask the participant if he or she remembers anything in that spot. For example, in the case of a machine label, your questioning might proceed as shown in Figure 9.2.

Test Monitor:	When you opened the cover to replace the transverse hippleklammer, did you notice anything in the vicinity?
Participant:	Why yes, I vaguely remember seeing a label.
TM:	Great, what was on the label?
P:	I haven't any idea. I didn't really look at it carefully, or even read it.
TM:	So you didn't feel it would be helpful in replacing the hippleklammer?
P:	Well, I suppose if you are asking me, it probably means that it would have helped, but at the time, I guess I was just really focused on the hippleklammer. Remember that it was stuck. So, what did the label say?
TM:	Oh, nothing that important. Let me read it to you. WARNING: Replacing the hippleklammer before checking that the tootenpleeber is securely fastened can result in serious injury.
P:	AHHHHHHHHHHHHHHH!!

Figure 9.2 "What Did You Remember" Dialogue

Note: *All kidding aside, in reality, you would never place the participant in jeopardy during the test, and you would explain that at the appropriate moment during the test if asked. However, on the job, it's a different story. There is a real problem to be solved here, and if the label is not working, you need to know that.*

Here is how I used this technique recently while conducting a test. A crucial part of the test was whether a participant would notice a label attached to a print cartridge on a printer, which helped the end user to insert the print cartridge correctly. I was testing the effectiveness of two different types of labels: graphic labels and word labels. I wanted to see whether one of these types was more effective than the other. After finishing the test, I would hide the print cartridge in my hand and ask the participants whether they remembered seeing the label and, if they did, what was on it. I found that for this particular situation words were remembered much more often than graphics—a somewhat counterintuitive finding. Users tended to ignore the graphic version.

I have found that this technique and line of questioning is extremely valuable in ascertaining which design elements are actually being noticed and having an effect, if simple observation does not reveal the answer. So often developers spend inordinate amounts of time refining elements that the end user does not even notice.

"WHAT WOULD YOU DO IF?" TECHNIQUE

Another very important aspect of questioning during a debriefing session, and one that unfortunately is misused, is exploring the hypothetical situation. For example, after a participant has performed incorrectly because he or she did not notice an error message, the test monitor often asks a question such as, "Well, what if we had placed the error message at the top of the screen? Would that have been better?" Whereupon the participant answers, "Definitely, much better." or "Sure, I think so." In either case the test monitor duly notes on the data collection form that, "Joan preferred error message at top." I am sure you are familiar with this type of interrogation. There is a problem here, though. In the early stages of product development, asking participants for their opinions about hypothetical situations is a major element of exploratory or concept testing. It is an excellent technique for establishing end user preferences for early models of products, and points one in a *general* direction. *However, a broad-brush technique meant for concepts is not necessarily a reliable one for very specific or fine points.*

In the scenario described previously, I am afraid that one cannot take much stock in Joan's answer. We humans are often poor predictors of what we would do in hypothetical situations. Furthermore, it is difficult to gauge one's own reactions after a critical piece of information is already known. In this case Joan is already aware of the error message and its purpose. *The only sure way to test the error message location is to have multiple user groups perform with the label in different locations.*

My advice then is not to invoke the "what would you do if?" technique when the intent is to gather very specific information, or, if you do, to take the results with a grain of salt. *Asking the participants what they would have done hypothetically may have nothing to do with what they **really** would have done.* In some cases it may lead you completely astray.

"DEVIL'S ADVOCATE" TECHNIQUE

There are times when you really want to challenge the intellectual positions of the participants on a particular issue to establish just how strongly they feel about it. It may be a particularly critical or vulnerable aspect of the product, and you might feel that a particular participant is not being completely candid.

This last technique, which I used originally on an experimental basis and now use rather consistently, is one of my favorites. It is also one of the more advanced data collection techniques. In this technique the test monitor drops his or her neutral demeanor and takes a position diametrically opposed to the participant's, in order to ascertain the participant's true feelings about a product. The main reasons for adapting this technique are that

- Your participants seem reluctant to criticize the product, even if they have experienced difficulty using it.
- You are testing a particular feature/section that is known to be problematic or controversial and that may jeopardize release of the product depending on the severity of the problem. In other words, there is a lot riding on the outcome of the usability test, and you have to be extra sure that the test is "exposing all the bad news" before release.

If either of these situations is the case, then the "devil's advocate" technique can be very helpful in providing that extra bit of confidence in your results. It is normally done during the debriefing session, after the participant has completely finished the usability test. It is especially appropriate to use this technique if the participant had a difficult time during the test, but downplays these problems during the debriefing.

HOW TO IMPLEMENT THE "DEVIL'S ADVOCATE" TECHNIQUE

The technique is simple but should be used with discretion. Here is how it works.

1. **Mention that you are surprised at the discrepancy between performance and the participant's comments.** Ask the participant for specific reasons for his or her feelings. Tell the participant that you sense a reluctance on his or her part to offer criticism, and you want to make sure the participant is not just "being kind."

2. **An even more assertive approach is to tell a "white lie" and mention that other participants have offered quite opposite criticism to this particular participant's comments, and you want to be absolutely sure how he or she feels.**

Following are some examples of the types of questions you might ask or the types of statements you might make:

- I'm rather surprised by your answer, are you sure you don't consider this unusually difficult to perform?
- Gee, other people we've brought in here have responded in quite the opposite way.
- You're the first person that has felt this way.

- Don't you think that the manufacturer of this product is doing you a disservice with this design?

Sometimes just asking these questions will cut through a participant's hesitation, and the participant will say that he or she has been reluctant to criticize, almost with a sigh of relief. More often than not, though, participants will simply restate their position because that is the way they truly feel about the product. Being challenged, however, forces them to look more closely at why they feel as they do and often results in a more thoughtful and comprehensive rationale. However, *it is very good news indeed* when participants continue to respond positively even after being challenged in this way.

EXAMPLE OF THE "DEVIL'S ADVOCATE" TECHNIQUE

Let me provide an example of this technique in action. I was recently testing a hardware product for a client. The product required a participant to run a manual adjustment routine (a fix) to overcome a problem on the assembly line. The routine adjustment would take an end user about three minutes to run and would need to be performed every three months or so. The manufacturer did not want to delay release of the product, which would be very costly, but would do so if the usability test showed a strong adverse reaction to the fix. The manufacturer was very concerned that the adjustment would be seen as a blemish on the company's sterling reputation.

The results of the performance test were very positive. Participants were able to perform the fix, and even enjoyed implementing it. Since the true feelings of the participant were so crucial in this case, I began to challenge each participant by intentionally asking *extremely* leading questions, such as, "Don't you find it insulting that the manufacturer is making you perform a fix that should have been resolved at the factory?" I gave them every possible opportunity to change their position.

Time and again, the participants said that performing the fix was not insulting because they appreciated that the company was advising them of the problem and providing them with an easy fix that was even fun to do. This reaction convinced both myself and my client that the fix was truly acceptable. In fact, so strong was the positive reaction that, by the time testing was complete, the company was ready to market the new routine as a "feature" rather than a fix.

Perhaps you are thinking, "Isn't it a bit risky to challenge participants this directly since you might cause them to 'cave in' and change their minds?" Certainly that is possible, but if the interrogation is conducted assertively but without aggression, using the appropriate target participant, it is very rare when you will intimidate the participant. If you do, it becomes rather obvious anyway, and you can back off and factor that into the person's comments.

In reality, it is much more likely during a test that the product will get treated with "kid gloves," and go out the door with a better reputation than it deserves. I am afraid that many organizations, even those committed to testing, are still loath to admit the truth about product problems until it is too late. Also, any risk of biasing the participant's *performance* data is negated by the time this technique is conducted, since the participant has finished that portion of the test already. You can only affect the participant's comments.

There are, however, some participants on whom this technique will not work well, since their opinions are more easily swayed:

- Very young participants
- Participants who are overly ingratiating
- Participants who mistakenly see the testing situation as a possible job opportunity and will say anything to please you.

One final note is in order here. If you should use this technique, be sure to warn observers and team members about your intentions beforehand. They may misunderstand your intentions, and get downright testy when they feel the test monitor is taking sides.

TRANSFORMING DATA INTO

FINDINGS AND RECOMMENDATIONS

10
_____

INTRODUCTION

Finally. You have completed the testing and are now ready to dive in and transform a wealth of data into recommendations for improvement. Typically, the analysis of data falls into two distinct processes with two different deliverables.

The first process is a preliminary analysis and is intended to quickly ascertain the *hot spots* (i.e., worst problems), so that the designers can work on these immediately without having to wait for the final test report. This preliminary analysis takes place as soon as it is feasible after testing has been completed. Its deliverable is either a small written report or a verbal presentation of findings and recommendations.

The second process is a comprehensive analysis, which takes place during a two- to four-week period after the test. Its deliverable is a final, more exhaustive report. This final report should include all the findings in the preliminary report, updated if necessary, plus all the other analyses and findings that were not previously covered.

A word of caution is in order regarding preliminary findings and recommendations. Developing and reporting preliminary recommendations creates a predicament for the test monitor. Your recommendations must be timely so that members of the development team, such as designers and writers, can begin implementing changes. However, you also need to be thorough, in the sense of not missing anything important. Once preliminary recommendations are circulated for public consumption, they quickly lose their *preliminary* flavor. Designers will begin to implement changes, and it is difficult to revisit changes at a later time and say, "Oops, I don't really think we should change that module after all."

You could simply avoid producing preliminary recommendations, but if designers viewed the tests they are sure to act on what they saw prior to your final report. Therefore, not providing *any* preliminary recommendations is not a satisfactory option. The best compromise is to provide preliminary findings and recommendations, but be cautious and err on the conservative side by providing too little rather than too much. Stick to very obvious problems that do not require further analysis on your part. If you are unsure about a finding or a recommended solution without performing further analysis, simply say so.

In my own situation, as an outside consultant, I will typically meet with the development team immediately after the test for a debriefing and informal report, and then follow up with a formal report later. My informal report will only include obvious items that do not require further analyses. In addition, I always qualify my preliminary recommendations as "*preliminary*," and if I leave any paperwork behind, it is clearly marked **PRELIMINARY** in large letters. I feel that this gives me the option of changing a recommendation later based upon further analysis.

Now let's move on and discuss the steps involved in analyzing test data and developing recommendations. There are four major steps to the process.

1. Compile and summarize data.
2. Analyze data.
3. Develop recommendations.
4. Produce the final report.

COMPILE AND SUMMARIZE DATA

Let's look at the process of compiling and summarizing the data you have collected. The following is a step-by-step process for compiling data, although in all honesty it never goes as smoothly and as linearly as described here.

BEGIN COMPILING DATA AS YOU TEST

The process of compiling involves placing all the data collected into a form that allows you to see patterns. The compilation of data, whether you are creating a preliminary report or not, should go on throughout the test sessions. Not only does this speed up the overall analysis process, but it also serves as a checkpoint to see that you are collecting the correct data and that the data matches the problem statements in the test plan. Compiling data as you test also helps you to see if you are missing anything important, and that you understand what you have collected during one day before moving on to the next day.

At the end of each day, gather all the data for that day's session. Make sure that all data is legible, especially if others will be helping you. If observers are assisting with collection, make sure that you can read their notes, too, and that they are collecting data as you expect. Begin to get tapes backed up and audio tapes transcribed. It is much easier to work with a transcription than with the tape itself.

Transfer handwritten notes to a computer, and transfer times and other quantitative data onto a master sheet or computer spreadsheet. If you like, keep a running summary of the data, which you update each night. For example, compute average times for each task on a spreadsheet and recompute the average after each day's data has been added.

This ongoing compilation of data takes advantage of the fact that the test is still fresh in your mind so that you will remember odd quirks and events that happened during the day. Even with the best note taking, keystroke recording, and so on, some events simply will not get captured except in your memory, and they will fade unless you record them. That is why I favor talking into a tape recorder immediately after a session. I find that I capture the highlights as well as the more mundane results much more consistently. The ongoing compilation also prepares you to move faster on any preliminary analysis that you will be providing.

If you happen to be conducting an iterative, fast-turnaround test (e.g., changes are made to the product after every few sessions), compiling data each night will be a necessity. You and the design team will have to decide which changes to the product will be implemented for the next day's session.

CREATE SUMMARIES

After all sessions have been completed, finish compiling data and, if you have not already, generate descriptive summaries for the quantitative data as explained next. Transfer information from data collection sheets onto summary sheets. Or, if you are using an automated data logger that summarizes data for you, print out those files and review them. *The intention of the statistical summaries is to provide a snapshot of what happened during the test; where participants performed well and where they performed poorly.* Statistical summaries are also used to indicate if there were differences in performance of different groups, such as novice and experienced users, or differences in performance of different versions of a product, such as two different styles of manuals.

SUMMARIZE PERFORMANCE DATA

You will want to summarize performance data in terms of task timings and task accuracy. The most common descriptive statistics for performance data are shown next. All of the statistics use simple formulas that are available on most computer spreadsheet programs.

TASK TIMINGS. Task timings relate to how much time participants required to complete each task. Common statistics used to describe task timings include mean, median, range, and standard deviation, each of which is explained in the following discussion.

- **Mean time to complete.** For each task, calculate the average time required by all participants to complete it, using the following formula:

$$\text{Mean} = \frac{\text{Sum of All Participants' Completion Times}}{\text{Number of Participants}}$$

  The mean time to complete is a rough indication of how the group performed as a whole. It can be compared to the original time benchmark developed for the task to see if users, in general, performed better or worse than expected. If it turns out that task times are very skewed either left or right, that is, the highest or lowest times are very different from the other times, then consider using the median score, instead of the mean, as a comparison tool.

- **Median time to complete.** The median time to complete is the time that is exactly in the middle position when all the completion times are listed in ascending order. For example, if the times to complete a task (in minutes) for nine sessions were:

Session Number	Completion Time (in minutes)
1	2.0
2	2.3
3	2.3
4	3.0
5	3.0
6	3.2
7	3.8
8	4.0
9	16.0

then the mean time to complete would be 4.4 minutes. However, the *median* time to complete would be 3.0 minutes (shaded above), which due to the aberration of session #9, seems more typical of the scores.

- **Range (high and low) of completion times.** Show the highest and lowest completion times for each task. This statistic can be very revealing if there is a huge difference between these two times. Especially for small sample sizes, where each participant's performance is crucial, you would like to know why there is such a huge difference between the high and low scores. Did the poorest performer view the task in an unusual way, one that might be shared by a significant minority of the target population? Or, did that participant simply lack some important skills possessed by the target audience?

I recently encountered such a situation. The very last participant of eight performed much more poorly than the other participants on a task, yet fit the user profile exactly. The design team was forced to decide if this poor performance was an aberration or if other end users might perform the task similarly.

- **Standard deviation (SD) of completion times.** The standard deviation, like the range, is a measure of variability—to what degree the times differ from each other. It reveals how closely the scores, in this case the completion times, are clustered around the mean time. Since the SD takes into consideration the middle as well as the end times, it is a more accurate indicator than simply using the longest and shortest completion times. The basic formula for calculating the standard deviation for a group of scores is as follows:

$$\text{Standard Deviation (SD)} = \frac{\sqrt{\Sigma x^2 - \frac{(\Sigma x)^2}{n}}}{n-1}$$

where Σx^2 = the sum of the squares of each of the scores
Σx = the sum of all the scores
n = the total number of scores

As an example of a calculation, let's assume that you have the following series of four completion times, where x is the value of each time:

x (minutes)	x^2
6.0	36.00
5.5	30.25
4.0	16.00
5.0	25.00
$\Sigma x = 20.5$	$\Sigma x^2 = 107.25$

Then the standard deviation would be calculated as follows:

$$\text{SD} = \frac{\sqrt{107.25 - \frac{(20.5)^2}{4}}}{3} = \frac{\sqrt{107.25 - 105.06}}{3} = 0.73 \text{ minutes}$$

The SD is always stated in the original measurement units, in this case, minutes. Fortunately, the SD formula is included on almost any current computer spreadsheet program.

How can you use the SD? Suppose that you calculate a mean time of 6.0 minutes for a task, with an SD of 0.5 minutes. This represents a tightly clustered distribution around the mean, which implies that users performed very similar to each other. If, however, the SD is 3 minutes with the same mean time of 6 minutes, that represents a much broader distribution of times. This much broader distribution could warrant a second look at user's performance to understand why they performed so differently from each other. Were there identifiable differences in experience that could cause this wide variation in scores? Or did some users simply miss an important piece of information?

TASK ACCURACY

For task accuracy, you have several different statistics at your disposal. You could simply count the number of errors made per task. Or, you could go further and categorize the errors by type, such as errors of omission, errors of commission, and so on. Or, as described in the following discussion, you could track the number of participants who performed successfully, either within the time benchmark expected or outside of it. You can also track those participants performing successfully but requiring some assistance. This statistic, however, is not all that helpful unless you have kept the type of assistance consistent from session to session.

Following are three types of statistics that relate to task accuracy:

1. **Percentage of participants performing successfully within the time benchmark.** This task accuracy statistic is an indication of correct performance. If 7 of 10 participants achieved success within the allotted time, then the task accuracy would be 70 percent.

2. **Percentage of participants performing successfully, regardless of the time benchmark.** This is a more inclusive task accuracy statistic. It indicates the percentage of participants who were at least able to muddle through the task well enough to complete it successfully, even if not within the expected time. If the participants made errors, you know they were eventually able to correct themselves and perform successfully.

3. **Percentage of participants performing successfully, regardless of the time benchmark, including those who required assistance.** This last task accuracy statistic is the most inclusive, since it includes every participant who completed the task successfully, whether before or after the maximum time allotted and whether or not they required assistance. If this number is very low, say 50 percent it indicates *very* serious problems with the product because participants could not perform successfully even with assistance and extra time.

Figure 10.1 shows an example of a combined summary of task timings and task accuracy scores from a hypothetical test.

Module	Tasks	Percentage of Participants Performing Correctly (within benchmark)	Mean Time (minutes)	Standard Deviation (minutes)
A	Set temperature and pressure.	83	3.21	4.38
	Set gas flows.	33	12.08	10.15[1]
	Ignite the QRC.	83	2.75	2.68
	Bake out column.	100	0.46	0.17
	Set oven temperature program.	66	6.54	2.56
	Run QRC checkout.	100	0.83	0.34
	Program pressure and temperature.	66	5.17	3.46
	Rerun checkout.	100	0.29	0.09
B	Load the sample tray.	100	0.88	0.28
	Create a subdirectory.	33	8.00	3.92
	Create a sequence.	66	9.42	7.70
	Start the sequence.	66	1.00	0.92
	Stop the sequence.	100	1.30	0.89
	Check the report.	100[2]	1.38	0.58
	Reintegrate and print report.	66	11.67	5.15
	Modify the method.	100[3]	2.67	1.86
	Save the method.	83	2.92	5.41
	Modify the sequence.	66	3.46	3.96
	Restart the sequence.	83	1.08	0.89

[1] Participant 4's timings are not included. Participant had great resistance to performing the task and had not attempted it on the job in more then 18 months. Participant was also given misinformation during the task.

[2] Participant 4 did not perform this task due to running the wrong method and having the test plot run.

[3] Participant 1 did not perform this task due to time constraints.

Figure 10.1 Performance Score Summaries and Mean Times ($N = 6$)

Note that one can look across any line on the table and see the timings and score for each task. For this particular summary, a score was considered correct only if it was performed within the benchmark. Note also the use of footnotes to indicate any discrepancies that occurred during the test. This provides a historical record without having to reference a second table or the raw data itself.

SUMMARIZE PREFERENCE DATA

In addition to summarizing performance data, you will also want to summarize the preference data that you collected. Preference data may come from multiple sources such as surveys, posttest questionnaires, and posttest debriefing sessions. Following are some guidelines for summarizing different types of preference data.

- **For limited-choice questions.** Sum the answers to each individual question, ranking, rating, and so forth, so that you can see how many participants selected each possible choice. You may also want to compute the average scores for each item, but for a small sample size this may not even be necessary in order to view trends.
- **For free-form questions and comments.** List all questions and group all similar answers into meaningful categories. For example, sum all positive and negative references to a particular screen or particular section of a document. This method will enable you to scan the results quickly for a general indication of the number of positive and negative comments.
- **For debriefing sessions.** Have all interviews transcribed and pull out the critical comments. It is always better if you can have interviews transcribed because it is so much easier to scan written comments and pull out the essential information from a transcription than it is to listen and categorize the information while you are listening to the tape. In addition, a written record of these interviews makes the information much more accessible for later reference by someone other than yourself.

List the comments and observations from data collection sheets, both your own and those of participants. Organize these comments and observations in some workable form that makes sense for your test. For example, group them by task or by product component, such as a screen or section of a manual.

Figure 10.2 shows an example of a preference data summary. The summary includes the questions and choices that were provided to participants, as well as a summary of their responses.

Figure 10.3 provides another example of a preference data summary. The data in this example is even more compressed because, instead of including partici-

Usability Survey (N=6)

1. Overall, I found the Series 7 analyzer easy to use. (Check One)

    Strongly Disagree __ Disagree __ Neither Agree nor Disagree _1_
                   Agree _3_ Strongly Agree _2_

2. I found the double-function method an easy to use method for accessing
    additional functions on the keypad.

    Strongly Disagree __ Disagree __ Neither Agree nor Disagree _1_
                   Agree _2_ Strongly Agree _3_

    Please explain the reasons for your answer below. **(Note: Each new
    paragraph represents the comments of a new subject.)**

    *"I use shift key functions on a computer on a daily basis, however keypad
    programming is new to me."*

    *"The double function keypad reduces the number of keys that would make
    the keyboard confusing."*

    "This is a common practice for calculators, etc., so it is not a new concept."

    *"This was easy. It only took one look at the book and the included card and a
    couple of times–if my settings were done correctly, and it was not hard to do."*

    *"I am familiar with the keypad operations using a blue key, and I found this
    easier to use."*

    "Blue key is found in many other applications, so I am used to it."

3. I found the following aspects of the Series 7 Analyzer particularly easy to use.
    (Please list from 0 - 3 aspects.)

    "Oven temp programming. On/Off buttons for detectors, oven, etc."

    "Keys are arranged in order you would logically use them."

    *"Setting pressures through the keyboard. Getting to the end of the detectors
    to measure flow. Air and H_2 settings were easy to set."*

    *"Pressure programming - nice added feature. More temp programs available.
    The QTP sensitivity is selected on the front panel instead of on top by
    cables."*

    *"Single keystrokes necessary to access or edit set points. On/Off gas
    controls with easily accessed flow adjustors."*

Figure 10.2   Usability Survey Data Summary

4. I found the following aspects of the Series 7 Analyzer particularly difficult to use. (Please list from 0 - 3 aspects.)

"Setting flow rates and use of manuals."

"Temp programming for on-column (prompts look the same). Rate X/Y: I assumed 'Y' came after the initial rate, etc. No indication if tracking is on or not in run mode."

"Additional time functions operated through blue key seemed redundant (although I didn't get to use them). Fine metering valve for make-up gas could have a pressure gauge like Series 6."

"I assumed the initial set points in a multi-rate program would be designated 'X,' but not the case."

5. Please add any comments below that you feel will help us to evaluate the Series 7. Some suggested topics are:

   · Functions you found especially helpful or problematic.
   · Aspects that are either better or worse than competitor's products.
   · Features you'd like to see on future products.

   "Helpful function - mouse and windows
   Problematic function - manual organization"

   "The use of the graphic interface will make it easy to use for the novice, but can be confusing to someone not used to Windows. The file naming process does not make enough differentiation between the files run on one sequence and the ones run on the next (they will be the same). This could lead to confusion when archiving the data."

   "Needs: Well labeled histograms (name, method, field labels).
   *   Ability to view part of a histogram.*
   *   Archiving of data.*
   *   Ability to export to an electronic notebook."*

   "Send the yellow book (the test tutorial) along as part of the documentation. Could there be an expanded version of the main menu quick reference card showing where the secondary choices lead to? Maybe reference it to a page in the manual."

   "I like being able to have multi-task functioning on the keypad, but I found running two instruments confusing. I was never sure if I was running the process that I set up."

   "Takes 2 keystrokes to exit a screen report, safety feature that may not be worth it."

Figure 10.2   (*Continued*)

6. Using the rating sheet below, please circle the number nearest the term that most closely matches your feelings about the Series 7 Analyzer.

```
Simple. . . .3 . . 2 . . 1 . . 0 . . .1 . . 2 . . 3 . . . Complex          (a)
High Tech . .3 . . 2 . . 1 . . 0 . . .1 . . 2 . . 3 . . . Low tech         (b)
Reliable . . .3 . . 2 . . 1 . . 0 . . .1 . . 2 . . 3 . . . Unreliable       (c)
Easy to use .3 . . 2 . . 1 . . 0 . . .1 . . 2 . . 3 . . . Complex to use   (d)
Friendly . . .3 . . 2 . . 1 . . 0 . . .1 . . 2 . . 3 . . . Unfriendly       (e)
Professional.3 . . 2 . . 1 . . 0 . . .1 . . 2 . . 3 . . . Unprofessional   (f)
Safe . . . . .3 . . 2 . . 1 . . 0 . . .1 . . 2 . . 3 . . . Unsafe           (g)
Durable . . .3 . . 2 . . 1 . . 0 . . .1 . . 2 . . 3 . . . Fragile          (h)
Attractive . .3 . . 2 . . 1 . . 0 . . .1 . . 2 . . 3 . . . Unattractive     (i)
High quality .3 . . 2 . . 1 . . 0 . . .1 . . 2 . . 3 . . . Low quality      (j)
I like . . . . .3 . . 2 . . 1 . . 0 . . .1 . . 2 . . 3 . . . I dislike      (k)
Clear  . . . .3 . . 2 . . 1 . . 0 . . .1 . . 2 . . 3 . . . Confusing        (l)
              (1)   (2)   (3)   (4)   (5)   (6)   (7)
```

(Note: **The rating scales are intended to gather subjective data. Subjects were instructed to put down the "first thought that comes to mind" for these rating scales, and not to unduly analyze.**)

The mean scores for the rating scales were as follows:

Term to be Rated	Mean Scores (Series 7)
Simple / Complex	3.2
High tech / Low tech	2.0
Reliable / Unreliable	1.5
Easy to use / Complex to use	2.5
Friendly / Unfriendly	2.5
Professional / Unprofessional	1.7
Safe / Unsafe	1.2
Durable / Fragile	1.3
Attractive / Unattractive	2.3
High quality / Low quality	1.0
I like / I dislike	2.0
Clear / Confusing	2.2

(Note: **Scores could range from 1.0 (most desirable characteristic) to 7.0 (least desirable characteristic) with 4.0 being a neutral choice.**)

Figure 10.2   (*Continued*)

Usability and Design Survey (N=12)

1.　　　Overall, I found the printer easy to use. (Check one.)

　　　　Strongly Disagree __ Disagree __ Neither Agree nor Disagree _4_
　　　　　　　Agree _6_ Strongly Agree _2_

2.　　　I found the following aspects of the printer particularly easy to use.
　　　　(Please list from 0 - 3 aspects.)

　　　　**(Note: On questions 2, 3, 5, and 6, the number to the left represents
　　　　the number of subjects who mentioned that topic. Where no
　　　　number is shown, only one subject made that comment.)**

　　　　2　Print Cartridge
　　　　2　Control Panel
　　　　7　Paper Loading
　　　　2　Changing fonts
　　　　4　Setup
　　　　2　Correcting paper jams
　　　　2　Manual answered *most* questions
　　　　　　Printing envelopes and labels
　　　　　　Assembly instructions
　　　　　　Quality of Print
　　　　　　Selecting Quality of type

3.　I found the following aspects of the printer particularly difficult to use. (Please
　　list from 0 - 3 aspects.)

　　　　4　Configuration Switches
　　　　3　Lining up the paper for letterhead
　　　　2　Cables seating
　　　　　　Lines overwriting other lines (bug)
　　　　　　Manual hard to follow
　　　　　　Book didn't explain fonts

4.　Overall, I found the printer well-designed. (Check one.)

　　　Strongly Disagree __ Disagree _2_ Neither Agree nor Disagree _2_
　　　　　　　Agree _4_ Strongly Agree _4_

Figure 10.3　Usability and Design Survey-Compressed Data Summary

5. I like the following aspects of the printer's design. (Please list from 0 - 3 aspects.)

    <u>6</u>   Small and compact
    <u>2</u>   Easy to assemble, with good directions
    <u>2</u>   Controls on front
    <u>2</u>   Like the neutral color
        Keypad on front
        Paper tray easy to insert
        Number of character sets available
        Fast printing
        Lights easy to see without standing

6. I dislike the following aspects of the printer's design. (Please list from 0 - 3 aspects.)

    <u>2</u>   Not seeing where the printer head is going to print
        No way to pre-set advance for letterhead
        Plastic felt thin
        Circular design not solid-appearing
        Doesn't take tractor feed paper
        Would like more detailed instructions
        On/Off switch should be up/down, not side to side
        Configuration switches are too small

Figure 10.3   (*Continued*)

pants comments, it shows only the number of times that a particular product component or aspect was referenced by participants. Especially for tests with more than 10 participants, this more compressed summary gives you a quick means of identifying those aspects that are of greatest concern and those that are of least concern.

Figure 10.4 summarizes the data from an icon evaluation that was given orally by the test monitor. Participants were asked whether they noticed and understood the eight icons located on the machine. If they had not noticed the icons, they were given the opportunity to look them up after the test to see if they understood their meaning at that time.

COMPILE AND SUMMARIZE OTHER MEASURES

Above and beyond the standard set of descriptive statistics just discussed is a variety of other measures that may be of use. For example, depending on your

Icon Evaluation (N=10)

1. Envelope Loading Icon

Noticed?	<u>6</u> Yes <u>4</u> No
Understood?	<u>7</u> Yes <u>3</u> No

2. Paper Loading Icon

Noticed?	<u>8</u> Yes <u>2</u> No
Understood?	<u>8</u> Yes <u>2</u> No

3. Paper Size Lever Icon

Noticed?	<u>8</u> Yes <u>2</u> No
Understood?	<u>5</u> Yes <u>5</u> No

4. Configuration Switch Icon

Noticed?	<u>9</u> Yes <u>1</u> No
Understood?	<u>7</u> Yes <u>3</u> No

5. Interface Cable Icon

Noticed?	<u>5</u> Yes <u>5</u> No
Understood?	<u>3</u> Yes <u>7</u> No

6. Security Device Icon

Noticed?	<u>2</u> Yes <u>8</u> No
Understood?	<u>1</u> Yes <u>9</u> No

7. Power Cord Icon

Noticed?	<u>7</u> Yes <u>3</u> No
Understood?	<u>8</u> Yes <u>2</u> No

8. Paper Support Tray Release Icon

Noticed?	<u>5</u> Yes <u>5</u> No
Understood?	<u>6</u> Yes <u>4</u> No

Figure 10.4 Icon Evaluation, Data Summary

particular test design, you may want to note the following:

- Number of times help was accessed
- Number of times the manual's index was accessed
- Points of hesitation in the manual

Compile and summarize these measures in your report, as needed, to diagnose problems and address test objectives.

SUMMARIZE SCORES BY GROUP OR VERSION

If your test design included more than one user group, you will want to summarize the data separately for each distinct group to see whether one group is performing differently from the other. For example, Figure 10.5 shows a comparison of task accuracy scores (e.g., percentage of participants completing a task successfully) for two groups—novices and experienced users.

Similarly, if you tested different versions of a product or materials, you should compile summaries of performance on each different version. For example, Figure 10.6 shows a comparison of the number of errors made by participants on three different versions of a manual.

Figure 10.7 shows a more comprehensive comparison summary from an exploratory usability test that compared two product prototypes, one a "radio button" type interface and the other a graphic representation of the product.

Group	Task 1 Accuracy Score	Task 2 Accuracy Score	Task 3 Accuracy Score
Novice users	88%	50%	66%
Experienced users	66%	100%	100%

Figure 10.5 Task Accuracy Scores, Compiled by Group

Group	Version A Number of Errors	Version B Number of Errors	Version C Number of Errors
Novice users	6	6	15
Experienced users	9	20	12

Figure 10.6   Number of Errors, Compiled by Version

Participant	Group	R # Tasks Correct	G # Tasks Correct	Liked Best	Would Prefer to Teach a Novice	R Ease of Use (1–5)	G Ease of Use (1–5)
P1	M	*12/15	11/15	R	G	4	3
P2	M	12/15	*11/15	G	G	3	5
P3	M	*12/15	10/15	R	G	5	2
P4	M	10/15	*13/15	G	G	2	4
P5	C	*11/15	10/15	G	R	4	3
P6	C	11/15	*13/15	G	R	5	4
P7	C	*12/15	10/15	G	G	3	4
P8	C	13/15	*11/15	G	G	4	3
					Avg.	3.8	3.5

Key:
C = Clerical   M = Manager
G = Graphic Interface Prototype   R = Radio Button Prototype
* = Prototype first shown to customer

Figure 10.7   Summary of Performance and Preference Rankings

ANALYZE DATA

After you have transformed the raw data into more usable summaries, it is time to make sense of the whole thing. Please note that the decision to summarize by task was a deliberate one, since the task represents the viewpoint or goal of the users and what they would like to achieve. Staying task oriented while summarizing and analyzing the data forces you to look at the situation from the viewpoint of the users, which is the ultimate reason for testing. Can the users perform their tasks using your product? If they cannot, you then need to determine which component or combination of components is the culprit and to what extent. To begin the analysis, identify the tasks on which users had the most difficulty. That will keep you focused on the worst problems.

IDENTIFY AND FOCUS ON THOSE TASKS THAT DID *NOT* MEET CRITERION

Simply put, a task that does not meet criterion is one that a predetermined percentage of participants did not complete successfully within the time benchmark, if one was specified. As mentioned in Chapter 2, I have come to use a 70 percent success criterion for a typical assessment test. If 70 percent of participants do not successfully complete a task, then I label it as "difficult" or "problematic," and focus on that task in my analysis, recommendations, and report. Essentially, such tasks represent the vulnerable portion of the product and its support materials. If you do a preliminary report, these noncriterion tasks are the ones on which you should focus first.

The 70 percent criterion represents a reasonable balance between being too demanding and too lax. Eventually, you would like users to approach a 95 percent success rate, but if you demand that for the usability test, you will often flag almost all tasks. The difference between 95 percent and 70 percent is what the design team has to bridge by its improvements to the product. Conversely, if you make the criterion too low, such as 50 percent, then too many product deficiencies are being assigned to a lower priority.

In Figure 10.8 I have shaded the eight noncriterion tasks, that is, the eight tasks from the data summary (originally shown in Figure 10.1) that have success rates below 70 percent. If this data had been collected during a validation test, you would flag these eight tasks in exactly the manner shown in Figure 10.8.

While the 70 percent criterion rule works quite well for providing a snapshot of problem areas, you may have a completely different method for identifying the most difficult tasks. For a test with few participants, for example, the most difficult tasks will usually jump right out at you, without need for much analysis. However you do it, you must make a distinction between levels of performance, rather than just listing and lumping all the results together into

Module	Tasks	Percentage of Participants Performing Correctly (within benchmark)	Mean Time (minutes)	Standard Deviation (minutes)
A	Set temperature and pressure.	83	3.21	4.38
	Set gas flows.	33	12.08	10.15[1]
	Ignite the QRC.	83	2.75	2.68
	Bake out column.	100	0.46	0.17
	Set oven temperature program.	66	6.54	2.56
	Run QRC checkout.	100	0.83	0.34
	Program pressure and temperature.	66	5.17	3.46
	Rerun checkout.	100	0.29	0.09
B	Load the sample tray.	100	0.88	0.28
	Create a subdirectory.	33	8.00	3.92
	Create a sequence.	66	9.42	7.70
	Start the sequence.	66	1.00	0.92
	Stop the sequence.	100	1.30	0.89
	Check the report.	100[2]	1.38	0.58
	Reintegrate and print report.	66	11.67	5.15
	Modify the method.	100[3]	2.67	1.86
	Save the method.	83	2.92	5.41
	Modify the sequence.	66	3.46	3.96
	Restart the sequence.	83	1.08	0.89

[1] Participant 4's timings are not included. Participant had great resistance to performing the task and had not attempted it on the job in more then 18 months. Participant was also given misinformation during the task.

[2] Participant 4 did not perform this task due to running the wrong method and having the test plot run.

[3] Participant 1 did not perform this task due to time constraints.

Figure 10.8   Noncriterion Tasks Shaded

one long table. Distinguishing between different performance levels will allow you to focus on the problem areas.

IDENTIFY USER ERRORS AND DIFFICULTIES

After you highlight the noncriterion tasks, identify the errors that caused the incorrect performance. An error in this case is defined as any divergence by a user from an expected behavior. For example, the user was supposed to enter a customer ID in field 10, but instead entered it into field 11. Or, the user was supposed to delete a backup file, but instead deleted a working file. Or, the user simply omitted a step. These all represent errors that resulted in unsuccessful completion of a task.

CONDUCT A SOURCE OF ERROR ANALYSIS

Now the real fun begins. Identify the source of every error, if possible, by noting the responsible component or combination of components, or some other cause. *This is your transition point from task orientation to product orientation*. This type of analysis is the ultimate detective work and is the most labor-intensive portion of the posttest regimen. Your objective is to attribute a product-related reason for user difficulties and/or poor performance. Essentially, one has to be clear about why user errors occurred, otherwise the recommendations cannot be accurate. Therefore, take your time and do a thorough job here. This is the point at which you would go back and review the tapes and possibly talk to others who had observed the test.

Of course, some sources of error will be *dead-on* obvious, and will take very little probing. For example, if a user's task was to enter a 20-character customer record within a field on a screen and the field was only long enough to contain 11 characters, the reason for the problem is obvious.

Other determinations will be much more challenging. For example, if users were unable to perform a complex data analysis that took them through three main screens, four different sections of a manual, and two help screens, identifying the source of error is an order of magnitude more difficult. Each of the aforementioned components probably contributed in its own way to the problem. However, there is usually a primary and a secondary culprit and you should so note. For example, when multiple components are involved, a confusing screen may be the primary problem, followed by the document, and last by the "help." Clearing up the primary problem invariably simplifies the changes required to the second sources.

To perform the source of error analysis, you have many areas to review and consider. You have your notes and memory, the notes and memories of others, the video tape record, your understanding of how the product works, and, equally as important, your understanding of user-centered design. You also need to consider the background of the users who made errors. For particularly

Task	Source of Error
Specify the hard drive from which the program should search for applications to configure.	1. Language on the specifications screen was too technical. The user did not recognize the icon for a hard drive and was familiar with the term "directory." The knowledge level of users was overrated. Users had little understanding of MS-DOS. 2. The user guide provided no explanation of why the program needed to search the hard drive.

Figure 10.9 Excerpt from Source of Error Analysis

challenging or critical errors, it is wise to review the videotapes of several users who erred. You may have missed something important during the actual test.

Try not to solve the problem prematurely and recommend a fix before you have identified *all* the sources of error. In terms of thoroughness, you should ideally perform a source of error analysis for every task performed by every user. In this way, you will account for every deficiency and recommend action for each one as well. Figure 10.9 shows an excerpt from a source of error analysis. Note that there are two sources of error, the screen and the user guide.

PRIORITIZE PROBLEMS BY CRITICALITY

After you identify the specific sources of errors, the next step is to prioritize these problems by *criticality*. Criticality is defined as the combination of the severity of a problem and the probability that the problem will occur. If you represented criticality as an equation, it would look like this:

$$\text{Criticality} = \text{Severity} + \text{Probability of Occurrence}$$

The reason for prioritizing problems by criticality is to enable the development team to structure and prioritize the work that is required to improve the product. Obviously, you want the development team to work on the most critical problems first. Here is one way to prioritize problems by criticality.

First, categorize a problem by severity. Severity is measured on a four-point scale, with each problem ranked as shown in Figure 10.10.

Severity Ranking	Severity Description	Severity Definition
4	Unusable	The user either is not able to or will not want to use a particular part of the product because of the way that the product has been designed and implemented. Example: Product crashes unexpectedly whenever a file is appended to an already existing file.
3	Severe	The user will probably use or attempt to use the product here, but will be severely limited in his or her ability to do so. The user will have great difficulty in circumventing the problem. Example: File naming scheme of program is lengthy, very technical, and causes users to forget where information is located. The scheme cannot be overwritten, is not mnemonic, and will be forgotten by infrequent users.
2	Moderate	The user will be able to use the product in most cases, but will have to undertake some moderate effort in getting around the problem. Example: The file naming scheme is lengthy and hard to understand, but the user can create a translation table that links a file name of his or her choice to the one recognized by the program.
1	Irritant	The problem occurs only intermittently, can be circumvented easily, or is dependent on a standard that is outside the product's boundaries. Could also be a cosmetic problem. Example: Each file name is limited to eight characters based on DOS restrictions, requiring users to come up with cryptic file names.

Figure 10.10   Problem Severity Ranking

Frequency Ranking	Estimated Frequency of Occurrence
4	Will occur ≥90% of time product is used.
3	Will occur 51–89% of time.
2	Will occur 11–50% of time.
1	Will occur ≤10% of time.

Figure 10.11   Frequency of Occurrence Ranking

Next, rank the problem by estimated frequency of occurrence. That is, estimate the probability that a problem will occur in the field, and convert that estimate into a frequency ranking. See Figure 10.11 for a table of frequency rankings. (Don't get nervous if this is hard—this is only an estimate.)

To arrive at your estimated frequency of occurrence, you need to account for two factors: the percentage of total users affected and the probability that a user from that affected group will experience the problem. Therefore, if you feel that 10 percent of the target population will encounter this problem about 50 percent of the time, then there is only a 5 percent estimated frequency of occurrence ($0.10 \times 0.5 = 0.05 = 5\%$). Do not worry about the exact precision for your estimated frequency of occurrence. Your best guess will still be quite meaningful.

Ascertaining a problem's criticality is then a simple matter of adding the severity ranking and the frequency ranking for that problem. For example, if a particular problem is ranked unusable (severity ranking = 4), but will only occur 5 percent of the time (frequency ranking = 1), then that problem would receive a priority of 5 (4 + 1). Similarly, if there were a problem that was simply an irritation but affected almost *everybody*, that would also get a 5. Using this method, the very highest priority would be assigned to problems that made the product unusable for everyone. These priorities can then help you decide how to focus resources, with the development team concentrating on fixing the more critical problems first if there is a time constraint. In an ideal situation every problem would be fixed before release, but that rarely happens. Keep in mind that you can develop your own hierarchy and definitions for criticality based on your organization's objectives and the particular product you are testing.

For simple tests, there is an easier way to ascertain which problems are most critical and in most need of attention. *That is to simply ask participants during the debriefing session to tell you what was the most problematic situation for them.* If you find that several participants are in agreement about priorities, then that is an important indication about where to focus your resources.

ANALYZE DIFFERENCES BETWEEN GROUPS OR PRODUCT VERSIONS

If you have conducted a comparison test, you may want to compare the differences between groups or between different versions of your product. For example, you might compare the difference between the use of an old vs. a new format for a manual or the difference between the performance of novice and experienced users.

You will do this by analyzing the amount types, and severity of errors that users made for the two (or more) versions or groups, as well as users' preference ratings, rankings, and general comments. This analysis can be very challenging especially if there is no clearcut "winner," as in the following example.

Figure 10.12 summarizes the results of a comparison test of two prototypes (previously compiled in Figure 10.7). A simple review of the number of errors and the ease-of-use rankings reveals that the two prototypes are very close in user performance and preference. There is a slight advantage in performance for the R (radio button) prototype and a clear advantage in preference for the G (graphic prototype). That much is clear.

What is not clear and what can only be deciphered from notes and observations are the *types* of errors that participants made, the assumptions they made even when they did perform correctly, and what they said about using the product. As it turns out, the reason that the graphic interface prototype did not perform as well as the radio button prototype was because it was unfamiliar to this group of participants. The participants were much more familiar with interfaces with radio buttons, which will also be true for the intended customers.

However, the graphic interface prototype resulted in more positive comments, especially as users mastered its subtleties. It also seemed more intuitive for new users. Almost all of the participants said they would prefer to teach the graphic interface to a novice, due to its more literal representation of the product. Participants felt that novices could see relationships of different pieces of equipment on the graphic interface, while these relationships were only inferred on the radio button interface.

Lastly, the source of error analysis was very revealing. Most of the graphic interface errors occurred because of the poor quality of the graphics. The participants simply misinterpreted the graphic representations of equipment,

Participant	Group	R # Tasks Correct	G # Tasks Correct	Liked Best	Would Prefer to Teach a Novice	R Ease of Use (1–5)	G Ease of Use (1–5)
P1	M	*12/15	11/15	R	G	4	3
P2	M	12/15	*11/15	G	G	3	5
P3	M	*12/15	10/15	R	G	5	2
P4	M	10/15	*13/15	G	G	2	4
P5	C	*11/15	10/15	G	R	4	3
P6	C	11/15	*13/15	G	R	5	4
P7	C	*12/15	10/15	G	G	3	4
P8	C	13/15	*11/15	G	G	4	3
					Avg.	3.8	3.5
Key: C = Clerical G = Graphic Interface Prototype * = Prototype first shown to customer				M = Manager R = Radio Button Prototype			

Figure 10.12   Summary of Performance and Preference Rankings

such as inlets and columns. Had the graphics been more realistic, the error rate might have been nil.

For all these reasons, the decision was made to move to a graphic interface for the initial top-level screen, with radio buttons used for lower-level selection screens.

The previous example illustrates how such comparisons usually work. There are many types of data to analyze and sift through before solid conclusions and recommendations can be formulated. Typically, the source of error analysis is especially important for comparisons. This is because each version usually has distinct advantages and disadvantages. Only by understanding the types and sources of errors in depth is it possible to ascertain the best version.

USING INFERENTIAL STATISTICS

To this point, you have analyzed the test data using simple descriptive statistics. For example, the means, medians, and ranges of times all *describe* the characteristics of your data in ways that help to see patterns of performance and preference and ascertain usability problems. You have also reviewed the strictly qualitative data such as specific comments made by participants. For the vast majority of tests that I conduct for my clients, and for the vast majority of readers of this book, such analysis is sufficient to make meaningful recommendations.

Occasionally though, the development team or whomever has commissioned the usability research may insist that one obtain statistically significant results. Most often, this situation arises when two versions of a product are being compared with each other, and much is riding on the outcome. To obtain statistically significant results requires the use of inferential statistics. That is, we *infer* something about a larger population from the smaller sample of test participants. If the results of a test are statistically significant, then one can assume that if you conducted the study over again with different people with similar experience and background, you would get the same results. However, the use of inferential statistics opens a huge can of worms, and I recommend extreme caution.

First of all, many of those conducting usability tests have not been sufficiently trained in the use and interpretation of inferential statistics. Even among seasoned professionals, there can often be much disagreement about exactly which statistical test to use, and what the results imply afterward. Deciding which statistical technique to use is not trivial and depends on the following five factors [124]:

1. The scale or measurement used for the conditions (variables) being tested
2. The number of conditions and the number of levels in each condition
3. The number of conditions that will be analyzed at the same time
4. The way in which participants were assigned to groups
5. What you will infer from the statistical method

Secondly, those using the results of the test to make decisions about the product are rarely trained in interpreting such statistics, and can easily misinterpret the results. It is important that they receive an explanation of what the statistical results "prove" and "disprove."

Thirdly, and probably most relevant, the way in which you conduct the test will vary greatly depending on whether you are trying to obtain statistical results or not. Obtaining statistical results requires a more rigorous design.

For example, when comparing two or more versions of a product, you must have rigorously controlled the conditions that differ in each version during the test. If you were testing to see if the *format of* a new version of a document was easier to use than the format of an old version, but in addition to a revised format, the new document had additional content and an improved index, you would find it very hard to isolate the effects of format on performance. To support a hypothesis that one format will result in improved performance, the versions should differ in *format* alone and nothing else.

Also, if you conduct a test with much probing and interaction between test monitor and participants, then it is very easy to bias the results of one of the versions to the detriment of the other for the purpose of proving a hypothesis.

Your sample size is also crucial. If your sample size is small, as in the previous example of the two prototypes (Figure 10.12), you will have difficulty obtaining statistical proof that the results were not due to chance. As a very general rule, all things being equal, you should have sample sizes of at least 10 to 12 participants per condition before considering the use of inferential statistics [124].

In sum, the appropriate use of inferential statistics is both a complex and subtle topic. While there certainly is a place for their use in usability research, I suggest that only those with a thorough grounding in experimental design and statistical theory make use of this tool. For the vast majority of practitioners, I suggest avoiding the use of such statistical techniques for the reasons mentioned previously. If you would like to learn more, I recommend reading one of the following introductory books on probability and statistics.

- *Introductory Statistics* by Prem S. Mann
- *General Statistics* by Warren Chase and Fred Brown

Also, the article by Jan Spyridakis [124] is an excellent introduction to conducting research using true experimental designs.

An even better plan, if you are genuinely interested in learning more, is to enroll in a university course on statistics offered through either the university's social science or behavioral sciences department.

DEVELOP RECOMMENDATIONS

At last we come to the raison d'être for the entire process of usability testing. It is time to take all the information you have analyzed and translate it into recommendations for action. This is neither a simple process nor a precise scientific one in the sense of a cookbook approach. In fact, it is similar to that stage in product development where one moves from characterization of the user and development of functional specifications to the design of the system. At that point, 20 different designers might conceivably come up with 20 different interpretations of the specifications resulting in 20 different designs. This process is similar, in that any single individual might read the implications of the test a bit differently, and make slightly different recommendations.

The recommendation process is one area that can benefit immensely from user-centered design expertise and knowledge of usability principles. The whole is often more than the sum of the parts, and it is not always obvious which component is responsible for problems. Even if one identifies the problem source, solutions are often extremely subtle. Knowledge of how people read and learn, how they process information, how human performance is affected by short-term memory limitations, and so on, are all critical in making accurate recommendations. Therefore, if you have not already done so, this is an excellent time to confer with someone experienced in human–computer interaction.

While the compilation of data should occur immediately after the testing process, I advise the opposite for making recommendations. The testing and analysis process can be arduous. It is very labor intensive, requires long periods of concentration, and, in general, tends to wear you down—not exactly the ideal frame of mind for thinking creatively and in new ways.

Therefore, before developing recommendations, I suggest that you get away from the project for a few days. Work on something else and do not even think of the project. Of course, if a great idea strikes you, write it down. But let it go after that. I have found that providing this "gap" helps me to recharge and approach problems from a fresh perspective.

The other important point about making recommendations is that doing so should not be a solo effort. While one person has primary responsibility for the report, the design team should be an integral part of the process. This is true whether one is part of the organization or an outside consultant, although the degree of collaboration will vary. Here is why a group effort is beneficial.

- **Different perspectives are essential.** As I mentioned earlier, there is no "right" answer when it comes to design recommendations. Rather, there will always be a variety of alternatives as seen from different perspectives. The development team will be composed of experts from a variety of disciplines, such as engineering, technical communication, marketing, and hopefully human factors. Each discipline will provide a unique perspective, which can help to make informed judgments. Often, if you can simply and clearly identify the issue, the design team can help you to come up with an elegant solution.

Also, I am constantly amazed how the same test can be viewed so differently by several different observers. I am not just referring to observers who have a clear vested interest in the product being tested. Even impartial observers will interpret what they see differently. Very often, this will result in a unique perspective or insight that triggers a creative recommendation. However, let me add that ultimately this process is not a democratic one. It is important that those who only saw a session or two do not have a major say in recommendations. Seeing only one or two sessions, while helping to provide a sense of value to the testing process, does not provide a wide enough perspective to interpret results. The test monitor who attended each session clearly has the broadest perspective.

- **You need buy-in.** *For optimum success, it helps if designers have a personal connection with the results and recommendations.* Recommendations are only as good as the degree to which they are embraced by the people who must implement them. Simply reading a recommendation in a report will rarely convince anyone to make a dramatic change. The most sterling ideas will sit on the shelf or in someone's drawer if they do not make sense to the people who incorporate them into products.

Therefore, it behooves you to find out what those people who will be affected by the report think of the preliminary test results and possible recommendations, prior to the final report. It is better to have discussions of conflicting perceptions and opinions and identify shortcomings of certain recommendations before the final report rather than afterwards. Also, remember that it is much easier to ignore a report than it is to ignore a flesh-and-blood person making a particular point. Do not underestimate your ability to persuade people to your point of view by holding discussions.

FOCUS ON SOLUTIONS THAT WILL HAVE THE WIDEST IMPACT ON THE PRODUCT

Obviously, recommendations will interact with each other. A recommendation to change a field on one screen will have very limited impact. A recommendation to change the navigation scheme for the entire user interface will have a decidedly greater impact. Similarly, a recommendation to change the wording of a paragraph will have limited impact, but the decision to change the entire format for procedural instructions has a far greater effect. The point is, global changes affect everything and need to be considered first.

Therefore, in determining solutions to problems, begin by looking at the global usability level first to make sure that those bases have been covered. For example, shown in Figures 10.13 and 10.14 are some global usability issues/principles for software and for documentation. These high-level issues will have profound and wide-ranging effects on the usability of the whole

The organization of the manual reflects the user's on-the-job tasks rather than the product's organization.

The layout and format are conducive to scanning information quickly.

Accessibility devices such as indices, tabs, major headings, and table of contents enhance rather than inhibit the search for information.

Graphics are at the correct level of detail and located at the point where required while on a task.

Figure 10.13   Example of Global Issues for Documentation

The overall logic of the program reflects user tasks, not the internal logic of the program.

Navigation cues and rules are intuitive and simple. User is able to move easily from screen to screen.

Rules of navigation are consistent from screen to screen.

Color coding of terms, messages, fields, etc., are intuitive and helpful. Color coding schemes are obvious to the user, and do not require explanations such as help or documentation.

Cues for informing the user of the screen's relation to the larger product are in place on each screen. User does not get lost in the program.

Figure 10.14   Example of Global Issues for User Interface

product. In a sense these are the foundation or building blocks of usability. Addressing such issues first will provide the most leverage for improving the product. That is why conferring with a usability specialist can be so helpful at this point. He or she will be familiar with the common global issues.

There are also global usability issues that are not necessarily associated with a broad principle, but rather are due to discovering a finding with broad implications. For example, on a recent software test that I conducted, I discovered through testing that users were divided into three distinct levels of expertise, with a huge difference in abilities and knowledge, almost a chasm, between the least and most sophisticated level. This discrepancy had not been known before the test, and had the most profound implications of all test results.

We found that it was impossible to adequately support all users from the same screens. Therefore, it was decided to have two distinct *tracks* for the product. The least sophisticated users would use the simple track which simplified decision making drastically and the functionality of the product as well. The second and third user groups, who were more sophisticated, would use a more comprehensive track with different screens, different choices, and full functionality. This finding set the stage for all other findings and recommendations, since the implications affected every screen and, of course, the documentation as well.

The main point is to recognize and begin developing recommendations at an aerial rather than ground level. In the anecdote just discussed, the finding had little to do with a specific difficulty on a certain screen or even with a certain task. Rather, it affected the entire approach to using the product. I suppose the best way to summarize this point is not to lose sight of the forest for the trees.

IGNORE ''POLITICAL CONSIDERATIONS'' FOR THE FIRST DRAFT OF RECOMMENDATIONS

By political considerations, I mean what may or may not be possible, doable, and acceptable to management and the team, and whether or not your recommendations are a major departure from the past. You *will* need to consider political issues later, since there is little point in making recommendations that have no chance of being implemented. However, if you concern yourself with politics prematurely, you lose your objectivity, limit your recommendations, and get sidetracked.

Proceed initially as if there is only one concern, the user. This approach results in the most creative solutions, and avoids presupposing that some constraint is in effect, either financial, time, or otherwise. If you are creating recommendations to be reviewed with the team, by all means include solutions that are clearly the right thing to do, but may not be politically correct for one reason or another. At the review session, it is amazing what happens when seemingly unacceptable solutions are discussed, rather than immediately suppressed. Solutions often get revised but end up further along than if you had simply avoided including them. It is important to remember that usability testing is one of the most potent forces for change within organizations, since the user is able to influence the process. By all means, take advantage of that opportunity.

PROVIDE BOTH SHORT-TERM AND LONG-TERM RECOMMENDATIONS

This point is related to the previous one. A test will often result in recommended changes to the product that cannot be addressed in time for the scheduled release. Do not be satisfied with just recommending band-aids for deep-seated problems, simply because there is no time to implement full-blown solutions. Instead, state in the report that your recommendations fall into two sections. In one section (short-term recommendations) are the types of changes that can be made without slipping the schedule. In the other section (long-term recommendations) are the types of changes that are really required for long-term success. It is important that the organization be aware that stop-gap changes are just that, an attempt to get the product out on schedule with minimal problems.

INDICATE AREAS WHERE FURTHER RESEARCH IS REQUIRED

Usability testing, as with almost all research, often results in many questions that require answers. This should not be considered a *defeat*. Rather, it is simply the norm if you are doing a good job, and you should not shy away from raising these questions. The questions might require further testing or the application of a different research technique, such as a formal experiment, survey of the user population, or on-site observation. Ambiguity is the wellspring of change, and no one will fault you if you honestly point out the limitations of the current study. You might even have a section in the report entitled *Future Research* to emphasize the point.

BE THOROUGH

Cover all bases. Even though you begin by focusing on the most critical problems, eventually you will want to cover everything. Make sure that each problem identified has been addressed. Remember that the final report becomes a historical document, referred to by others who were not privy to your constraints. You want to make sure you have addressed all the objectives and captured all the revisions required.

PRODUCE THE FINAL REPORT

It is typical of most development environments that the development team begins revising the product well before the final test report is distributed. However, this is no excuse for not producing a report or for doing less than a stellar job on its content. Always produce a report, even if it is brief and even if its recommendations are after the fact. The report will serve as the only historical record of what occurred for years to come.

PURPOSE AND INTENT

The quality of the report and how it is viewed will be a direct reflection of how you view it. If you see the creation of the report simply as a *mopping-up* exercise intended to pull together all the loose ends, then that is what it will be. If you view it as a vehicle for impressing others with the sheer volume of statistics and minutiae collected, it will impress no one but yourself and the two other coworkers in your organization who revel in reading such documents.

What the test report *should* do is support and initiate change, direct action, provide a historical record, and educate—all at the same time. Above all else, it should *communicate* to people. There is no reason that reports need to be stuffy, boring, and overly technical. Do not use the report as a way of creating job security for yourself, by ensuring that you are the only one who can decipher its mysterious findings and revelations. I guarantee you that this approach will backfire in the long run. Think a moment about the incongruousness of receiving a report on a usability test that itself is hard to use. Such a report sends a very mixed message indeed, and one that you should avoid.

When writing the report, approach it as if you were basically telling a story, and make sure that all the sections of the report relate to that story. Thinking of it in this way makes it easier to pull the disparate sections together so that they make sense and support each other.

There should be a threefold logic to the report. That is, the report should have a beginning, a middle and an end. The beginning is composed of why you did the test, and how you prepared, the middle is composed of what happened during the test, and the end is composed of the implications of what happened, that is, what you recommend doing about what happened. Following is a suggested format for a report, showing the major sections and each section's intended purpose.

MAJOR REPORT SECTIONS

- **Executive summary section.** This section should contain a brief synopsis of the test logistics, the major findings and recommendations, and further research required, and the overall benefits of the test. Keep it to one page if you can, as its purpose is to enable readers to quickly scan for high-level information.

- **Method section.** In this section describe the nature of the research, how it was set up, user profiles, and the data collection methods used. If this sounds suspiciously like the test plan, go to the head of the class. If your test plan is comprehensive, simply paste it in as is, with one exception. Update it with exceptions to the original plan. That is, describe any events that occurred that forced you to change your procedure, such as the system crashed repeatedly, no participants showed up one day, and so on. Of course, since you were so diligent about noting this information as it happened, you will have no trouble documenting it now.

- **Results section.** In this section display both the quantitative and qualitative summaries, using the most concise and readable form possible. Quantitative summaries are timing, task completion percentages, and so forth. Qualitative summaries are free-form questions, types of errors, and the like. You need not include the raw data (e.g., copies of individual questionnaires or data collection sheets), although you could place these in an appendix. However, I have found it useful to leave out the raw data, and I suggest that you do the same. Simply mention in the report the name of the person who holds the raw data, for those interested in perusing it. Also, mention where the videotapes are stored.

- **Findings and recommendations (discussion).** In this section are the findings and recommendations, along with a discussion and explanation of them. The design of this section should enable someone to quickly pick out the findings and recommendations *without* having to read the supporting text. Especially design this section for usability, by having the findings and recommendations in boldface or italics or separated by space from the discussion. Just as with good documentation, do not make people read through a whole lot of extraneous information to get to the things they need quickly.

Having said that though, I must add that the critical element is usability, not brevity. It is not necessary to leave out anything important, and you should explain findings in as much detail as is required to make your point. But do lay out the information so that readers can easily bypass explanations if they choose to.

You may find that you want to divide this section into *general findings and recommendations* followed by *specific findings and recommendations*. The general findings and recommendations section would include a high-level discussion of important global issues, possibly in paragraph form. For example, this section might include a discussion about what you learned about the abilities and expectations of the end user from viewing the participants at work. The specific findings and recommendations section would contain a listing of the nitty-gritty changes that are required, usually organized by product component.

Figures 10.15, 10.16, and 10.17 contain three suggested formats that you can use for showing specific findings and recommendations, which is probably the most important part of the report. The format you choose will depend on the amount of explanation you provide, your personal preference, and your intended audience.

Data Analysis Module

1. Finding and Explanation:

    The process for creating a sequence table on the Sample Entry Table screen is tedious and not consistent with other similar tables. Users found the combination of the "Insert" command and the necessity of having to move the "Final Line" out of the way to be nonintuitive and confusing.

    Recommendation:

    Use a simpler, consistent method already in use on other tables, such as the "Edit Log Table." That table seems to work more simply, completely foregoing the "Insert" command altogether. After the user enters the last entry, the mouse cursor moves to the next line of the table. The user is ready at that point to add another line without having to move the "Final Line" out of the way.

Figure 10.15   Sample Format 1 (Data Analysis Module)

Installation Screen

Findings and Explanations:

1.   First finding and explanation.
2.   Second finding and explanation.
3.   Third finding and explanation.

Recommendations:

1.   First recommendation.
2.   Second recommendation.
3.   Third recommendation.

Figure 10.16   Sample Format 2 (Installation Screen)

Setup Help Screen

1. First recommendation:

    Explanation for first recommendation:

2. Second recommendation:

    Explanation for second recommendation:

Figure 10.17   Sample Format 3 (Set Up Help Screen)

Task	Source of Error	Recommendation
Specify the hard drive from which the program should search for applications to configure.	Language on the specifications screen was too technical. The user did not recognize the icon for a hard drive, nor was familiar with the term "directory." The knowledge level of users was overrated. Users had little understanding of MS-DOS. The user guide provided no explanation of why the program needed to search the hard drive.	Revise the task so that the system automatically asks to search on the user's C: drive for applications with which it will set up to use with the analyzer. If the user answers no, then the user will be asked to choose from a list of alternative drives. Add explanations in help about this process in simple language explaining what is happening. Add information in the manual explaining this process and that for most users, the default choice of the C: drive is the correct one.

Figure 10.18   Format 4 (Three-Column Format)

Format 1 shown in Figure 10.15 is the format I favor because of its cause-and-effect logic. It lets me reveal the specific finding (the cause), and follow it with a recommendation (the effect). Figures 10.16 and 10.17 are variations on the same theme.

Figure 10.18 shows a fourth format that takes advantage of your source of error analysis by simply adding another column—Recommendation—to that analysis.

- **Appendices section.** The *appendices* section is the place to include raw data compilations, samples of test materials, such as questionnaires, scripts and the like, and any other items that you feel belong with the package, with one exception. In the interest of providing additional protection for the identity of participants, I would not list their actual names in the report, simply their backgrounds and other important information. Their names are of no importance, and this is simply an added precaution against misuse. Anyone needing to contact a participant can contact the test monitor directly.

REFINING THE REPORT FORMAT

If you will be conducting tests on an ongoing basis within your organization, it is important to get feedback on how well your test report is communicating to people. You need feedback not only on the content, but also on the report's usability and value. Ask the readers of the report such questions as:

- Were you able to get at the information you needed?
- Was the type of information you needed all there?
- Was the format easy to use?

Then incorporate that feedback into later reports until you come up with a format that really works in your organization. Once you do, stick to it as a template for future tests and reports, and let it guide your analysis as well as the writing of the report. Why reinvent the wheel if you have found something that works?

In addition to the report, you may want to make a presentation of your findings, especially if your efforts are part of an overall usability program. Setting up such a program is the focus of the next chapter.

PART FOUR

EXPANDING USABILITY

ESTABLISHING A USABILITY PROGRAM:

STRATEGIES AND TACTICS

11

INTRODUCTION

Up to this point, we have covered the technical aspects of planning, designing, conducting, and reporting the results of a usability test in great detail. We have also placed usability testing within the context of a user-centered approach to product development. In this final chapter I would like to revisit the larger picture and discuss how to expand the influence of usability engineering within an organization. Specifically, I would like to discuss the strategies and tactics for establishing such a program within an organization new to the discipline of user-centered design. These suggestions are primarily intended for an individual who has been given (or would like to take) primary responsibility for usability within his or her organization, with minimal formal training in usability engineering.

I have placed my suggestions within the context of a phased program, extending over months or more likely, years, to emphasize the need to build such a program gradually. Let me be very clear. Implementing a user-centered approach to product development for organizations that have not embraced such a program previously is a major undertaking, fraught with the same difficulties, risks, excitement, and political intrigue of any major shift in the corporate culture. It requires much forethought and attention to the "human" issues within your own organization. However, depending on the degree of management support and the amount of resources assigned to usability, you may want to move faster or slower, implement these suggestions in a different order, or avoid those that simply do not make sense for your organization. The important point is to understand and account for the dynamics operating within your own organization and to act accordingly. There is no magic formula that can be adapted in "cookie-cutter" fashion to every organization, and any attempt to do so will jeopardize a program.

PHASE I: GETTING STARTED

Appraise the current situation within your organization and search for opportunities to contribute. The overall goal at the beginning is to make steady progress while educating the organization about the benefits of usability engineering.

BEGIN YOUR EDUCATION

Begin your education by becoming familiar with the abundance of information available. Although much of it tends to be quite technical and overwhelming for the beginner, you should start with those publications that teach usability principles and guidelines in simple English. The following books are excellent for an introduction to the field of usability engineering, either for yourself or for those you wish to educate.

- *The Design of Everyday Things* by Donald Norman
- *Elements of Friendly Software Design* by Paul Heckel
- *The Human Factor: Designing Computer Systems for People* by Richard Rubinstein and Harry Hersh

Another excellent introduction is the colloquium offered by the University of Michigan each summer for budding human factors specialists. This two-week seminar spends the first week on basic issues of human psychology, and the second week on system design issues. Either week may be attended separately.

DEVELOP A PLAN

How you begin, in terms of setting expectations and establishing an overall philosophy, will go a long way toward determining ultimate success. Even if you are just starting to work with usability issues, it behooves you to think of the long term at the very start. Therefore, begin by developing a usability plan that extends over a two to three-year period. Sit down with management and talk about the long-term vision of the organization as it pertains to usability. Jointly ascertain where you see the organization moving in the future, the types of usability engineering techniques and methods that need to be implemented, hiring needs, physical plant requirements, modifications and additions to the product life cycle, types of usability tests and evaluations to be performed, educational opportunities to be pursued for both yourself and the organization, and outside services required, such as market research firms, usability consultants, and so forth. The plan can suggest guidelines for projects, such as usability checkpoints in the life cycle, when to develop usability objectives, and types of tests to conduct at different phases.

Develop the plan for either your own use or to show others, depending on your position and the amount of responsibility you are given within the organization. Why this emphasis on a plan at such an early stage? Because without a plan, usability, as with any other organizational and cultural change, will sputter and languish. As the organization becomes more serious about implementing a usability program, it will need to grapple with and address many of the issues in your plan. Even though you may be starting from scratch, assume that the techniques you implement will be successful and have people clamoring for more. It is important to stay one jump ahead and be prepared for success.

Your plan should take into consideration the political realities of the organization and management's commitment or lack thereof. In other words, find the right balance of stretching the organization, yet not proposing impossible endeavors. Also, remember that any plan is revisable as circumstances change. It's a living document.

START SLOWLY AND CONSERVATIVELY

As mentioned earlier, usability engineering is a complex undertaking within an organization, and there is a danger in just simply "jumping on the usability bandwagon" in an unskillful way. It is important to build a usability program slowly, success upon success, rather than suddenly reinventing the organization. Usability, like its counterpart, *quality*, cannot simply be mandated from above. It needs the support of everyone in the organization so that it can enter the organization's bloodstream, rather than existing as some superficial "user-friendly" flag that everyone waves, but which brings very little results.

Consider an approach of gradual infiltration of the organization, rather than simply an all-out attack on usability problems. As mentioned in an earlier anecdote concerning the premature implementation of a fully equipped usability lab, beginning *too* ambitiously can undermine a long-term program. Initially, usability will often be seen as a threat and loss of control by those you would like to help. On the other hand, usability's most vociferous adversaries will often turn into its most ardent supporters, once they see that the user-centered process makes sense as a logical, cost-effective way to conduct business, and that it is not a threat.

CHOOSE THE FIRST PROJECT CAREFULLY

If you have been charged with selecting or carrying out an initial "kick-off" project, choose one with moderate to high visibility within the organization and with a high probability of success. Success will come easier if the first project has a champion(s) besides yourself and if there are minimal obstacles for carrying out a test or evaluation. A champion is one who is committed to the philosophy of usability and has a personal interest in seeing such a program blossom and flourish.

A documentation project is often an excellent kick-off project with which to begin, since it is seen as less threatening to the hardware and software community. Begin with manageable objectives, such as testing only a portion of a manual or user interface. An assessment test midway through the development life cycle is probably the simplest, most straightforward test for the beginning usability specialist to conduct. Even though earlier involvement will have the greatest effect on the product, later involvement seems to be more politically acceptable and initially less threatening. Once the project is completed, play up and publicize the initial success as much as possible.

BUILD ON INITIAL SUCCESS

Resist the temptation to go for the home run. Instead, go for singles and doubles. Opt for steady, incremental progress on both specific products and on the overall program. You will be amazed when you review a product at a later date and see how all the "minor" revisions add up to a greatly improved product. Try to avoid setbacks, which, during the early stages of developing a usability program, can create doubt in the program itself.

As you proceed from one project to the next, focus your efforts on earlier and earlier involvement, for that is where the greatest usability benefits can be shown. More on that later.

LEVERAGE YOURSELF AND "VOLUNTEER" YOUR SERVICES AS MUCH AS POSSIBLE

While you need to proceed slowly, do not be a shrinking violet either. Usability is "hot" right now, and there has never been a better time in which to assert yourself. Look for opportunities to leverage your efforts. For example, if you are assigned to test the documentation of a product, that is an opportunity to positively affect the user interface as well. In your test report, include, as a "courtesy," problems originating from nondocumentation sources, such as the product's software interface or an inaccurate characterization of the end user. Offer to expand on these findings personally and to help with overcoming them.

Take on *any* usability project, even if it is one that occurs very late in the life cycle, with limited benefits. While a test conducted very late in the life cycle may have little bearing on the current release of a product, it will have effects on the next release 18 months from now. Therefore, keep the long-term vision in mind. Even for small projects, go the extra mile by creating a well-thought-out, professional report. Your methodology and approach will be scrutinized by others wishing to learn what this "usability" stuff is all about.

CONSIDER A COMBINED TOP-DOWN AND BOTTOM-UP STRATEGY

In establishing usability engineering within the organization, work from the bottom up and from the top down simultaneously. Usability needs commitment from both the troops *and* management. Work "bottom up" by conducting actual projects and showing results. Work "top down" by educating management about the benefits of usability testing and user-centered design and by getting management involved. Obviously, you will need to enlist the help of any usability champions to take on such a comprehensive effort.

SELL YOURSELF AND WHAT YOU ARE DOING

Tell people what you do and how what you are doing helps the organization. In the course of a week, you might have dozens of conversations with people in your organization. View these as opportunities to plant seeds and educate people about the benefits of usability engineering. Eventually, two or three seeds will take root and you will find people requesting you to help them out.

Especially at the beginning, you need to *sell*, *sell*, *sell* at every opportunity. Expect it. Take every opportunity to make presentations to those with a vested interest and those who are simply interested. An obvious presentation to make is one comprised of usability test results. Such presentations are most effective when you show videotape excerpts of a test; sort of a "greatest hits" tape with emphasis on the most dramatic, cost-saving, embarrassment-preventing events that occurred. Nothing is as effective in bringing home the reality of and need to address usability deficiencies as seeing actual customers or representative users struggle. Never be defensive about modest test results. Five "minor" inconsistencies can equal one big headache to a user.

CHOOSE YOUR BATTLES CAREFULLY

Initially, usability is often an uphill effort, as you attempt to overcome old habits in the organization. If you are doing your job properly as usability specialist, you *will* find yourself in adversarial positions. Expect it. The key is in how you handle these situations. Save your energy for major issues, and do not get caught up with petty controversies. Major issues are those with larger implications for future projects; for example, a documentation format strategy that will be used by all future projects. This is one of the characteristics of an experienced usability specialist, he or she knows the issues that are worth fighting for and when to give in on minor points.

PHASE II: EXTENDING FURTHER

Once initial seeds begin to bear fruit and you begin to establish the benefits of usability engineering, begin to formalize the process. Create both physical and organizational structures to support usability engineering.

ESTABLISH A CENTRAL RESIDENCY
FOR USABILITY ENGINEERING

It is important how you position usability engineering support in the organization. There are two major appproaches you can take. Usability support can reside at the project level with a dedicated usability specialist working on a single project and reporting to the same project manager as everyone else. Or, usability can be centralized with one or more specialists supporting multiple projects and reporting to a centralized manager, either within the marketing or quality function, or the like. The former approach is often used by "usability-mature" organizations that employ many human factors specialists, with each one assigned to a specific project and reporting to that project's manager.

While both approaches can be successful, for the organization that is new to usability I recommend the centralized approach for two reasons. One, usability advocacy can be a very difficult and lonely position, with the usability specialist often placed in an adversarial position on a project. Since support by others is so crucial for one's confidence, outlook, and success, it helps when one has a manager who has usability as a major concern. In addition, if there are multiple usability specialists reporting to the same manager rather than separate ones, then the reporting structure enables them to help support, reinforce, teach each other, and develop a genuine espirit de corps. This is very important in organizations new to usability engineering.

Second, when a usability specialist reports directly to a project manager on a specific project, it is easy to become unduly influenced by the goals of the project team, which may conflict with usability goals. One may find it difficult to be honest about a particular design because revising it may cause more work for the developer(s), your very close peers. This hesitation eventually threatens one's autonomy and user advocacy. Reporting to a manager outside the project, as well as working on multiple projects, can help to retain one's autonomy and objectivity, and especially one's user advocacy because there is less peer pressure associated with this reporting structure.

ESTABLISH A ''PERMANENT'' RESEARCH LAB

Once you have established some momentum, with usability tests occurring regularly, then it makes sense to commandeer or construct a permanent space. Until then, consider using an electronic observation setup or a traveling or mobile lab. One advantage of the traveling lab is that your test need not wait until a specific room is free. A second is you can easily move to another location, to a customer site, or even to a local hotel's conference room if need be.

Be aware though that constructing a fully equipped lab takes everything to a new level, and I do not advocate setting one up until you are ready to use it on an ongoing basis. The lab should be the tool of a well-organized program and not the program itself. If it is set up before it can be used on an ongoing basis or before usability has gained widespread acceptance, management may find other users for it or even question the value of a usability program altogether when times are tough. It is better to be too late with a full-blown lab than too early.

Remember that the lab can be extremely simple; the main requirement is that it be available to conduct studies as required. Alternately, if you work for a company with a household name, you may want to arrange to have a secondary laboratory setting off site from which to run "anonymous" studies. For an excellent overview of how several corporations have set up their laboratories, see [42a].

BEGIN TO ADD USABILITY-RELATED ACTIVITIES TO YOUR COMPANY'S PRODUCT LIFE CYCLE

To succeed beyond the superficial level, usability has to become incorporated into the fabric of the organization's development process. Ultimately, it should be viewed as a completely ordinary activity, much as any other development activity. It needs to be seen simply as the appropriate way to develop and build a first-class product.

Therefore, beware of developing a *separate* life cycle; one for the usual development activities and a different one for usability activities. To the degree that usability is thought of as being separate from other activities is the degree to which it can be undermined. When activities such as establishing usability objectives, formally characterizing the user, conducting a task analysis, and establishing testing checkpoints simply become the way to conduct business, you will know that usability has arrived, and it will be difficult to sabotage.

EDUCATE OTHERS WITHIN YOUR ORGANIZATION

This suggestion is multifaceted. Here are some specific ways to spread the word about usability, as well as to expand your own horizons.

- **Take the time to explain usability decisions to colleagues at every turn, for example, why one design is potentially better than another.** When making recommendations, do not just expect developers to respond to your title or greater sense of what is better for users. Instead, take the time to explain your proposed changes and their benefits, as well as the dangers that exist if such changes are not implemented. Listen to their concerns and address them in your recommendations.

- **Hold seminars on usability engineering.** But make sure that they are appropriate and tailored for the audience. Not everyone needs to know the details of usability testing—some just need to understand the benefits and the appropriate time to conduct a test. Others need to hear about success stories, what the process involves, or expected cost benefits. Bring in professionals to conduct short presentations on a particular subject of interest to the troops or management for added credibility and a less insular approach. This could range from a simple lunch-time meeting to a full-blown seminar.

- **Start a usability resource area consisting of a library of books and articles on usability, as well as project-related usability materials.** Set up such a space, even if it is merely one cubicle in an area, where anyone is free to go and borrow materials. The project-related materials can be test plans and test reports that can be used as reference materials by others who are testing.

  Start a bulletin board and post articles of interest from newspapers, journals, magazines, product reviews, and so forth. Post product reviews that highlight usability as a key issue, either negative or positive. Encourage everyone to donate materials of interest, especially on success stories. Send articles and reports to those who require education, both advocates and adversaries.

- **Place an article in your company's in-house newsletter espousing the virtues of usability testing.** Better yet, report the results of the most recent test including the implications for the customer/user. Focus on benefits that go beyond just the product tested and that have implications for other related products as well. Many organizations are composed of groups who develop similar products for similar customers, yet because of politics, do not take advantage of each other's research efforts.

CONTINUE YOUR EDUCATION

For more pithy information, there are many usability-related journals and proceedings. The following periodicals and proceedings all feature information related to usability and usability engineering. Those marked with an asterisk, are more technical in nature.

- *Behavior and Information Technology**
- *Common Ground* (the newsletter of the Usability Professionals Association)
- *Human-Computer Interaction**
- *International Journal of Human–Computer Interaction**
- *International Journal of Man–Machine Studies**
- *Journal of the Human Factors and Ergonomics Society**
- *Newsletter of the Computer Systems Technical Group* (CSTG) *of the Human Factors and Ergonomics Society*
- *Proceedings of CHI** (a special interest group on Computer–Human Interaction of the ACM)
- *Proceedings of the Human Factors and Ergonomics Society**
- *Proceedings of the International Professional Communication Conference*
- *SIGCHI Bulletin* (a special interest group of the ACM on Computer–Human Interaction)
- *Technical Communications* (a journal of the Society for Technical Communication)

IDENTIFY AND CULTIVATE USABILITY CHAMPIONS THROUGHOUT THE ORGANIZATION

Who in the organization will benefit from usability testing? Who is chafing at the bit to get at usability information? Find out the answers to these questions. For those projects without formal usability support, use your influence to establish a usability champion on each project team; someone whose job it is to watch out for the customer/user. An advocate would at minimum be responsible for raising usability issues at meetings, ensuring that usability is included in all design documents and specifications, and helping—if only with the administration—to perform specific usability engineering methods such as testing. Without such champions, progress is slower, and "business as usual" continues.

As appropriate, find a way to unite these champions, as a task force, for example. The task force would hold periodic meetings to compare notes on how work is progressing on the different usability fronts, and would exchange ideas and support each other's efforts.

PUBLICIZE THE USABILITY SUCCESS STORIES
OF COMPETITORS OR EVEN
OF OTHER INTERNAL DEPARTMENTS

Take advantage of the natural competitiveness of different departments and product lines with each other. No department wants to feel that someone else in the organization or an outside competitor has an edge. In particular, let others know if you are falling behind your competition.

LINK USABILITY TO ECONOMIC BENEFITS
WHENEVER POSSIBLE

Whenever possible, establish and report on the cost benefits of studies and tests that you perform. Take the attitude that usability engineering should at a minimum pay for itself. One way to establish this link is to use a particular economic-based objective within the organization as the basis for a usability engineering project. For example, an objective might be to "cut down on the number of usability-related hotline calls currently received." That means you would have to begin with research as to the nature and frequency of calls to see how many are caused by usability-related issues. Then you need to determine what the hotline calls are costing the company and what proposed savings might be in terms of lost sales, additional customer support, and the need to send out "fixes." Here's such a calculation.

Suppose you know that each hotline call costs the company about $22.00 in salary, phone costs, fixes sent to the field, and so on. You also know through some stellar detective work that of the 18,000 calls taken each month, about 40 percent (or 7200) are directly attributed to usability issues. Therefore, about $158,400 of hotline costs are directly attributed to usability problems. If you can reduce usability-related calls by 50 percent, you can save the company about $79,200 dollars per month or almost $1 million per year.

This type of analysis will go a long way toward establishing the benefit of usability engineering in everyone's mind, and will create a very specific target. You can analyze the nature of the problems that are causing the calls, why they are occurring, and develop a strategy for solving them. Also, see Claire-Marie Karat's article on cost–benefit analysis [67] for a means of computing the value of iterative usability studies.

As an alternative, you might also pursue more indirect economic benefits. Propose as an objective to "raise the rating for documentation that is produced" or cut down on the number of pages in documentation without loss of effectiveness.

Once you begin to approach problems in this way, you will be amazed at the treasure chest of problems that exist within the organization just waiting to be mined and analyzed. Pool the efforts of marketing and research and development to work on solving a specific problem. Quite often, this may be the first time these departments have worked together to address a specific usability issue or objective.

Review reports of product problems from all groups with a vested interest in the product, for example, marketing, training, and so on. Sources of problems can be internal to the organization, such as hotline reports, warranty cards, letters from customers, and marketing surveys, or external, such as product magazine reviews, beta site reports, and the like. With just a little emphasis on collecting and categorizing problem information, you can move from a shotgun approach to a more pointed, focused approach to usability.

More specifically, begin projects that consist of a "follow-on" product to an existing product by first gathering information about any usability problems of the existing product. Then address these problems by incorporating their improvement into the usability objectives for the new product. For example, if you know that the current product has on-line error messages that are cryptic and also lacks clear explanations of the errors in the user guide, then cleaning up the error messages should be an automatic usability objective for the new project. While this seems like the most basic commonsense logic, it is amazing how often politics gets in the way and prevents such an analysis from happening.

JOIN USABILITY-RELATED SOCIETIES AND ATTEND THEIR ANNUAL CONFERENCES

As this book goes to press, the following associations and societies are concerned with usability testing:

- Usability Professionals Association
  c/o Janice James
  American Airlines/STIN
  P. O. Box 619616 MD4230
  DFW Airport, Texas 75261-9616

- Society for Technical Communication
  901 North Stuart St.
  Arlington, VA 22203

  The STC offers a Professional Interest Committee (PIC) on usability.

- Human Factors and Ergonomics Society
  P.O. Box 1369
  Santa Monica, CA 90406-1369

The Computer Systems Technical Group of the Society emphasizes usability issues of computer-based systems and products.

- Association for Computing Machinery's Special Interest Group on Computer–Human Interaction (ACM SIGCHI)
P. O. Box 12115
Church Street Station
New York, NY 10249

Become involved by attending presentations at a society's annual conference, or, better yet, make a presentation about your efforts and what you have learned.

PHASE III: SOWING THE SEEDS

After usability has begun to take root and there are many champions within your organization, you can extend yourself further, knowing that your efforts are not threatened by a single setback.

PURSUE MORE FORMAL EDUCATIONAL OPPORTUNITIES

If you are serious about usability engineering as a career and do not have a formal education in the discipline, I would suggest pursuing a degree program in one of the behavioral sciences (such as psychology or sociology), industrial design, or human factors. Alternately, there are also certificate programs being offered in human factors at some universities, such as Stevens Institute in Hoboken, New Jersey. Also, work with an experienced usability specialist who can serve as an advisor and help on the more technical aspects of projects.

STANDARDIZE PARTICIPANT RECRUITMENT POLICIES AND PROCEDURES

Formalize your relationships with your different sources of participants, such as temporary agencies and colleges as discussed in Chapter 6, so that recruitment is easy to carry out. Create and refine a database of participants, listing the who, what, where, and when of their participation. Remember that you may want to use people more than once if you require experienced participants. As the need for participants grows, you may want to assign one person to be in charge of acquiring them and maintaining the database.

ALIGN CLOSELY WITH MARKET RESEARCH AND INDUSTRIAL DESIGN

If your organization is large enough and fortunate enough to have a market research and/or an industrial design function, work closely with these disciplines during the life cycle. There is a natural alliance of the three disciplines of usability/human factors, market research, and industrial design. For example, work closely with the marketing organization to characterize the user. Or, use marketing to help line up participants and acquire or conduct field research. The industrial design specialist(s) can help with solutions for hardware and software problems, graphic design, and an overall user-centered approach.

EVALUATE PRODUCT USABILITY IN THE FIELD AFTER PRODUCT RELEASE

This evaluation expands the usability life cycle beyond the typical product life cycle which ends at product release. Conduct studies of the usage of your company's product out in the workplace and outside the lab. This could take several forms. You could observe the product being used and question users directly. Or, you could gather information on how the product is being used via either telephone or written surveys. Fold this information back into the development of the next product by making it widely available to the follow-up product's development team. So often a development team simply moves to another project as soon as the team completes and releases the current product. This creates a major gap in the feedback chain, since new ideas and implementations, while tested in the lab, are never seen in the light of day-to-day usage. Consequently, any problems experienced by users are simply carried over to the next product.

A good example of such field research was conducted by one of my clients, a human factors specialist whose company had just developed a software product. During product development, there had been much controversy over the inclusion of some fields and the exclusion of others on software screens. While the product had been tested for usability, many questions about on-the-job usage remained. My client conducted a postrelease phone survey of 200 customers, whereby each customer was asked questions about how he or she used the product. The nature of the research was to evaluate which options and fields on the screen were both understood and used. The phone survey brought closure to many open questions, and the results were then applied to the follow-up product.

EVALUATE THE VALUE OF YOUR USABILITY ENGINEERING EFFORTS

To ascertain the effects of usability engineering, conduct "before" and "after" studies. First, conduct studies in the field of a current product—how it sizes up on ease of use, satisfaction, and so on. Then conduct a similar study on the next-generation product that has been subjected to usability testing or other techniques, and compare the results. This is an excellent way to establish a real foothold for usability within the organization and to find out which techniques are most effective. Of course, publicize your results, and refine your process based on what's working and what's not working.

DEVELOP DESIGN STANDARDS

This activity certainly need not wait for Phase III, but many organizations have great difficulty standardizing prior to the development of an ongoing program of usability testing. The standards here refer to consistent methods for representing operations of the user-interface design, or standards for documentation formats, or the layout of a control panel; *within your own organization*. The idea is to ensure that similar design principles are being implemented in identical ways across all product lines. For example, Microsoft tries to ensure that all software products for a Windows environment work in the same way so that a user will know how to use the software from one package to another without having to relearn basic navigation and operations. While standards cannot account for every situation, they certainly can account for the most common situations, which frees developers to worry about the more creative aspects of new product development.

FOCUS YOUR EFFORTS AS FAR BACKWARDS INTO THE PRODUCT LIFE CYCLE AS POSSIBLE

Without question, the greatest benefits can be reaped by early involvement in the product life cycle. Always strive to influence products at the earliest possible moment, although typically one needs to prove the value of usability engineering in the later stages before this is possible. Focus on early exploratory tests of multiple design concepts. Take the time to interrogate users about the validity of your usage assumptions. For example, have as one of your objectives for an exploratory test to document how users perform specific tasks on the job. This is a very different objective from merely seeing if your design is usable. This early research has many times the payoff of a test conducted after much of the design is frozen. Do not be put off by developers who insist that there needs to be a more tangible product before research can take place. It is never too early in the product life cycle to consider usability.

CHARACTERIZE AND DESCRIBE THE USERS OF YOUR PRODUCT AND THE TASKS THEY PERFORM AND MAKE THIS INFORMATION WIDELY AND EASILY AVAILABLE

This might be the most important research you conduct, with the most impact to your organization, and, if you can do it before Phase III, by all means do so. There are many ways to do this research, and you can be extremely creative.

Visit customer sites, observe users in their workplace, and analyze and document the tasks they do. While many organizations do this, it must be performed systematically and consistently. Then present your results in a compressed accessible format. Usually, it is not for a lack of needing the information, but because the information is in a form that makes people's eyes glaze over, that sabotages this process. Let's face it—reviewing a typical task analysis can put anyone to sleep.

One of the ways to overcome this obstacle is to use the power of video to bring this research alive. One client that I have been working with, a new usability specialist, volunteered to document the tasks and process used at one of her company's large customers, an environmental testing lab. In return for this, her company equipped the lab with some new equipment to try, as well as advice on how to make its process more efficient. She and an associate visited the lab for a week, to videotape and analyze in great detail the steps required to test an environmental sample for contaminants.

After the research, which consisted of much observation and interrogation, she reduced over 8 hours of tape into a 15-minute professionally produced video with an accompanying booklet that documented the 90 steps in the lab's environmental sampling process (essentially a task analysis). The video was engaging and grabbed people's attention, while the booklet captured the required details. Together the package, a combination of video and booklet, is being used by marketing specialists, the sales force in the field, and development teams to design products to meet this very typical customer's need. The rest of the raw footage of the videotapes that did not make it into the final cut is also being used by individual developers interested in understanding specific aspects of the customer's process in greater depth.

PHASE IV: NEW HORIZONS

Phase IV is a fruitional phase and the point at which things really become interesting and fun. It is also the point at which I will end this book. Once your organization reaches this level of acceptance of the value of usability engineering in developing products, further efforts will be limited only by your imagination and by what the future will bring in the form of new technology. For example, usability engineering need not be limited to the product development life cycle, but can be expanded to include the entire product *ownership* life cycle. (Thanks to Carolyn Gazely, a marketing specialist, for first presenting this concept to me.) Much value can be achieved by taking a user-centered approach to these prepurchase and postpurchase phases.

In terms of new developments in the field of usability engineering, we can certainly expect two current trends to evolve further. One will be the proliferation of automated usability evaluations built directly into software products. These evaluations will provide feedback about customer usage, preferences, and difficulties, gathered more quickly and on a much larger scale than ever before. We need to be careful that the process does not become too rote.

Second, we can expect to see the continued demise of manual programming skill as a prerequisite for designing software interfaces. Many software prototyping tools have already made the development of mocked-up interfaces quick and simple, without the need for comprehensive programming skills. Soon, the writing of program code will be completely automated, with developers needing only to specify desired design parameters and the computer automatically writing the code to implement the design. At that point, usability and communication expertise will be the critical requirements for developing interfaces rather than programming skills, and usability specialists will play ever more prominent roles in the product development process.

We can also expect to see usability research explode as more firms assign resources to exploit the economic advantages of usable products (money talks) and as more educational institutions expand their programs to meet this need. Regardless of how the future unfolds and how tools and technology evolve, we can take heart that the following time-tested tenets of user-centered design in all their wonderful simplicity will remain inviolate.

1. **Analyze and understand the user's skills, knowledges, expectations, and thought process.**

2. **Analyze, understand, and document those tasks and activities performed by the user which your product is intended to support and even improve.**

3. **Design your product in iterative phases based on your analysis of user and usage. Evaluate your progress at every stage of the process.**

Any organization that truly takes these principles to heart will be well on its way to successful products and a host of satisfied customers.

HUMAN FACTORS AND ERGONOMICS SOCIETY CODE OF ETHICS

Appendix

Article IV—Subject Precautions from the Human Factors and Ergonomics Society Code of Ethics.

Article IV—Subject Precautions

Human factors scientists and engineers have the responsibility of treating both human and animal subjects humanely and in accordance with federal, state, and local laws or regulations, as well as the generally accepted procedures within the scientific community.

Principle 1

Members determine through consultation with colleagues or institutional review committees, that the exposure of human or animal research subjects to hazards, stress, divulgence of history or preferences, or tedium is commensurate with the significance of the problem being researched.

Principle 2

Members determine the degree of hazard present in the exposure of human or animal research subjects, avoiding any exposures to human subjects that may result in death, dismemberment, permanent dysfunction or extreme pain, and utilize the lowest levels of exposure to both human and animal subjects consistent with the phenomenon under consideration.

Principle 3

Members ensure the ethical treatment of human and animal research subjects by collaborators, assistants, students, and employees.

Principle 4

Members establish an informed consent with the human research subjects when required by institutional, state, or federal codes or regulations, making explicit in plain language the terms of participation, particularly with respect to any elements of risk or stress involved, and adhere to those terms throughout the experiment. One of these terms must be that the subject has the right to terminate participation at any time without prejudice.

Principle 5

Members do not coerce potential human research subjects to participate as subjects, nor do they use undue monetary rewards to induce subjects to take risks they would not otherwise take.

Principle 6

Members preserve the confidentiality of any information obtained from human research subjects that, if divulged, may have harmful effects on those subjects.

REFERENCES

1. Aaronson, A. & Carroll, J. "The Answer Is in the Question: A Protocol Study of Intelligent Help," *Behavior and Information Technology* **6**(4), 1987, pp. 393–402.
2. Abelow, D. "Wake Up! You've Entered the Transition Zone." *Computer Language*, 1993, pp. 41–47.
3. Anderson, M. & Mahan, G. "Usability Testing: What It Is and What It Can Do for Your Documentation," *STC Proceedings*, 1991, p. WE 48.
4. Asahi, T. & Miyai, H. "A Usability Testing Method Employing the 'Trouble Model'," *Proceedings of the Human Factors Society*, 1990, pp. 1233–1237.
5. Atlas, M. A. "The User Edit: Making Manuals Easier to Use." *IEEE Transactions on Professional Communications*, **PC-24**, 1981, pp. 28–29.
6. Babbie, E. *The Practice of Social Research*, 4th ed. Belmont, CA: Wadsworth, 1986, pp. 208–209.
7. Bailey, Robert W. *Human Performance Engineering: A Guide for System Designers*. Englewood Cliffs, NJ: Prentice-Hall, 1982.
8. Bandes, H. "Defining and Controlling Documentation Quality: Part I." *Technical Communication*, First Quarter, 1986, pp. 6–8.

9. Bell, B., Rieman, J., & Lewis, C. "Usability Testing of a Graphical Programming System: Things We Missed in a Programming Walkthrough," *Proceedings CHI '91*, pp. 7–12.

10. Benel, D. C. R. & Pain, R. F. "The Human Factors Usability Laboratory in Product Evaluation." *Proceedings of the Human Factors Society*, 1985, pp. 950–952.

11. Bergfeld Mills, C. "Usability Testing: User Reviews." *Technical Communication*, Fourth Quarter, 1985, pp. 40–44.

12. Bergfeld Mills, C., Bury, K. F., Reed, P., Roberts, T. L., Tognazzini, B., Wichansky, A., & Gould, J. "Usability Testing in the Real World." *CHI '86 Proceedings*, 1986, pp. 212–215.

13. Bethke, F. J. "Measuring the Usability of Software Manuals." *Technical Communication*, Second Quarter, 1983, pp. 13–16.

14. Bethke, F. J., Dean, W. M., Kaiser, P. H., Ort, E., & Pessin, F. H. "Improving the Usability of Programming Publications." *IBM Systems Journal*, **20**(3), 1981, pp. 306–320.

15. Booth, Paul. *An Introduction to Human–Computer Interaction*. London: Lawrence Erlbaum Associates, 1989.

16. Brown, C. Marlin. *Human–Computer Interface Design Guidelines*. Norwood, NJ: Ablex, 1988.

17. Brown, D. "How to Get Started in Usability Testing." *STC Proceedings*, 1989, pp. RT 165–168.

18. Brown, D. C. "Training Writers in Usability Testing: A Step-by-Step Approach." *STC Proceedings*, 1991, pp. ET 159–162.

19. Buchanan, C. "The Workplace as Laboratory: Beta Testing Software User's Guides on the Job." *STC Proceedings*, 1992, pp. 155–158.

20. Burnham, K. "Marketing Usability: How to Sell Usability Testing to Your Company or Clients." *Common Ground*, **2**(2), Fall 1992, pp. 1–4.

21. Bury, K. F. "The Iterative Development of Usable Computer Interfaces." In B. Shackel (Ed.), *Human Computer Interaction—Interact '84*, *Proceedings of the First IFIP Conference on Human–Computer Interaction*, Amsterdam: North-Holland, 1984.

22. Bush, R. "The Human–Computer Technology Group at Bellcore." *Proceedings CHI '92*, pp. 283–284.

23. Card, S. K., Moran, T. P., & Newell, A. *The Psychology of Human–Computer Interaction*. Hillsdale, NJ: Lawrence Erlbaum Associates, 1983.

24. Carroll, J. M., & Rosson, M. B. "Usability Specifications as a Tool in Iterative Development." In H. R. Hartson (Ed.), *Advances in Human–Computer Interaction*, Vol. 1. Norwood, NJ: Ablex, 1985, pp. 1–28.

25. Chaboya, H. L. & Bolden, M. A. "Usability Testing and You: Improving Your Product for Your Customer." *STC Proceedings*, 1988, pp. RET 96–98.

26. Chin, J. P., Diehl, V. A., & Norman, K. L. "Development of an Instrument Measuring User Satisfaction of the Human–Computer Interface." *Proceedings CHI '88*, 1988, pp. 213–218.

27. Coe, M. A. "Is Usability Testing Worthwhile?" *STC Proceedings*, 1991, pp. WE 154–156.

28. Cohen, S. "User-Centered Design in Manufacturing Applications: The Development of a Capacity Planning Tool." *CSTG Bulletin*, 1992, pp. 17–21.

29 Conklin, James. "The Next Step: An Integrated Approach to Computer Documentation." *Technical Communication*, First Quarter, 1993, pp. 89–95.

30. Constantine, L. "Going to the Source." *Computer Language*, December 1992, pp. 110–112.
31. Cummings, M. & Kolesar, K. "Testing the Product: Usability and Liability." *STC Proceedings*, 1991, pp. ET 163–166.
32. Dayton, T. "Cultivated Eclecticism as the Normative Approach to Design." Printed in John Karat (Ed.), *Taking Software Design Seriously: Practical Techniques for Human–Computer Interface Design*, 1991, pp. 21–44.
33. del Galdo, E. M., Williges, R. C., Williges, B. H., & Wixon, D. R. "An Evaluation of Critical Incidents for Software Documentation Design." *Proceedings of the Human Factors Society—30th Annual Meeting*, 1986, pp. 19–23.
34. Dieli, M. "A Problem-Solving Approach to Usability Test Planning." *Proceedings International Professional Communication Conference*, 1988, Seattle, pp. 265–267.
35. Dieli, M. "The Usability Process: Working with Iterative Design Principles." *Proceedings International Professional Communication Conference*, 1989, pp. 272–278.
36. Dieli, M., Wagner Navarro, N., & Brown, D. C. "Training for Usability Testing: Giving Writers a Tool They Can Use." *STC Proceedings*, 1991, p. ET 158.
37. Doheny-Farina, S. "Current Research in Technical Communication." *Technical Communication*, Fourth Quarter, 1987, pp. 289–291.
38. Dorazio, P. A. & Winsberg, F. Y. "Usability Testing of Online Information." *STC Proceedings*, 1988, p. ATA 41.
39. Dumas, Joseph. "Conducting Usability Tests." *Designing User Interfaces for Software*, 1988, pp. 25–30.
40. Dumas, Joseph S. *Designing User Interfaces for Software*. Englewood Cliffs, NJ: Prentice-Hall, 1988.
41. Dumas, J. S. "Stimulating Change Through Usability Testing." *SIGCHI Bulletin*, 1989, pp. 37–42.
42. Dumas, J. S. "On Usability Testing." *Common Ground*, **1**(2), November 1991.
42a. Dumas, Joseph S. & Redish, Janice C. *A practical guide to usability testing*. Norwood, NJ: Ablex, 1993.
43. Eason, K. D. "Towards the Experimental Study of Usability." *Behavior and Information Technology*, **3**(2), 1984, pp. 133–143.
44. Engel, D. C. & Lewis, K. K. "Building a Better Mousetrap Whilst the Mouse Evolves (Or Searching for Accuracy in Documentation)." *STC Proceedings*, 1989, pp. MG 121–123.
45. Ericsson, K. A. & Simon, H. A. "Verbal Reports as Data." *Psychological Review*, **87**(3), 1980, pp. 215–251.
46. Frey, T. J. & Stults, J. "Workstation Prototypes: A Human Engineering Approach." *Proceedings of the Human Factors Society*, 1990, pp. 547–551.
47. Goubil-Gambrell, P. "A Practitioner's Guide to Research Methods." *Technical Communications*, Fourth Quarter, 1992, pp. 582–591.
48. Gould, John D. "How to Design Usable Systems." *Human–Computer Interaction*, 1987, pp. 35–41.
49. Gould, J. D. & Lewis, C. "Designing for Usability: Key Principles and What Designers Think." *Communications of the ACM*, **2**(3), March 1985, pp. 300–311.
50. Green, P. & Wei-Haas, L. "The Rapid Development of User Interfaces: Experience with the Wizard of Oz Method." *Proceedings of the Human Factors Society—29th Annual Meeting*, 1985, pp. 470–474.
51. Greenbaum, Thomas L. *The Practical Handbook and Guide to Focus Group Research*. MA: D.C. Heath, 1988.

52. Greene, S. L. "Prototyping: An Integral Component of Application Development." *Proceedings of the Human Factors Society*, 1990, p. 266.

53. Greene, S. L., Gould, J. D., Boies, S. J., Rasamny, M., & Meluson, A. "Entry and Selection-Based Methods of Human–Computer Interaction." *Human Factors*, 1992, pp. 97–113.

54. Grice, R. A. "Tis a Gift to Be Simple: Aim to Be Simple." *STC Proceedings*, 1992, pp. 139–154.

55. Grice, R. A. & Ridgway, L. S. "A Discussion of Modes and Motives for Usability Evaluation." *IEEE Transactions on Professional Communication*, 1989, pp. 230–237.

56. Guillemette, R. A. "Usability in Computer Documentation Design: Conceptual and Methodological Considerations." *IEEE Transactions on Professional Communication*, 1989, pp. 217–229.

57. Hackos, J. T. "Establishing Quality Benchmarks for Technical Publications." *STC Proceedings*, 1992, pp. 684–685.

58. Heckel, Paul. *The Elements of Friendly Software Design*. New York: Warner Books, 1982.

59. Herring, R. D. "Evaluative Methods for Rapid Prototypes." *Proceedings of the Human Factors Society*, 1990, pp. 287–290.

60. Hewett, T. T. "The Role of Iterative Evaluation in Designing Systems for Usability." In M. D. Harrison and A. F. Monk (Ed.), *People and Computers: Designing for Usability. Proceedings of the Second Conference of the BCS HCI Specialist Group*. Cambridge: Cambridge University Press, 1986.

61. Hewett, T. T. & Meadow, C. T. "On Designing for Usability: An Application of Four Key Principles." *CHI '86 Proceedings*, 1986, pp. 247–251.

62. Hubbard, S. E. "A Practical Approach to Evaluating Test Results." *IEEE Transactions on Professional Communication*, **32**(4), 1989, pp. 283–288.

63. Human Factors Group, Compaq Computer Corporation. "The Human Factors Group at Compaq Computer Corporation." *Proceedings CHI '92*, pp. 285–286.

64. Isakson, C. S. & Spyridakis, J. H. "A Study of Survey Methodology." *STC Proceedings*, 1989, pp. RT 32–35.

65. Jacobs, V. "Conducting the Test—Who Does What?" *Proceedings International Professional Communication Conference*, 1987, Winnipeg, pp. 131–134.

66. Jones, J. "Not Just Manuals: The Newsletter Challenge." *STC Proceedings*, 1992, pp. 84–86.

67. Karat, C. "Cost–Benefit Analysis of Usability Engineering Techniques." *Proceedings of the Human Factors Society*, 1990, pp. 839–843.

68. Keister, R. S. & Galloway, G. R. "Making Software User Friendly: An Assessment of Data Entry Performance." *Proceedings of the Human Factors Society's 27th Annual Meeting*, 1983, pp. 1031–1034.

69. Knox, S. T., Bailey, W. A., & Lynch, E. F. "Directed Dialogue Protocols: Verbal Data for User Interface Design." *Proceedings CHI '89*, May 1989, pp. 283–287.

70. Kodimer, M. & Tullis, T. "Lab/Group Profile: Human Factors at Canon Information Systems." *Computer Systems Technical Group Bulletin*, **19**(1), August 1992, pp. 10–12.

71. Krauss, D. A. "Usability Testing For Lotus Documentation." *ITCC Proceedings*, 1988, pp. RET 165–167.

72. Lee, J. "To See Ourselves as Others See Us: Evaluating Software Documentation." *Asterisk*, Association for Computing Machinery, SIGDOC Newsletter, **13**, 1987, pp. 8–11.

73. Leedy, P. *Practical Research: Planning and Design*, 3rd ed. New York: Macmillan, 1985, pp. 135–140.

74. LeGrand Fairbourn, E. "Competitive Evaluation on Technical Documentation." *IEEE Transactions on Professional Communication*, 1986, pp. 127–130.

75. Lewis, J. R. "The Iowa Silent Reading Test's Comprehension Section: Local Norms and Predictive Validity for Usability Studies." *Proceedings of the Human Factors Society*, 1990, pp. 922–926.

76. Marshall, Chris "Ergonomics Is Dead." *Human Factors Society Bulletin*, March 1991, pp. 4–6.

77. Mason, E. F. "Case Study: A Software Designer and Documentation Developer Team Up to Get Customer Feedback." *STC Proceedings*, 1992, pp. 81–82.

78. Mayhew, D. J. "Cost-Justifying Human Factors Support—A Framework." *Proceedings of the Human Factors Society*, 1990, pp. 834–838.

79. Maynard, J. "A User-Driven Approach to Better User Manuals." *IEEE Transactions on Professional Communication*, **PC-25**, 1982, pp. 16–19.

80. Miller-Jacobs, H. H., Kurys, D. J., Campbell, S. E., Couture, R. G., & Murphy, M. J. "Panel Session: Rapid Prototyping on Graphics Workstations: User's Perspective of Tools." *Proceedings of the Human Factors Society*, 1990, pp. 305–307.

81. Milligan, C. "Designing Documentation That's Easy to Use." *STC Proceedings*, 1989, pp. WE 95–96.

82. Mills, C. B. "Usability Testing in the Real World." *SIGCHI Bulletin*, **19**(1), 1987, pp. 43–46.

83. Mills, C. B. & Dye, K. L. "Usability Testing: User Reviews." *Technical Communication*, **32**(4), 1985, pp. 40–44.

84. Mirel, B., Feinberg, S., Allmendinger, L., Mead, P., & Theodos, R. "Designing Levels of Information for User Manuals." *STC Proceedings*, 1989, pp. RT 170–172.

85. Mitta, D. & Ellis, N. C. "Human Factors Data: Knowledge Sources for Intelligent Design Associates." *Proceedings of the Human Factors Society*, 1990, pp. 308–311.

86. Montgomery, D. "Documenting the Documentation Process." *STC Proceedings*, 1988, MPD 88–90.

87. Mulligan, R. M., Altom, M. W., & Simkin, D. K. "User Interface Design in the Trenches: Some Tips on Shooting from the Hip." *Proceedings CHI '91*, pp. 232–236.

88. Mulligan, R. M., Dieli, M., Nielson, J., Poltrock, S., Rosenberg, D., & Ehrlich Rudman, S. "Designing Usable Systems Under Real-World Constraints: A Practitioners Forum." *Proceedings CHI '92*, pp. 149–152.

89. Mumau, C. Personal Correspondence, December 1992.

90. Myers, Brad A. *Creating User Interfaces by Demonstration*. San Diego: Academic, 1988.

91. Myers, B. A. & Rosson, M. B. "Survey on User Interface Programming." *CHI 92 Conference Proceedings*, 1992, pp. 195–202.

92. Navarro-Boomsliter, M. L. "Usability Testing—Expectations Versus Reality." *STC Proceedings*, 1992, p. 83.

93. Neal, A. S. & Simons, R. M. "Playback: A Method for Evaluating the Usability of Software and Its Documentation." *IBM Systems Journal* **23**(1), 1984, p. 82.

94. Nielsen, Jakob (Ed.). *Coordinating User Interfaces for Consistency*. San Diego: Academic, 1989.

95. Nielsen, J. "Finding Usability Problems Through Heuristic Evaluation." *Proceedings CHI '92*, pp. 373–380.

96. Norman, D. A. & Draper, S. W. (Eds.). *User Centered System Design: New Perspectives on Human–Computer Interaction*. Hillsdale, NJ: Lawrence Erlbaum Associates, 1986.

97. Penn, D. "Prototyping in he User Interface Design Process." *Proceedings of the Human Factors Society*, 1990, p. 265.

98. Planeta, L. S. "Major Issues in Usability Testing." *STC Proceedings*, 1992, p. 335.

99. Plumb, C. & Spyridakis, J. H. "Survey Research in Technical Communication: Designing and Administering Questionnaires." *Technical Communications*, Fourth Quarter, 1992, pp. 625–638.

100. Prail, A. "cf. Observation vs. Interpretation." *Common Ground*, March 1992, **2**(1), pp. 2–3.

101. Prasse, M. J. "The Video Analysis Method: An Integrated Approach to Usability Assessment." *Proceedings of the Human Factors Society*, 1990, pp. 400–404.

102. Ramey, J. "Broadly Applicable Information from Product-Specific Usability Testing." *IEEE Transactions on Professional Communication*, 1986, pp. 113–116.

103. Ramey, J. "A Self-Reporting Methodology for Rapid Data Analysis in Usability Testing." *Proceedings International Professional Communication Conference*, 1988, pp. 147–150.

104. Raven, M. E. "Comparative Read-and-Locate Tests: Online and Hardcopy." *STC Proceedings*, 1992, pp. 341–344.

105. Raven, M. E. & Beabes, M. A. "Redesigning a Help Menu Based on Usability Testing." *STC Proceedings*, 1992, pp. 159–162.

106. Rieman, J., Davies, S., Hair, D. C., Esemplare, M., Polson, P., & Lewis, C. "An Automated Cognitive Walkthrough." *Proceedings CHI '91*, pp. 427–428.

107. Rosenbaum, S. "Selecting the Appropriate Subjects: Subject Selection for Documentation Usability Testing." *Proceedings, International Professional Communication Conference*, 1987, Winnipeg, pp. 135–142.

108. Rosenbaum, S. "Usability Evaluations Versus Usability Testing: When and Why?" *IEEE Transactions on Professional Communication*, 1989, pp. 210–216.

109. Rosenbaum, S. & Walters, D. "Design Requirements for Reference Documentation Usability Testing." *Proceedings International Professional Communication Conference*, 1988, Seattle, pp. 151–155.

110. Rubinstein, R. & Hersh, H. *The Human Factor: Designing Computer Systems for People*. Digital Equipment Corporation, 1984.

111. Schell, D. A. "User Friendly Documentation: What Writers Need to Know About Usability Testing." *IEEE Transactions on Professional Communication*, 1986, pp. 117–120.

112. Schell, D. A. "Testing Online and Print User Documentation." *IEEE Transactions on Professional Communications*, **29**(4), 1986, pp. 87–92.

113. Schell, D. A. "Review of a Typical Usability Test." *IEEE Transactions on Professional Communication*, 1987, pp. 117–119.

114. Schell, D. A. "Overview of a Typical Usability Test." *Proceedings International Professional Communication Conference*, 1987, Winnipeg, pp. 117–125.

115. Schell, D. A. "Laboratory-Based Usability Testing of Online and Printed Computer Information." *Human Factors Society Bulletin*, **30**(3), 1987, pp. 1–3.

116. Schriver, K. A. "Evaluating Text Quality: The Continuum from Text-Focused to Reader-Focused Methods." *IEEE Transactions on Professional Communication*, 1989, pp. 238–255.

117. Shackel, B. "Ergonomics in Design for Usability." In M. D. Harrison and A. F. Monk (Eds.), *People and Computers: Designing for Usability. Proceedings of the Second Conference of the BCS HCI Specialist Group*. Cambridge: Cambridge University Press, 1986.

118. Shneiderman, B. *Designing the User Interface: Strategies for Effective Human–Computer Interaction*. Reading, MA: Addison Wesley, 1987.

119. Skelton, T. M. "Testing the Usability of Usability Testing." *Technical Communication*, Third Quarter, 1992, pp. 343–359.

120. Smith, G. L. "How Writers Can Improve the Usability of Programming Specs." *STC Proceedings*, 1989, pp. RT 156–158.

121. Smith, S. & Mosier, J. "Guidelines for Designing User Interface Software." Technical Report ESD-TR-86-278, 1986, Hanscom AFB, MA: USAF Electronic Systems Division.

122. Soderston, C. "The Usability Edit: A New Level." *Technical Communication*, First Quarter, 1985, pp. 16–18.

123. Spencer, R. *Computer Usability: Testing and Evaluation.* Englewood Cliffs, NJ: Prentice-Hall, 1985.

124. Spyridakis, J. H. "Conducting Research in Technical Communication: The Application of True Experimental Designs." *Technical Communications*, Fourth Quarter, 1992, pp. 607–624.

125. Stovall, J. C. & Fisher, J. R. "Usability Testing with a Vendor." *STC Proceedings*, 1992, pp. 469–472.

126. Strange Reitman, P. & Reitman Strange, C. "Streamlining Your Documentation Using Quick References." *STC Proceedings*, 1989, p. WE 58.

127. Sullivan, P. "Beyond a Narrow Conception of Usability Testing." *IEEE Transactions on Professional Communication*, **32**(4), 1989, pp. 256–264.

128. Sullivan, P. "Future Writers and the Practice of Usability: Questions for Educators and Trainers." *STC Proceedings*, 1991, pp. WE 123–126.

129. Sullivan, P. & Spilka, R. "Qualitative Research in Technical Communication: Issues of Value, Identity, and Use." *Technical Communications*, Fourth Quarter, 1992, pp. 592–606.

130. Suzuki, S. *Zen Mind, Beginner's Mind: Informal Talks on Zen Meditation and Practice.* New York: John Weatherhill, 1970.

131. Tanabe, K. "Hear a Cry from the Audience." *STC Proceedings*, 1992, pp. 461–464.

132. True, J. *Finding Out: Conducting and Evaluating Social Research.* Belmont, CA: Wadsworth, 1983, pp. 189–223.

133. Trungpa, C. *Shambhala: The Sacred Path of the Warrior.* MA: Shambhala Publications, 1984.

134. Tuchman, B. W. *Conducting Educational Research*, 2nd ed. New York: Harcourt Brace Jovanovich, 1978, pp. 196–245.

135. Tullis, T. "High-Fidelity Prototyping Throughout the Design Process." *Proceedings of the Human Factors Society*, 1990, p. 266.

136. Velte, C. E. "Document Usability Through Objectives." *IEEE Transactions on Professional Communication*, 1989, pp. 279–282.

137. Virzi, R. A. "Low-Fidelity Prototyping." *Proceedings of the Human Factors Society*, 1990, p. 265.

138. Virzi, R. A. "Streamlining in the Design Process: Running Fewer Subjects." *Proceedings of the Human Factors Society*, 1990, pp. 291–294.

139. Vogt, H. "Designing the Test—Writing the Scenarios." *Proceedings International Professional Communication Conference*, 1987, Winnipeg, pp. 121–125.

140. Vogt, H. E. & Helms, A. D. "Information-Usability Workshop." *STC Proceedings*, 1988, p. WE 107.

141. Vreeland, J. & Grice, R. "How We Used Data from Our Quality Program to Revise Our Process." *IEEE Transactions on Professional Communication*, 1986, pp. 163–166.

142. Wagner, C. B. "Quality Control Methods for IBM Computer Manuals." *Journal of Technical Writing and Communication*, **10**, 1980, pp. 93–102.

143. Wagner Navarro, N. & Moretto, L. "Changing Roles: A Survey of Technical Communicators as Usability Specialists." *STC Proceedings*, 1991, pp. MG 86–89.

144. Warren, T. L. "Research in Technical Communication: Who's Doing What in the U.S.?" *STC Proceedings*, 1992, pp. 450–452.

145. Wasserman, A. I. & Shewmake, D. T. "The Role of Prototypes in the User Software Engineering (USE) Methodology." In H. R. Hartson (Ed.), *Advances in Human–Computer Interaction*. Norwood, NJ: Ablex, 1985.

146. Weiss, E. *How to Write a Usable User Manual*. Philadelphia: ISI Press, 1985.

147. Weiss, E. "Usability: Stereotypes and Traps." In *Text, ConText and HyperText*. Cambridge: MIT Press, 1988.

148. Wenger, M. J. & Spyridakis, J. H. "The Relevance of Reliability and Validity to Usability Testing." *IEEE Transactions on Professional Communication*, **32**(4), 1989, pp. 265–271.

149. Wharton, C., Bradford, J., Jeffries, R., & Franzke, M. "Applying Cognitive Walkthroughs to More Complex User Interfaces: Experiences, Issues, and Recommendations." *Proceedings CHI '92*, pp. 381–388.

150. Whiteside, J., Bennett, J., & Holtzblatt, K. "Usability Engineering: Our Experience Evolution." In M. Helander (Ed.), *The Handbook of Human–Computer Interaction*. Amsterdam: Elsevier Science Publishers B.V., 1988.

151. Winbush, B. & McDowell, G. "Testing: How to Increase the Usability of Computer Manuals." *Technical Communication*, **27**, 1980. pp. 20–22.

152. Woodson, Wesley E. *Human Factors Design Handbook: Information and Guidelines for the Design of Systems, Facilities, Equipment, and Products for Human Use*. New York: McGraw-Hill, 1981.

153. Zirinsky, M. "Usability Testing of Documentation." *IEEE Transactions on Professional Communication*, 1986, pp. 121–125.

INDEX